D1295368

The Chartist Movement

A new annotated bibliography

The Chartist Movement

A new annotated bibliography

Edited by
Owen Ashton, Robert Fyson
and Stephen Roberts

MANSELL

First published 1995 by
Mansell Publishing Limited, *A Cassell imprint*
Villiers House, 41/47 Strand, London WC2N 5JE, England
387 Park Avenue South, New York, New York 10016-8810, USA

British Library Cataloguing in Publication Data
The Chartist Movement : a new annotated bibliography
  I. Ashton, Owen R.
  016.322440941

  ISBN 0-7201-2177-9

Library of Congress Cataloging-in-Publication Data
The Chartist movement : a new annotated bibliography/edited by
  Owen Ashton, Robert Fyson and Stephen Roberts.
      p.   cm.
   "This bibliography is intended to supplement, rather than
  replace, J.F.C. Harrison and Dorothy Thompson, *Bibliography of
  the Chartist movement 1837–1976* " — Editorial note.
   Includes index.
   ISBN 0-7201-2177-9
   1. Chartism—Bibliography. I. Ashton, Owen R. II. Fyson,
  Robert. III. Roberts, Stephen, 1950–
  Z7164.L1C543   1995
  [HD8396]   94-37219
  016.3224'4'094109034—dc20   CIP

Printed and bound in Great Britain by
Biddles Ltd, Guildford and King's Lynn

Contents

For
Edmund and Ruth Frow
in recognition of their dedication
to the preservation of labour
movement records

Editorial Note

This bibliography is intended to supplement, rather than replace, J.F.C. Harrison and Dorothy Thompson, *Bibliography of the Chartist Movement 1837-1976*, Harvester Press, Hassocks, 1978. To include all of the entries in Harrison and Thompson, as well as the new information listed here, would have burst the bounds of a single volume. Only the Manuscript Sources section and the Chartist and Near-Chartist Periodicals section are intended to provide, as far as possible, a comprehensive survey of sources, including the bulk of those listed by Harrison and Thompson. The remainder of this bibliography lists printed material either published since 1978, or omitted by Harrison and Thompson. A small number of entries for printed material are preceded by an asterisk. This indicates that the entry also appears in the Harrison and Thompson volume. Generally, these entries correct small errors in the first bibliography or indicate that an item has been reprinted; for example, in Dorothy Thompson, ed., *Chartism: Working Class Politics in the Industrial Revolution*, Garland, New York, 1986. Occasionally, an item is listed again because we can provide a location; we believe this will be helpful to researchers. During the course of our work we have collected photocopies of a large number of contemporary pamphlets. These photocopies have now been deposited in the Library of Staffordshire University at College Road, Stoke on Trent, ST4 2XW; this is indicated as well as the location of the original. For all periodicals we have indicated wherever possible the location of one file of the original publication.

Valuable collections of secondary sources are to be found in the Marx Memorial Library, Clerkenwell Green, London EC1R 0DU, and the Working Class Movement Library, Jubilee House, 51 The Crescent, Salford, M5 4WX. Access to these two libraries is by appointment.

In view of the continuing widespread academic interest in Chartism, and the amount of new publications since 1978, we hope that this book in its turn -- despite errors or omissions -- will be a valuable tool for scholars, researchers, and all who are interested in Chartism.

Acknowledgements

In compiling this bibliography, the editors have received a great deal of help world-wide. Financial assistance from the Lipman Trust and the co-operation of staff in many different libraries, record offices and publishing houses has greatly eased our task. We would also like to thank the following individuals: Brian Barton; Clive Behagg; John Belchem; Joyce Bellamy; J.T. Boulton; Michael Brook; Raymond Challinor; Malcolm Chase; Gregory Claeys; John Cole; Michael S. Edwards; Marianne Elliott; James Epstein; Hywel Francis; Keith Flett; Edmund and Ruth Frow; Janice Ginn; David Goodway; Eileen L. Groth; Jill Hall; John Halstead; J.F.C. Harrison; Ron Heisler; Paul Hill; Joan Hugman; Tony Humphrys; the late Alfred Jenkin; Angela John; David J.V. Jones; Hugues Journès; Jaap Kloosterman; Hideo Koga; Takashi Koseki; Lord Lucas of Crudwell; David Mayall; Clare Midgley; the late Ralph Miliband; E. Ronald Morris; Tish Newland; Irina Novichenko; Alf Peacock; Paul Pickering; Archie Potts; Pat Preston; Douglas Reid; Paul Romain; Horst Rössler; Edward Royle; John Rule; Michael St. John; John Salt; John Sands; John Saville; Anne Scott; Roger Swift; Dorothy Thompson; Martha Vicinus; Philip Walmsley; David Walsh; Jan Webber; Roger Wells; Colin Williams; Keith Wilson; Michael Winstanley.

We would like to acknowledge the help of three individuals at Staffordshire University: Maggie Ellis and Lyn Hodgkiss in the School of Arts who, respectively, typed the manuscript and prepared it for camera-ready copy; and Debbie Roberts in the University Library for her assistance. Librarians and secretarial staff in the University of Birmingham have also given us a good deal of help and we would like to record our thanks to them.

Finally, Veronica Higgs at Mansell responded quickly to our enquiries and, in many other ways, has shown herself to be the most helpful of commissioning editors.

Introduction

Nearly twenty years ago J.F.C. Harrison and I put together our card indexes and published a bibliography of the Chartist movement (see item 11). We had both been working in the field for many years and had often been asked for guidance on sources by other researchers. Neither of us was a bibliographer by training, and the resulting volume left a good deal to be desired in many ways. Nevertheless it drew together some of the very disparate sources for the study of one of the most interesting movements of the nineteenth century. Since its publication errors have been pointed out to us, some of the material has been moved, re-calendared or more precisely catalogued, new material has been discovered, and a great deal of work has been done in the form of theses and of published books and articles. We were both therefore very pleased when the editors of the present volume proposed to correct and up-date the original volume. This has been done now in just over two years, without any but the most cursory assistance from either of us.

The work of the editors has underlined many of the problems which we found in preparing the original volume. One of the first and most difficult of these was and is the problem of where to draw the line. If every published and unpublished work which includes some reference to Chartism is to be included, then very few histories, biographies, or even works of literary criticism which cover the decades of the thirties and forties of the nineteenth century could be excluded. And since the historiography of Chartism is a subject which itself sheds a great deal of light on nineteenth and twentieth century thought, as well as on the development and change of historiographical techniques, a case could be made for including even the most ill-informed or casual references in text-books or standard histories. [1] Nevertheless the general principle has been followed here, as in the first volume, that work is only included which contains either research or re-interpretation. Those textbooks which still summarise Mark Hovell, or refer glancingly to Chartism as one among many problems with which the politicians at the centre of their narrative had to deal, have not been listed.

Other works have been passed over which have perhaps a weightier claim for inclusion. Chief among these are the biographies of major statesmen, including some of those who were in power during the various Chartist "crises". The treatment of

Chartism in such books varies considerably. Where the subject's dealings with the Chartist movement have been specifically studied, as in George J. Billy's *Palmerston's Foreign Policy: 1848*, [2] the work has been listed. Works in which the response of the authorities to Chartism has been only briefly considered, for example, the late J.T. Ward's biography of Sir James Graham, or not at all, have not been included. [3] Clearly anyone studying Chartism and other popular movements will need to consult the biographies and the unpublished papers of the politicians who were in power at the time. Papers and archives which contain relevant material are listed in the manuscript section.

The earliest historians of Chartism tended to fall into two main categories. On one hand historians like Mark Hovell saw the Chartists as the descendants of the seventeenth century Commonwealthsmen. For them the Charter was the restatement of the position of the country party, the democratic opposition to the crown and the court, and it stood in a continuous political tradition from at least the seventeenth century through Wilkes, Cartwright and the Association Movement to the reform agitation of the 1820s and 1830s. The adoption of the Charter by the desperate, disorganised and mindless labourers of the industrial districts took it out of the logic of political development and into the realm of mob violence. A second approach saw Chartism as part of economic history -- a kind of revolt against industrialism. As such, its political programme was accidental and to a large extent immaterial. What was really at issue was the breakdown of traditional labour patterns, the replacement of paternalist master-servant relationships by the cash nexus and the gut response of the displaced hand labour force to mechanisation and industrial expansion. Where the politically-minded historians saw the end of Chartism as coming when a reformed parliament allowed the state to become more liberal, the economically minded saw the end of Chartism as being associated with a drop in food prices and an expansion in employment opportunities -- particularly the beginning of the age of railway construction and the growth of large-scale industry in textiles, heavy metal and engineering works. Just as any student of Chartism has to be aware of the goings on at the level of high politics, so the development of particular industries is an essential component of the understanding of the pressures of the period as they bore upon the working people. However, to include works on the economic history of the Chartist years would again add extensively to an already full agenda. Apart from industrial and trade union histories, parliamentary enquiries into particular industries and into labour conditions contain not only information which places Chartism in context (and which was often drawn on by writers like Benjamin Disraeli, and Charles Kingsley when they were writing their "Chartist" novels) but also occasional references to Chartism, as do the social enquiries of Henry Mayhew at the end of the 1840s. [4]

The widespread interest in labour history which has grown since the end of the Second World War has produced many works on industrial and trade union history which again are a necessary element in the understanding of the context of Chartism, even where they do not refer directly to the movement. These too have not been listed here unless they contain a fair amount of original material about Chartism. [5] The running bibliography in the *Bulletin* of the Society for the Study of Labour History, now continued as the *Labour History Review,* is a most valuable service to all students of social and labour history and contains regular up-dates of published material, theses, dissertations and work in progress, as well as occasional accounts of manuscript sources and document collections as these become available.

G.D.H. Cole, one of the first serious historians of Chartism in modern times, saw both political and economic elements in Chartism, but saw them in a rather more sophisticated way than had Mark Hovell. Cole made a distinction between "Hunger Chartism" and the more rational political form of the movement. He did not see the power of the crowd as being destructive in the way that Hovell had seen it, but nevertheless he saw it as irrational and difficult for the more rational and political leaders to control. From the work of Cole and other historians in the 1930s and 1940s came another important category of works relevant to Chartism but not included here. They saw that the post-Napoleonic war years were alive with movements for reform of many different kinds, from the pragmatic and limited demands for a reduction in working hours in the factories, through the pre-Chartist demands for the extension of the franchise, to movements which implied a total restructuring of society like Owenism and other communitarian philosophies. All the other popular movements of the period overlapped with Chartism. Many Chartists had been followers of Henry Hunt and William Cobbett, many were or had been Owenites; they took part in the factory reform movements, trade union protests, demonstrations against the 1834 Poor Law Amendment Act and the attempts to implement it in the industrial north in the mid and late thirties; they supported the campaign for Catholic Emancipation and demonstrated against the 1801 Act of Union with Ireland. The story of these movements has been written, but although such stories are clearly very close to the history of Chartism, books about them have only been included if they also contain Chartist material or are written by Chartists. The same applies to the history of dissenting Christian groups and the rationalist and freethinking groups of the period.

The two volumes of the bibliography, then, have limited their contents to works specifically concerned with the Chartist movement, without suggesting that that movement can be understood without setting it in the broader political and economic context of its age.

The list of manuscript sources in this volume is as complete as possible, including almost all the items listed in the 1978 volume as well as additions and corrections. A full list of Chartist and near-Chartist periodicals is also provided, but the other sections on printed material contain only additions and a few corrections. Many of the recent writings on Chartism which are listed are local studies, and it is among these that the greatest amount of new information is to be found. Probably the most likely source for further discoveries about Chartism is still the local newspaper press in the second half of the nineteenth century. Provincial papers in those years abounded in reminiscences and obituary notices of former Chartists, and the correspondence which these often sparked off are rich sources which have by no means been fully explored. With a few exceptions, however, local studies have tended to be informative rather than analytical, often relying on assumptions about the nature of the movement which date from the earliest historians.

Recent years have seen new interpretations of Chartism from a number of different directions. The great amount of new material provided by local and regional studies has shifted the emphasis away from the small number of metropolitan figures who tended to monopolise the early accounts. Foremost among these were Francis Place, the major archivist of radicalism in the early years of the nineteenth century, but himself also an interested participator in the activity, and William Lovett, whose papers and autobiography were among the accessible sources available to the early historians.

As the focus shifted to the massive numbers involved in the movement outside the metropolis, the concentration on the personalities of a small number of metropolitan radicals was replaced by a broader canvas. The novel feature of Chartism was not its programme which was the almost traditional one of parliamentary reformers since the seventeenth century, but the scale of the movement and the social make-up of the supporters. Leaders who were not remarkable for the novelty of their ideas, but for the power of their writing and oratory as organising forces, have been restored to their dominant position. Chief among these, of course, is the movement's acknowledged leader Feargus O'Connor, who has to be seen as a much more skilful and dedicated leader than had hitherto been allowed. To recognise his qualities is not to assert any kind of moral superiority over those who disputed the leadership with him, but the fact is clear that he was the movement's recognised leader during the years of its greatest power and influence, and that his leadership was never seriously challenged. [6] Recent work has also brought out the great importance of the network of leaders and organisers who maintained the movement in the localities. [7]

Historians have taken some years to understand the politics and dynamics of crowd action. Studies of crowd activity and theoretical examinations of its nature which are not based on the example of Chartism have not been included in the bibliography, although again they may be thought to be essential to the study of the movement . Once it has become clear that hungry people do not form threatening crowds by some kind of spontaneous surge, but that demonstrations which bring out tens of thousands of people need a great deal of organising, the rationality of the popular movements of the period, of which Chartism was the greatest, presents itself in a new form. Local studies and the discovery of scraps of Chartist correspondence -- particularly the papers confiscated from Thomas Cooper in 1842 and lodged in the series T.S.11 at the Public Record Office [8] -- have given some glimpses of the hard work that was put in to Chartist organisation and propaganda.

Renewed interest in the politics of crowd activity , started by the work of George Rudé and others on French popular politics, has led to an interest in the make-up of the Chartist crowd and to the examination of sources which were not used at all in early histories. These include the listings of the National Land Company, [9] an extremely important source of information, since it is the only list available, apart from those of arrested or imprisoned Chartists, which includes names, addresses and occupations; and, at the level of close local research, the census enumerators' notebooks. [10] This kind of close analysis has called into question many of the earlier generalisations about the Chartist crowd from those of Frederick Engels onward. Examinations of working patterns have shown the limitations and constraints upon certain social groups -- textile factory workers were rarely able to observe Saint Monday, for example, and most mass meetings were held on that day. On the sabbath religious forms had usually to be observed, so that many camp meetings had an aura of Christianity which could be seen as something of a smokescreen. Crowd action has received more serious and analytical treatment, and the display of numbers has been seen as a much less spontaneous and more deliberately contrived form of political activity than was allowed for in earlier accounts.

Events of the 1970s, 1980s and 1990s have called into question many of the underlying teleologies of historical writing. These included, among economic historians, an underlying teleology of economic expansion and development, among labour historians that of a developing consciousness of class, and among political historians the old fashioned but nevertheless persistent whiggish teleology of the gradual unfolding of political parliamentary democracy. In the political sphere, Chartism was often written off patronisingly as a kind of premature liberalism, whilst in the economic it was seen, either as, along with Luddism, the protest of men made redundant by modern technology, or, conversely, as the first manifestation of a consciousness of class which would lead eventually to the development of forms of working class organisation which would overthrow the capitalist system altogether and replace it with a more equitable and more efficient means of production in which the working-class would at last be dominant before classes were altogether abolished.

Concern with the social and physical environment, the emergence of violent conflicts fuelled by religious, national and other forms of ethnic consciousness, the demands of colonial peoples for freedom and statehood have all called into question the structures of analysis which earlier historians had brought to popular movements. The analysis of the spoken and written language in which Chartist demands and arguments were set forth have suggested possible new ways of seeing both the causes and the effects of the movement. Most of these latter have been little more than a turn from a purely social and economic set of analytical terms back to the political

description of Chartism which had held sway from Gammage to Hovell. The two areas
in which new questions are being raised are those of class and of gender.

That Chartism was an intensely political movement has never been at issue. As George
Eliot wrote in her novel about political radicalism in the 1830s, that was a time when "
faith in the efficacy of political change was at fever-heat in ardent Reformers". [11]
Robert Blake in his biography of Disraeli, wrote of "the quasi-revolutionary forces
such as Chartism which the spirit of reform had conjured up". [12] As I wrote in the
introduction to a book of Chartist documents in 1971:

> It was no new experience for large sections of the people of Britain to
> feel hungry. What is of interest in the late 'thirties is why the British
> workers responded to hunger by forming a nation-wide movement
> around a political programme instead of by more traditional means of
> protest like food rioting, arson, begging, poaching or praying." [13]

The great belief in political reform and the attainment of the suffrage as the panacea
for all ills was specific to the period. The histories of earlier reform movements,
above all of the agitation which preceded the Catholic Emancipation Bill of 1829 and
the Great Reform Bill of 1832, are necessary components of the history of Chartism,
establishing, as they appeared to have done, the efficacy of extra-parliamentary crowd
activity and the power and influence gained by hitherto excluded constitutencies
when they achieved the suffrage. [14]   Unlike the earlier movements, or the
contemporary Anti-Corn-Law League, however, Chartism was almost entirely a
movement of the poor. A modern work which offers a typology which has relevance
to the study of Chartism in that it addresses specifically the organisational problems
of movements which have to be self-financing and are limited by the poverty and
comparative powerlessness of their members is Piven and Cloward, *Poor People's
Movements*. [15] Although the movements studied are American, the book is one of
the very few which takes account of the resources and problems of movements with
no guaranteed financial backing, rather than dealing entirely with their programmatic
and theoretical nature.

Conclusions and judgements about the nature of Chartism, the success or failure of its
aims, the extent to which it fulfilled its potential and the influence it had on later
movements, all depend on placing it in its historical context and on analysing the
evidence. The movement has been extensively used by sociologists, political

philosophers and social and political theorists. For example, the reminder that
Chartism was a movement which based its programme for change on the
achievement of a political programme has been used by Gareth Stedman Jones to
simplify the question of why Chartism failed and came to an end. In a conventional
Marxist analysis the undoubted presence of a high level of class consciousness among
the ranks of the Chartists was seen as a breakthrough in the developing struggle with
the capitalist system. It was therefore necessary to find reasons for the apparent
decline of class consciousness in the second half of the century when a more mature
capitalist system of production was developing which should have led to the
intensification of the class struggle. Two theories were mainly called on -- one the
development of a privileged stratum of the workers, an aristocracy of labour who
were in effect bought off by the employers and turned against their less-skilled
brethren, and the other, connected to it, that the enormous wealth brought into
Britain by the expansion of Empire enabled the British workpeople to live in
comfort at the expense of the colonial peoples. In these analyses the privileged class
or stratum joined in a consensus with the ruling class and deflected the fundamental
conflict between capital and labour. Stedman Jones proposed a simpler reason for
the decline of Chartism in the "liberalisation of the state". He suggests that the
Chartists saw the state softening in important ways without the attainment of universal
suffrage and so dropped their confrontational attitude. [16]

The wheel has in some ways come full circle. Stedman Jones has taken Chartism back
into the realms of political thought, and suggested that the struggle between classes
was mainly carried on in rhetorical terms. Once the rhetoric of bourgeois
government became tamed, neither the vagaries of the trade cycle, the displacement
of traditional craft practices, the squalor of expanding conurbations, or the continued
denial of the right of working men to participate as citizens in the processes of local
or national government, caused discontent or disturbance. John Saville, by contrast,
has suggested that far from becoming more liberal, the state in the late forties
presented a much tougher face to dissidence. Improved policing and crowd control,
the development of the telegraph system and of a rail network for rapid military
deployment, and the deliberate manipulation of the legal processes showed a tougher
response, illustrated by such legal changes as the "Gagging Act" of 1848 and by the
militarisation of the metropolis on 10th April. [17] In fact neither the aristocracy of
labour theory, nor the suggestion of a liberalisation of the state, goes very far towards

explaining the falling away from the political programme of Chartism. Some recent work indeed, and many local studies which have taken the story beyond 1850, suggest that support for suffrage extension did not die, that Chartists rarely if ever disavowed their commitment to the programme of the movement, and that many of the lesser movements which involved working men and women were informed by the strong class feelings and class rhetoric which had been present in Chartism. What went was the priority given to the suffrage as the necessary precursor of political and social change, and the unifying force which such a panacea had above local, craft , religious or temperamental differences. This may have been due to the liberalisation of the state -- or at least to the liberalisation of the rhetoric of inter-class communication. It may also be related to events in continental Europe, especially France, where confrontational politics and the achievement of universal male suffrage soon produced not a popular republic but a reactionary Empire. Former Chartists turned away from the macro-politics of a national movement to the establishment of power bases on a lower level. Some political campaigns which the Chartist leaders had declared would have to wait for universal suffrage, had broken through to the statute book, chief among them the Repeal of the Corn Laws and the Ten Hours Act. A short-term improvement in trade allowed for the successful take-off of practical extra-parliamentary forms of action which had been attempted by the Chartists throughout the decade -- the development of co-operative trading stores, the establishment of trade societies among the skilled and regularly employed, mutual improvement societies, home colonies, building societies and savings banks. In the age of liberal free trade ideology the ethics of self-help, albeit with a far greater degree of community involvement and mutuality than in its raw middle class version, developed among the regularly employed and thrifty working people. The history of these various movements has not always been closely studied by Chartist scholars. Where local studies have gone beyond the chronology of the movement itself, the close connection of the Chartists with these more practical and more limited projects becomes clear. [18] Sections of the provincial middle classes and the intelligentsia developed much greater communication with some of these more limited movements, and the rhetoric of class confrontation became modified on both sides. W.E. Adams, at the turn of the century, wrote:

> People who have not shared in the hopes of the Chartists, who have no personal knowledge of the deep and intense feelings which animated them, can have little conception of the difference between our own times and those of fifty or sixty years ago. The whole

governing classes -- Whigs even more than Tories -- were not only
disliked, they were positively hated by the working population. Nor
was this hostility to their own countrymen less manifest on the side of
the "better orders". [19]

The mid-century saw something of a shift in the rhetoric of inter-class
communication. Men such as George Dawson, Charles Kingsley, Henry Solly and
Frederick Robertson helped to open up the possibility of inter-class dialogue by
speaking without bitterness to working men and by supporting certain forms of
working class initiative. Their motives were mixed, from the radicalism of Solly to the
conservative Christian nationalism of Kingsley or Robertson, who opened a dialogue
with the local Chartists in Brighton in 1848 because "his loyalty to the race was
stronger than his sympathy with a class". [20] There is no doubt that in the third
quarter of the century this more relaxed attitude made possible the development of a
degree of cooperation between some former Chartists and some members of the
established parties, particularly the Liberals. Apart from the work of Royden Harrison
and more recently of Margot Finn, however, the extent to which Chartist influence
extended into this period in forms other than the demand for the franchise has not
been the subject of many studies. [21]

The Reverend Robertson wished to see England united by race rather than divided by
class. The growth of ethnic conflict in some areas -- particularly Lancashire -- has been
seen as exemplifying this move from the class loyalties of the Chartist period to a
more nationalistic populism which transcended class. [22] Margot Finn's work, on the
other hand, demonstrates a strong support for nationalism which was at the same
time closely associated with class loyalties. Recent years have seen explosions of
national, ethnic and communal conflicts throughout the world and may be sending
younger scholars to look more closely at these phenomena. For many in the
nineteenth and twentieth centuries these divisions had been seen either as
epiphenomenal relics of more ancient societies or as deliberate constructions
encouraged by dominant classes or nations to divide subject peoples.

The extent to which the Chartist movement managed to contain a representative
selection of the various ethnic groups in the British Isles has been discussed so far
mainly in relation to the Irish in mainland Britain. Work on Scottish Chartism has
suggested differences between Scotland and England, as has most of the work on
Welsh Chartism, but in the main the differences have been seen as no greater than the

considerable differences between regions within England, and no more of a bar to common action. Only among the Irish has the influence of national politics been seen as a limitation on participation in the Chartist movement. Recent work has raised the profile of the Chartists in Ireland itself, but has not resolved the disagreements between scholars as to the participation of the immigrant Irish on the mainland. [23] That the intense class conflict in Wales also contained a strong element of nationalism has been proposed by one study, but in general Welsh scholars have not seen inter-ethnic conflict as inhibiting cooperation between Welsh Chartists and those in the rest of the British Isles. [24] One major Chartist leader, William Cuffay, was black and another, John Taylor, had an Indian mother. These characteristics only ever seem to be mentioned either in hostile press comments or by the authorities at the time of an arrest. There may well be more to be discovered about the influence of ethnicity in the Chartist movement, but for the present we have a picture in which divisions due to nationality, religion, trade and region were of considerably less influence than the unifying force of the Charter, its national leadership and its national press.

Another area of study which has become of major importance to social historians in the last few decades is the study of gender. Here there has clearly been a good deal of revisionism in the story of the Chartist movement. The history of women has taken several forms. One of the more obvious has been gap-filling. It is clear that almost every study of the Chartist movement since the mid-nineteenth century has written out the women -- mainly because the Chartists did not have a specifically feminist agenda, and women were not seen to have had any weight or interest if they acted in support of a class agenda. It was indeed something of an embarrassment to historians seeking a respectable ancestry for the modern Labour Movement, to encounter the pipe-smoking, beer-drinking, stone-throwing females of the Chartist crowd. For some feminist historians the Chartist women have remained marginal because they were acting upon a "male" agenda. For those who want to extend their knowledge of the women's actions, the gap-filling has not been difficult -- the record is clear and the presence of women and young people in the Chartist crowd can be demonstrated without difficulty, although the problems of identification of individual women come up against all the problems of studying women in an age when they were almost invariably described in the record in terms of their marital or familial status in relation to men. Very few historians would now deny the female presence in Chartism. The interpretation of that presence and of the influence of women in general in the period is, however, an area of some contention. The fact that much of the Chartist action and rhetoric was in defence of the working class family can be seen as contributing to the withdrawal of women in the later part of the century into a more domestic environment, and as supporting the doctrine which became dominant in the second half of the century of "separate spheres". Far from contributing to an assertion of the right of women to take part in public activity, as many Chartist writers and speakers claimed, and as Chartist practice demonstrated, the women have been seen by some feminist historians to have been digging their own graves as independent beings at the behest of the dominant male agenda-writers. [25] On this question, as on many others, the argument has to be followed not only in works specifically on Chartism and therefore listed here, but in other studies of contemporary issues which are outside the scope of this volume but which, like Deborah Valenze's study of women preachers in the non-conformist sects, are clearly very relevant. [26]

One final category should be mentioned, which is the study of Chartism in comparison with similar movements in other parts of the world. The very great interest in the history of the British labour movement, which is demonstrated by the many languages into which the standard works have been translated, is not merely scholarly and antiquarian. In many ways, Britain was seen as the first nation to experience changes which were later to occur in all other "modernising" industrial nations. Comparative studies have tended to be based on this assumption, and to have concentrated on the socio-political and structural elements in the story. More modern approaches have opened the possibility of more complex comparative studies. The first volume of Neville Kirk's comparative study of British and United States labour movements is particularly valuable for the study of Chartism, and it is to be hoped that similar comparisons which are in hand with movements in other industrialised countries will soon be available. [27] Such comparisons enable us to set Chartism in a more exact context, not only by emphasising similarities of experience, but perhaps more by showing the particular elements which were unique to Britain. They may also help us to follow and to understand developments in the industrial nations of contemporary Asia, and other parts of the world, without making too many assumptions based on out of date teleologies.

Dorothy Thompson
Worcester, June 1994

Notes

1. For further development of this question see my "Chartism and the Historians" in *Outsiders,* [item 831] pp 19-34 and see also Diana Sinnott "This Strange Interlude ", item 1131

2. George J. Billy, *Palmerston's Foreign Policy,* item 555

3. J.T. Ward, *Sir James Graham* (1967) Many of the biographies, although not listed here, are essential reading at least in part for the study of Chartism, e.g. Robert Blake, *Disraeli* (1966) and for an excellent account of Disraeli as a political novelist, John Vincent, *Disraeli,* (1990)

4. For example, (among many others) *First Report of the Commissioners Appointed to Inquire as to the Best Means of Establishing an Efficient Constabulary Force in the Counties of England and Wales* (1839), *Reports of the Handloom Weavers Commissioners* 1840 etc. Henry Mayhew, *London Labour and the London Poor* (1861)

5. Thus Challinor and Ripley, *The Miners' Association* (1968) is included, but James Jefferys, *The Story of the Engineers* (1946) is not, although the latter does have a few references to Chartism

6. For the most recent studies of O'Connor see J. Epstein, *The Lion of Freedom,* item 609 and J. Belchem, "Feargus O'Connor and the Collapse of the Mass Platform", item 544

7. There are entries for local Chartist leaders in Saville and Bellamy (eds), *Dictionary of Labour Biography,* item 1335 and there will be some in the new *D.N.B.* See also Stephen Roberts, *Radical Politicians and Poets in Early Victorian Britain,* item 774

8. Public Record Office, series T.S.11, item 23.13

9. Public Record Office, series BT 41, item 23.4

10. Public Record Office, series HO 107, item 23.1

11. George Eliot, *Felix Holt, the Radical,* 1897 edition, p 162

12. Robert Blake, *Disraeli,* p 242

13. Dorothy Thompson, *The Early Chartists,* pp 11-12

14 There is a large literature on the 1832 Bill, summarised and listed in John Cannon, *Parliamentary Reform 1640 - 1832* (1972). For Catholic Emancipation see Oliver MacDonagh, *The Emancipist* (1989) and Angus Macintyre, *The Liberator* (1965)

15. Frances Fox Piven and Richard A. Cloward, *Poor People's Movements* (1977)

16. Gareth Stedman Jones, "Rethinking Chartism" in *Languages of Class,* item 814

17.   John Saville, *1848,* item 791

18.   For example, John Cole's study of Rochdale shows the connection of the local Chartists with the most important of the early retail cooperative stores. John Cole, *Conflict and Cooperation*, item 580

19.   W.E. Adams, *Memoirs of a Social Atom*, vol 1, p 237

20.   Stopford A. Brook (Ed), *Life and Letters of Frederick W. Robertson M.A.*, London 1866, vol 1, p 149

21.   Royden Harrison, *Before the Socialists* (1965), Margot C. Finn, *After Chartism*, item 615, see also Patrick Joyce, *Work, Society and Politics*, (1980) and Kate Tiller "Working-Class Attitudes and Organisation in Three Industrial Towns", item 1283

22.   See, for example, Neville Kirk, *The Growth of Working Class Reformism in Mid-Victorian England,* item 692, ch 7

23.   See two papers by Takashi Koseki, items 1037 and 1040, and a summary of the arguments on both sides in Graham Davies, *The Irish in Britain,* item 589

24.   For a study asserting a strong nationalist element in the Newport Rising of 1839, Ivor G.H. Wilks, *South Wales and the Rising of 1839*, item 863

25.   Anna Clark, "The Rhetoric of Chartist Domesticity", item 935; Jutta Schwartzkopf, *Women in the Chartist Movement*, item 795

26.   Deborah Valenze, *Prophetic Sons and Daughters, Female Preaching and Popular Religion in Industrial England* (1985)

27.   Neville Kirk, *Labour and Society in Britain and the USA*, item 693

The Bibliography

Bibliographies

1   Altholz, Josef L. *Victorian England 1837-1901*, Cambridge University Press, Cambridge, 1970, pp.100 (See Section V. pp.12-25, "Political History", for Chartist secondary sources)

2   Boddington, Mike *Labour History in the West Midlands : A Bibliography*, Wolverhampton, 1982, pp.19 (A compilation of 187 items including a number on Chartism in the trade unionism and politics sections)

3   Boddington, Mike 'A Bibliography of Theses and Current Research Relating to the West Midlands since 1800', *West Midlands Studies*, vol. 15, Winter 1982 (A compilation of 185 theses either completed or on-going in Shropshire, Staffordshire, Warwickshire and Worcestershire, of which ten relate to Chartism)

4   Burnett, J., Vincent, D., Mayall, D. (eds.) *The Autobiography of the Working Class, An Annotated Critical Bibliography, 1790-1945*, Harvester Press, Brighton, 3 Vols. Vol.I 1790-1900, 1984, pp.463 contains the bulk of Chartist leaders and activists; Vol. II 1900-1945, 1987 pp.435; Vol.III a supplement 1750-1945, 1987 pp.129

5   Chaloner, W.H. & Richardson, R.C. *British Economic and Social History : A Bibliographical Guide*, Manchester University Press, Manchester, 1976. Reptd. 1984, pp.208 (Section on Chartism pp.131-133)

6   Conway, Eddie et.al. *Labour History of Manchester and Salford: A Bibliography*, Manchester Centre for Marxist Education Pamphlets, Manchester, 1977, pp.34 (pp.13-16 for Chartist primary and secondary sources in the two cities)

7   Gilbert, Victor F. *Labour and Social History Theses, American, British and Irish University Theses and Dissertations in the Field of British and Irish Labour History presented between 1900 and 1978*, Mansell Publishing, London, 1982, pp.194 (Contains a number of entries under the headings "Chartism" and "Radicalism")

8   Gwent County Record Office *Chartism. A Guide to Documentary and Printed Sources*, Cwmbran, 1993, pp.14 (Includes manuscript collection, contemporary pamphlets, newspaper articles, broadsheets and directories relating to Chartism in Monmouthshire in general and to the Newport Rising in particular)

9   Hackett, Nan *Nineteenth Century Working Class Autobiographies: An Annotated Bibliography*, Ams Press, New York, 1985, pp.241 (Includes a small number of Chartists: S. Bamford, J. Barker, J.J. Bezer, J.D. Burn, T. Cooper, J. Gutteridge, G.J. Holyoake, W.J. Linton, W. Lovett, C. Shaw, B. Wilson)

10   Hambrick, Margaret *A Chartist's Library*, Mansell Publishing, London & New York, 1986, pp.266 (A compilation of the literary and historical works - 1,634

titles - owned by G.J. Harney and his family, and deposited in the Vanderbilt University Library, Nashville, Tennessee, USA. The collection includes books by such Chartists as W.E. Adams, T. Cooper, W.J. Linton, G. Massey and W. Thom)

11   Harrison, J.F.C. & Thompson, Dorothy *Bibliography of the Chartist Movement 1837-1976*, Harvester Press, Hassocks, Sussex, 1978, pp.214. (The companion to this volume)

12   *Harrison, Royden, Woolven, Gillian, and Duncan, Robert *The Warwick Guide to British Labour Periodicals, 1790-1970: A Checklist*, Harvester Press, Hassocks, Sussex, 1977, pp.685 (Over 4,000 entries; indicates the nature and location of nearly all Chartist periodicals; some locations are inaccurate)

13   MacDougall, Ian *A Catalogue of Some Labour Records in Scotland and Some Scots Records outside Scotland*, Scottish Labour History Society, Edinburgh, 1978, pp.598 (Section on primary and secondary sources, pp.109-111, relating to Chartism in Scotland)

13.A   Newcastle-upon-Tyne Public Libraries *The Harney Library: List of Books (Mainly Political) Presented by Mr and Mrs G. J. Harney, and placed in the Reference Department*, Newcastle-upon-Tyne, 1899, pp.9

14   Neville, Robert G. & Benson, John 'Labour in the Coalfields. A Select Critical Bibliography', *Bulletin of the Society for the Study of Labour History*, no.31, Autumn 1975 (Indicates the limited extent of the work on Chartism and the mining trades unions. Only a few entries)

15   Nicholls, David *Nineteenth Century Britain 1815-1914,* Critical Bibliographies in Modern History, Dawson, Archon Books, Folkestone, 1978, pp.170. (See pp.39-41, 94-101 for recent secondary works on Chartism, with comments on their usefulness)

16   Potts, A. & Jones, E.R. *Northern Labour History. A Bibliography.* The Library Association Reference, Special and Information Section, London, 1981, pp.122 (See pp.21-23 for Chartism and Radicalism)

17   Regan, Anne *A Guide to the Literature Concerning Joseph Rayner Stephens of Ashton (1805-1879), Methodist Minister and Political Agitator,* Manchester School of Librarianship, Manchester, 1972, pp.9. (Typescript in Tameside Local Studies Library, Stalybridge)

18   Shaaban, Bouthaina 'The Romantics in the Chartist Press', *Keats-Shelley Journal,* Vol.38, 1989 (A bibliographical list of 126 Romantic items, particularly by Byron, Coleridge, Keats and Shelley, in both the Chartist and Owenite press)

19   Smith, Harold *The British Labour Movement to 1970. A Bibliography*, Mansell Publishing, London and New York, 1981, pp.250 (Has seventy entries, pp.93-98, relating to Chartism in general and to local and special studies. All entries are for works published between 1945-1970)

20   *Warner, John & Gunn, W.A. *John Frost and the Chartist Movement in Monmouthshire. Catalogue of Chartist Literature, Prints and Relics*, Newport Chartist Centenary Committee, Newport, 1939, Reptd. Gwent County Council, Newport 1980, pp.39 (The second edition also includes a number of secondary works acquired in the 1970s)

21   Wiener, Joel H.   'The Radical and Labor Press' pp.45-57 in J. Don Vann and Rosemary T. Van Arsdel (eds) *Victorian Periodicals. A Guide To Research*, Vol.2, The Modern Language Association of America, New York, 1989, pp. 177 (See 'The Chartist Press', pp.49-51)

22   Wyke, T.J. 'Nineteenth Century Manchester: A Preliminary Bibliography' pp.218-271, particularly Section XIII "Labour history" pp.242-245 in A.J. Kidd and K.W. Roberts (eds.) *City, Class and Culture. Studies of Cultural Production and Social Policy in Victorian Manchester*, Manchester University Press, Manchester, 1985, pp.280

Manuscript Sources

23   PUBLIC RECORD OFFICE

The major depository of all official papers, legal records and the papers of
Government departments, the PRO includes the largest body of manuscript
material relevant to the study of Chartism. Listed below are records known to
be of value, but there may be others. (Nineteenth-century filing clerks were
not invariably accurate, and Chartist material may sometimes be found in
unexpected places.) Most of the relevant records are located in the main record
office at Kew, but there is also relevant material in the office at Chancery Lane,
and the location of this material is indicated below. However, the PRO plans to
close the Chancery Lane office and transfer all records to Kew at some time
during 1996. A complete list of the contents of the PRO may be found in the
PRO: *Current Guide*, 1992, available on microfiche.

23.1   *Home Office Papers: Correspondence and Papers, Disturbances.*

This series contains the largest number of items relating to Chartism, and is a
very rich source, including correspondence to the Home Office from
magistrates, Lord Lieutenants, informers and military reports, intercepted
Chartist letters, odd copies of Chartist posters, leaflets and newspapers. Most
bundles are arranged by county, subject and year.

HO40
Disturbances to 1840: in-coming correspondence for the early Chartist years,
e.g. *HO 40/48* includes Disturbances 1839 Staffordshire, bundle of 167
numbered items; *HO 40/53* has military correspondence and intercepted
Chartist letters, 1839, 275 numbered items.

HO41
Disturbance Entry books, copies of out-letters, Home Office replies to letters
in *HO40* and *HO45*.

HO45
Continuation of *HO41* - Disturbances from 1841 on, for the rest of the Chartist
period, including 1842 and 1848 (for which *HO 45/2410*, in five boxes, is the
essential source) and relevant material throughout the 1840s and 1850s.

HO52
         Counties Correspondence to 1840: a series which was parallel with, and
should be used in conjunction with, *HO40*, for the early years of Chartism.

OTHER RELEVANT MATERIAL IN THE HOME OFFICE PAPERS

HO6
Circuit letters 1816-1840: Returns of Judges and Recorders of persons
recommended for mercy, letters from governors of convict prisons.

HO9
Convict Prisons, Miscellaneous Registers, 1802-1849, including prison hulks.

HO10
Convicts, New South Wales and Tasmania, 1788-1859: Lists of convicts with some details of their sentences, employment, settlement in Australia and pardons granted.

HO11
Convict Transportation Registers, 1787-1870. Lists under respective ships of convicts transported in them, with dates of conviction etc.

HO12/2/81
Criminal Papers: interesting file including papers on Chartist prisoners of 1848 - lists petitions on behalf of prisoners; list of pardons, 1856. Material on Ernest Jones' imprisonment; two letters from Ernest Jones (1851, both about William Cuffay); two letters from John Frost (1856,1857).

HO13
Criminal Entry Books, correspondence and warrants for removal, transfer, transportation of prisoners.

HO16
Old Bailey Sessions, 1815-1849. Original returns by Clerk of Sessions of prisoners committed for trial, charges and result of trials.

HO20
Prisons: correspondence and papers 1820-1843, especially *HO20/10* - a file including detailed interviews with 73 Chartists serving prison terms in the winter of 1840-1, with statements by Chartists, inspectors' comments etc. (See Godfrey and Epstein, 1977; Godfrey, 1979, listed below in Published Secondary Material).

HO21
Prisons: Entry Books with copies of out-letters from Home Office.

HO24
Prison Registers and Returns, 1838-1875.

HO26
Criminal Registers: London - Lists of prisoners.

HO27
Criminal Registers: Counties - Lists of prisoners.

HO44
Correspondence and papers, Domestic and General, Original Letters 1820-1861. This miscellaneous category yields some interesting material including, for example:

HO44/31
Miscellaneous Correspondence 1838: poster, depositions etc. re anti-Poor Law riots in Todmorden and Huddersfield; folder of papers on trade unions, including O'Connor's agitation on behalf of the Glasgow Cotton Spinners; material on Working Men's Associations.

HO44/34
Folder re Socialists 1839.

HO44/38
Socialism, 1840, Owenite responses to persecution.

HO44/52
Police reports on meetings of the National Convention and the East London Democratic Association, 1839.

HO48
Law Officers' Cases and Reports 1792-1871. Includes some depositions, for example, *HO48/40* Case of the Queen v. John Wilde and others; deposition of John Latimer on plans for Chartist rising in Ashton-under-Lyne, 1848 (Reptd. in F.C. Mather (ed.), *Chartism and Society*, Bell and Hyman, London, 1980, pp.140-146).

HO49
Letters to Law Officers, entry books.

HO50
Correspondence and papers, military - letters from Commander-in-Chief re internal defence, 1782-1840.

HO51
Entry Books: Military, Commissions, Appointments etc. 1758-1855.

HO60
Police Courts, 1821-1865. Out-letters to magistrates and others concerning business of police courts.

HO61
Original letters relating to Metropolitan Police.

HO65
Entry Books: Metropolitan Police, Birmingham Police and Rural Police.

HO73
Expired Commissions: Records of Commissions of Enquiry, including some unpublished material. *HO73/52* has only known copies of *Northern Star,* no.3, 2 Dec. 1837; no.5, 16 Dec. 1837.

HO75
Hue and Cry and *Police Gazette*, 1828-1845. Bound volumes of printed journal.

HO79
Entry Books: Private and Secret, 1798-1864; letters relating to censorship, opening mail etc., including warrants to open the mail of Chartists.

HO100
Ireland, Original Correspondence, 1782-1871.

HO102
Scotland, Correspondence and Papers, 1782-1840.

HO103
Scotland, Entry Books, 1763-1871.

HO104
Scotland, Criminal Entry Books, 1762-1849.

HO122
Ireland, Entry Books, 1782-1871.

Census Records
HO107
Censuses, 1841 and 1851 enumerators' schedules. Names, addresses, ages, occupations and - in 1851 only - birthplaces of individuals and all members of their households. The essential tool in pursuing details of individual Chartists. Located at Chancery Lane. Microfilm copies only are available. Copies are usually also available for particular areas at local libraries and record offices.

OTHER RELEVANT CLASSES OF RECORDS

Admiralty

23.2   *ADM101*
Includes log books of surgeon-superintendents on convict ships to Australia, including some comments on Chartist convicts and their health and morale.

23.3   *Assizes*

ASSI
Assize records have only been retained for cases of particular interest. However, these include cases involving sedition, treason, riot and conspiracy to effect political change. e.g. *ASSI 6.6* includes depositions, with witnesses' statements and defendants' responses, for each of the 276 persons put on trial at the Staffordshire Special Assize of October 1842 (Located at Chancery Lane).

23.4   *Board of Trade*

BT41/136
Has some general documents on the Chartist Land Company.
BT41/474-476 contains lists, in roughly alphabetical order, (as required by law, for the unsuccessful attempt to register the Land Company as a Joint Stock Company or a Friendly Society) with names, addresses and occupations, of some 25-30,000 Land Company members, in 1847 and 1848. This is the largest single source of data on rank-and-file Chartist supporters.

23.5   *Chancery Records*

Land Company documents in *C35-6, C54* (maps of Chartist Land Colonies), *C101* and *C121* (Located at Chancery Lane).

23.6   *Colonial Office*

CO 904/8-9 : Ribbonism, and informers' reports on Irish Chartists.

23.7   *Foreign Office*

FO146/341-3
Has interesting material in correspondence between London and Paris in 1848.

23.8   *Metropolitan Police*

MEPO 1-8
These records include much valuable and relevant correspondence and papers.

23.9   *Ministry of Health*

MH12
Includes papers and correspondence from individual Poor Law Unions, with some references to Chartism and much valuable background information on social conditions.

MH13
Has similar correspondence with post-1848 local Boards of Health, sometimes including references to Chartist participation in local controversies about public health.

MH32
Consists of reports, papers and correspondence from Poor Law inspectors and Assistant Commissioners about the districts they visited.

23.10   *Palatinate of Lancaster*

PL26 Indictments/Pl27 Depositions
For Chartist trials in the area covered by the Palatinate of Lancaster. (Located at Chancery Lane).

23.11   *Prison Commission*

PCOM1
Sessions Papers, Old Bailey.

PCOM2
Prison Books, 1770-1894, with full lists of all prisoners: age, occupation, residence, sentence, conduct, literacy, dependents etc.

PCOM5
Court orders for imprisonment and transfer of convicts, with penal records and other particulars of prisoners.

PCOM6
Registers and indexes for *PCOM5*.

23.12   *Treasury*

T50
Documents relating to refugees, 1780-1856, including Polish refugees 1841-56, and others.

23.13   *Treasury Solicitor*

TS11
An important class of records, including papers relating to State Trials, preservation of the public peace etc., with a large number of prosecution briefs, material being used in evidence, miscellaneous letters and papers, concerning Chartist trials 1839-1848. (Located at Chancery Lane) The following are especially noteworthy:

TS11/596
Includes a small collection of notes and other items (12), including a notebook, belonging to John Richards, Hanley Chartist and confiscated on his arrest in 1842.

TS11/600-602
Includes over 300 letters confiscated from Thomas Cooper's house in Leicester after his arrest in 1842. This is the largest known collection of Chartist correspondence, being mainly letters received by Cooper during 1841-2. Many of the letters are concerned with Cooper's business as a Chartist newsagent and his successive Chartist newspapers, but they also include much general discussion of Chartist politics, as well as bills, poems and miscellaneous ephemera.

TS11/600
About 120 letters to Cooper: correspondents include P.M. Brophy, John Campbell, John Cleave, John Collins, T.S. Duncombe, G.J. Harney, William Jones, James Leach, John Markham, Jane Peddie, T.R. Smart, George White, Jeremiah Yates and a number of other Chartists, most from Leicestershire and the Midlands.
There are also copies of letters from Cooper in Stafford Gaol to William Freshney and Thomas Winters; letters from Mary Harney and Thomas Winters to Cooper; and a letter from H. Prince to John Neal, a Potteries Chartist, all Aug.-Oct. 1842.

TS11/601
Over 200 letters to Cooper: correspondents include P.M. Brophy,Thomas Clark, John Cleave, Susanna Cooper, G.J. Harney, R.G. Harney (brother), William Hill, Joshua Hobson, John Markham, P.M. McDouall, E.P. Mead, John Neal, James Sweet, Jeremiah Yates and others.

TS11/602
Includes about 12 Chartist letters, c. Aug.-Sept.1842, among them letters from Cooper to Susanna Cooper, G.J. Harney and Leicester Chartists; from Susanna Cooper to G.J. Harney; and to Cooper from Jonathan Bairstow, James Leach, John Richards and George White.

23.14 *War Office*

WO30/81
Miscellaneous Papers relating to Defence, 1776-1870, includes some 1848 material.

WO30/111
Correspondence and Papers, including bundle labelled "Chartist Riots 1848" with Duke of Wellington's disposition of troops in London.

23.15 The Public Record Office also holds a number of archives of individuals in the class *Public Record Office (Gifts and Donations)*. These include:
PRO 30/22 Lord John Russell Papers. These are not a rich source for Chartism, but include some relevant material, especially in Boxes 3^D (for 1839), 7^B and 7^C (for 1848).

24   **BRITISH LIBRARY**

24.1 *Linton Collection*
20 volumes of manuscripts, proofs, cuttings, pamphlets, magazines and placards, labelled "Prose and Verse written and published in the course of fifty years, 1836-1886", written and compiled by W.J. Linton, and presented by him to the British Museum in 1895. A rich source for the history of British and American radicalism.

24.2 *Place Collection*
The huge collection of newspaper cuttings and other printed material collected in scrapbooks by Francis Place includes a number of volumes relevant to Chartism, especially in the series "Reform 1836-47", comprising 29 volumes. There is a detailed catalogue in the British Library, but the following are especially relevant:

Set 9
Distress Riots 1842.

Set 47
Politics - Chartists 1848.

Set 48
Politics - Chartists 1849-52.

Set 55
Reform - Case of Lovett and Collins, 1839-40.

Set 56 Volume I
Newspaper cuttings and narrative of the early Chartist movement.

Set 66
The Charter. 1 Volume, January 1839-March 1840. Complete run of an early Chartist weekly newspaper.

BRITISH LIBRARY, DEPARTMENT OF MANUSCRIPTS.

24.3   *Place Papers*
These are the handwritten political narratives by Place, and other manuscript
material collected by him, which include a great deal of Chartist material,
constituting a major source.

The main volumes relating to Chartism are as follows:
(All references are prefixed by Add.MSS - Additional Manuscripts)

27,819 Historical narrative of the foundation of the (London) Working Men's
Association and its proceedings, 1836-7.
27,820 Continuation of the above, with proceedings of the Birmingham
Political Union, 1838.
27,821 Continuation of the above, concentrating chiefly on the National
Convention, to early July 1839.
27,835 Miscellaneous printed papers and manuscripts on working men's
political associations, 1799-1842: contains only a few items from the Chartist
period e.g. letter to Place from John Seal, Leicester, July 1841.
34,245 A and B: The essential source for the Chartist National Convention of
1839. Correspondence and papers, in two volumes, of the 1839 "General
Convention of the Industrial Classes" consisting of returns and lists of
delegates, reports from Chartist "missionaries" in the provinces, reports of
committees etc. The first volume includes original correspondence between
Lord John Russell and John Frost. The letters are mainly addressed to William
Lovett, Secretary of the Convention, and later to T.R. Smart, who took over
when Lovett was arrested. There is also a series of reports on Chartism in the
regions. (See D.J. Rowe's article in *Economic History Review*, 1969)

35,148-35,151 contain Place's political correspondence, 1827-50.
35,151 has letters from a number of Chartist correspondents including William
Carpenter, John Cleave, Mary Anne Cleave, John Collins, T.S. Duncombe,
William Lovett and Richard Moore.
37,773-6 consists of the minute books of the London Working Men's
Association, in the handwriting of William Lovett.
37,773 - 9 June 1836 - 30 April 1839.
(Gap, representing Lovett's time in prison)
37,774 - 12 October 1841 - 23 July 1844.
37,775 - 30 July 1844 - 4 July 1849.
37, 776 - Committee minutes, 30 March 1843 - 11 October 1847.

It is probable that the Place Papers contain further material relevant to
Chartism, not listed here.

24.4   *John Burns Papers*
46,345 - A collection of letters acquired by John Burns in 1909, including letters
to Richard Moore from T.S. Duncombe (1840, 1855) and John Frost (1867,
1873) and Francis Place (1839-41); other letters from Place, to Henry
Hetherington (1840) and William Lovett (1841); and letters to James Watson,
including letters from Thomas Attwood (1841) and Thomas Cooper (1848).

24.5   *Thomas Cooper Letters*
56,238 Seven letters from Cooper: 1 to Brogden from Leicester, Dec. 1842; 6
letters to William Freshney from Stafford Gaol, 1843-4, mostly about *The
Purgatory of Suicides*, with lengthy extracts from an early version of the poem.

24.6   *Ernest Jones' Album*
61,971 Album containing 19 sketches of landscapes, and family houses, done
from memory while Jones was in prison in 1849; five poems by Jones (1844-
9), birthday verses addressed to his wife and sons; some sketches by another
hand, two loose silhouettes, and five autograph poems by Jones' friend
Archer Gurney. A birthday present to Jones' wife.

24.7   *Papers of Sir Robert Peel*
40,181-40,617 A large and important collection of Prime Ministerial
correspondence and papers with many references to Chartism. For example,
40,434 for Peel's correspondence with Queen Victoria and Prince Albert in
1842; 40,447 for Peel's correspondence with Sir James Graham, Home
Secretary in 1842.

24.8   *Royal Literary Fund Archives*
These include files on applicants for assistance and beneficiaries of the fund;
among them are Ernest Jones (File 1360), Gerald Massey (File 1581), Thomas
Cooper (File 1717). (For the file on Ernest Jones, see T.W. Porter 'Ernest
Charles Jones and the Royal Literary Fund', *Labour History Review*, Vol.57,
No.3, Winter 1992).

24.9   *Joseph Sturge Papers*
43,845 Correspondence 1833-1858. Includes one letter from Feargus
O'Connor (1844). See also: 43,722 Richard Cobden's letters to Sturge, 1849-
59; 43,723 and 43,845 John Bright's letters to Sturge, 1842-59.

24.10   *Individual Letters*

There are also a great many letters scattered in various collections, of great
interest for the study of Chartism, which may be traced from the British
Library Index of Manuscripts under the names of individuals. Among them
are the following:

Joseph Barker
Letter to T.R. Horwood, 1845; letter to Secretary of Unitarian Association,
1850, both in 42,583.

Thomas Cooper
Letter to Richard Cobden, 1853 (43,668); letters to A.J. Mundella (44,258) and
W.E. Gladstone (44,471) both in 1881.
Benjamin Disraeli
Letter on his speech on Chartism, 1839 (37,053); notes by Gladstone on
Disraeli's *Sybil*, n.d. (44,792).

George Julian Harney
Correspondence with Lord Ripon, 1871 (43,623); letter to Mme. Laura
Lafargue, 1882 (45,345).

Isaac Ironside
Letters to Gladstone 1853-5 (44,374-5; 44,383).

Ernest Jones
Correspondence with Lord Aberdeen, 1842 (43,239); poem, "Italy and Her Masters", 1856 (43,909); letter to Jones, 1843 (52,477); letters to Jones, 1862-8 (52,484).

Charles Kingsley
Letter to J.J. Bezer, 1851 (43,798); notes by Gladstone on *Alton Locke*, n.d. (44,793)

William Lovett
Nine letters to him, 1837-43, mainly from MPs, including Bright, Cobden, Hume (47,663).

Sir Charles James Napier
Letter to Earl of Wharncliffe re unrest in Barnsley area, July 1839 (62,114M).

G.W.M. Reynolds
Letter to W. Guernsey, 1846 (43,382).

Thomas Southwood Smith
Draft memorial on behalf of Frost and other convicted Chartists, 1840 (44,919).

John Taylor
Letter by him, on his arrest, 1839. Printed. (40,427).

Henry Vincent
Letter to Cobden, 1848 (43,667).

25   GREATER LONDON RECORD OFFICE

Middlesex Sessions Records

WA/G4-6
References to Chartist prisoners in Westminster House of Correction, among minutes of visiting justices 1848-50.

WA/GP 1849/12; WA GP 1851/1
References to Ernest Jones' imprisonment.

26   CORPORATION OF LONDON RECORD OFFICE

Misc.Mss.244.5
Court of Aldermen Papers for 11 April 1848, with full details of measures taken for keeping peace in City of London on 10 April 1848.

PD75.12
Sir George Grey's letter to Lord Mayor of London, 12 April 1848 (Printed) .
See also Court of Common Council Minutes for 1848.

563B–C
Gaol Committee minute books refer to imprisonment of Chartists, 21, 28, April, 5 May 1849.

27   **UNIVERSITY OF LONDON LIBRARY (GOLDSMITHS' LIBRARY)**

ULAL43
Fragment of a letter from Richard Oastler, concerning Queen Victoria's reaction to a political meeting and Chartists (n.d.); letter from Thomas Cooper to Edward Smith re Smith's poverty, 1855.

ULAL56
Five letters from G.J. Harney to John Salkeld, bookseller, asking for books, 1888-1895.

28   **BRITISH LIBRARY OF POLITICAL AND ECONOMIC SCIENCE, LONDON SCHOOL OF ECONOMICS**

Allsop Collection: Coll.Misc.0525
Letters to Thomas Allsop from James Bronterre O'Brien (23 letters, 1836-62), Feargus O'Connor (25 letters, 1843-9) and Richard Oastler (13 letters, 1845-51).

Frederic Harrison Mss
Letter from Ernest Jones to Robert Applegarth, 1868.

Newspaper Cuttings: Coll.Misc.0208
Collection of press cuttings reporting the speeches and trials of Chartists in 1848.

Portrait Collection, 1800-1900: Coll.Misc.0717
Includes photographic, engraved or printed portraits of G.J. Holyoake, Ernest Jones, J. Baxter Langley, J.J. Merriman.

Solly Collection
Papers of Henry Solly. These papers concerning the life and work of an interesting middle-class Chartist include, in Vol.VII, Politics, an invitation card to a Chartist soirée and ball in Yeovil, March 1842.

Webb Trade Union Collection
There is some relevant material in the mass of information assembled by the Webbs about the history of particular trades in particular localities.

29   **BISHOPSGATE INSTITUTE**

Thomas Cooper Letters
3 letters from Thomas Winters to Susanna Cooper (1842); 69 letters from Thomas Cooper, 2 letters from Susanna Cooper to Thomas Tatlow (1848-60); 14 letters from George Jacob Holyoake, 2 letters from Austin Holyoake to Thomas Cooper (1856-74); 429 letters from Thomas Cooper to Thomas Chambers (1857-68).

Holyoake Collection
Mainly books and published material, but includes ms. diaries of G.J.
Holyoake, 1836-1900, and other ms. items, including some miscellaneous
correspondence, and a ms. "Record" giving a summary of over 5,000 letters
written by Holyoake, 1845-8. See also above entry for letters to Thomas
Cooper.

Howell Collection
The papers of George Howell include: Howell's unpublished ms.
autobiography, with a section on Chartism, and the Chartists he knew; ms.
"History of the Working Men's Association, 1836-50" (published 1970); and
ms. biography of Ernest Jones (serialized in the *Newcastle Weekly Chronicle*,
January-August 1898). There is also a collection of miscellanea concerning
Ernest Jones, including some ms. items, and, in Howell's correspondence,
some letters from Ernest Jones (1866-7). The materials, assembled for
Howell's life of Jones, include complete transcripts of Jones' diaries, 1839-47.

National Secular Society - Charles Bradlaugh Collection
Includes 2 letters from Eliza Sharples Carlile to Thomas Cooper, July 1849 and
April 1850; 2 letters from Charles Bradlaugh to Thomas Cooper, October
1855. (These letters are not listed in Edward Royle, *The Bradlaugh Papers: A
Descriptive Index*, 1975).

30   **CHURCH OF ENGLAND RECORD CENTRE, SOUTH BERMONDSEY**

National Society for Promoting Religious Education
Correspondence with local Anglican clergy, in 15,000 files relating to individual
schools. Some of these files include letters referring to Chartism, but these
are not easy to locate.

31   **LIBRARY OF THE RELIGIOUS SOCIETY OF FRIENDS, FRIENDS' HOUSE,
EUSTON ROAD**

Clare Taylor Mss. (Temp. Mss. 191)
This mainly anti-slavery collection of letters has occasional references to
Chartists and Chartist meetings. The letters of Elizabeth Pease to Wendell and
Anne Phillips, especially, include interesting references to Joseph Sturge and
the Complete Suffrage Union, women and Chartism. Uncatalogued collection;
access by permission only.

ENGLAND, OUTSIDE LONDON

32   **BARNSLEY PUBLIC LIBRARY**

John Hugh Burland, Annals of Barnsley
Ms. record of local history by a Barnsley Chartist: 2 vols. covering period 1839-
54, including newspaper cuttings of articles in local press, late 1870s to early
1880s.

Joseph Wilkinson Collection
Volume of mss. and newspaper cuttings relating to local history and Barnsley
Chartism by another Barnsley Chartist. Also a volume of Barnsley Obituaries,
including mss. and press notices of deaths of local figures, including Chartists.

33   BEDFORD COUNTY RECORD OFFICE

Earl de Grey, "The Memoirs of My Own Life"
CRT 190/45/2 Typed transcript of the memoirs of Thomas, Earl de Grey,
Conservative politician, containing account of his role as leader of special
constables for the parish of St. James', Piccadilly, in 1848. (Original in private
possession of the Right Honourable Lord Lucas).

34   BIRMINGHAM PUBLIC LIBRARY

Lovett Collection
Archives Ms. 753. 2 volumes of cuttings, leaflets, posters, ms. letters, mainly
1836-43, collected by William Lovett. Largely relating to the 1839 Convention,
but also useful for the London Working Men's Association, National
Association, Complete Suffrage Union; and People's League, 1848-9.

Complete Suffrage Union
662611. Letters from Joseph Sturge to Francis Place.
129666 and 129668. 2 vols. minute-books of the Complete Suffrage Union, and
its Committee for General Purposes, 1842-6.
1675/2/9. Ms. draft speech by Rev. Thomas Swan advising electors of
Nottingham to vote for Joseph Sturge, 1842.

Birmingham Borough Council Minute Book, 1839-40
Includes ms. copy of report of Committee appointed to investigate causes of
1839 Bull Ring riots, with evidence of witnesses, 40pp., 1840. See also
Birmingham Police Order Books, 1839-1856.

Robert Martineau Correspondence
Archives Ms.1412 (Accession 98/66). Letters from Martineau's term of office
as Mayor of Birmingham 1846-7: includes petition with 80 signatures calling on
mayor to convene town meeting to petition for Charter, and copy of mayor's
letter of refusal, both November 1846.

35   BOLTON PUBLIC LIBRARY

Robert Heywood Papers
Heywood was Mayor of Bolton in 1839-40. His papers for 1839 include his
journal of events during the Bolton Chartist riots, August 1839, *(ZHE 35/58)*,
his statement concerning riots at Little Bolton Town Hall *(ZHE 35/61)*, two
anonymous letters to him about Chartism in Bolton *(ZHE 35/43 and 57)*, and a
few other relevant items. His papers for 1842 include copies of letters from
Heywood about the suppression of rioting in Bolton in August *(ZHE 38/37)*
and commenting on the refusal of Henry Ashworth to assist due to religious
scruples *(ZHE 38/39)*, and a letter from Ashworth *(ZHE 38/38)*. There are also
two letters from Heywood's sister in Southport, referring to the disturbances
(ZHE 38/60 and 62).

John Warden
A single letter from John Warden, Bolton Chartist, to David Urquhart, Southampton, seeking help in finding employment, February 1841 *(ZZ/576)*.

36   **BRADFORD DISTRICT ARCHIVES**

Bradford Reform Societies
Records 1835-1867, including Great Horton Chartist Association membership and contributions book, 1840-66; Bradford Reform Society minute book, 1835-41; Bradford Operative Conservative Society minute book, 1837-9; Bradford United Reform Club minute book, 1841-5, order book 1841-48 and members' proposition book, 1841-50 *(DB4 C1)*.

37   **BURNLEY PUBLIC LIBRARY**

Radicalism and Chartism in Colne
Letter from Colonel J. Wemyss to Home Office re despatch of troops to Colne, July 1837; letters from clerk to Colne magistrates, and others to Earl of Derby and Lord John Russell, re working-class unrest and Chartism in Colne, April-August 1838; magistrates' examinations of witnesses against Colne Chartists, April 1839; extract from PRO *PL27/11* re Chartist meeting at Pendle Hill, June 1842. (All these are transcripts of papers held elsewhere.)

38   **CAMBRIDGE UNIVERSITY LIBRARY**

Sir James Graham Papers
The papers cover the years c.1820-c.1860. Graham was Home Secretary 1841-6; especially relevant are Bundles 52A and 52B (August 1842), 53A (September 1842), 54A, (October 1842). On microfilm. Original in private hands.

Madden Ballads Collection
Vol.23 contains political and miscellaneous pieces Nos. 403-553, printed by Thomas Willey, Cheltenham Chartist.

39   **CASTLE HOWARD, YORKSHIRE**

Carlisle Papers
Papers of George William Frederick Howard, 7th Earl of Carlisle, Liberal politician, and, as Lord Morpeth, MP for the West Riding of Yorkshire 1832-41, 1846-8. Records likely to include relevant material are:
J 19/1 Letters - 111 volumes, with alphabetical index.
J19/8 Diary - 40 volumes, 1843-64.
J 19/14 Papers relating to Parliamentary Reform.

40   **CHELTENHAM PUBLIC LIBRARY**

C.A. Probert Papers
Includes brief mss. notes on John Goding, Cheltenham Chartist, by Probert, a nineteenth century local historian.

41   **CHESTER : CHESHIRE RECORD OFFICE**

Joseph Shawcross
Letter from Shawcross, Chartist awaiting trial at Chester, to his daughter, and
her reply, both 1849.

42   **COLCHESTER BRANCH, ESSEX RECORD OFFICE**

Autobiography of John Castle
Ms. autobiography of Colchester silk-weaver who was also a Chartist. Covers
years 1819-1871, written c.1871, but no mention of Chartism, apart from
references to several individuals who were active in the Colchester Co-
operative Society, founded 1861 *(D/DDU 490)*.

43   **COLCHESTER MUSEUM**

Diary of William Wire
Wire was a Colchester watchmaker who had been a Chartist in 1838-9, but was
no longer actively involved in the movement in the period covered by the
diary, April 1842-March 1857. (See A.F.J. Brown, *Essex People*, 1972, for
extracts from Castle and Wire, and the same author's *Chartism in Essex and
Suffolk*, 1982, for background information).

44   **COVENTRY: UNIVERSITY OF WARWICK LIBRARY, MODERN RECORDS
CENTRE**

Fortnightly Return, Operative Stonemasons' Friendly Society
This fortnightly newsletter (1834-1910) with detailed reports from branches,
includes useful references to Chartist activities *(MSS. 78/05/4/1/1-98)*.

45   **DERBY LOCAL STUDIES LIBRARY**

The Chartist Movement in Derby, 1841
Bound volume of ms. papers, formerly in possession of Town Clerk of Derby.
Includes requisition for use of Town Hall, March 1841, signed by 54 Derby
Chartists; Mayor of Derby's letter to Home Office (copy) and reply, May-June
1841; detailed reports by police and informers on Chartist sermons and
speeches by Jonathan Bairstow (March-August 1841), Dean Taylor (August
1841), P.M. McDouall (Sept. 1841) and other visiting Chartist speakers; one
report on meeting in pub room re Chartist election strategy, June 1841.
About 25 items. *(Ms. BA909/16186)*.

46   **DUDLEY LIBRARIES: ARCHIVES AND LOCAL HISTORY SERVICE, COSELEY**

Samuel Cook Papers
The letters and family papers of the leading Dudley Chartist include:
Z44: One bundle of letters, bills, papers, rough drafts of letters by Cook,
1822-1860, including material on his trials and imprisonments in 1840 and 1842
Z38: Letter from Cook re mining accidents, with cuttings, to Home Secretary,
1846

Z5: Reply to above, from Home Office

Z111: Copy of Cook's letter to Garibaldi, with Garibaldi's reply, and translation, July and September 1861
Acc.8748: Further material on Cook family, 1810-1891, includes: letter from Cook to his father (1810); letter from Thomas J. Wooler, draft petition and two letters from John Cartwright (1823); 4 draft letters from Cook to Joseph Hume (1824, 1835) and 5 letters and notes from Hume to Cook (1834-5); Queen v. Samuel Cook, Dudley, August 20 1842: deposition of C.C. Brettell, and copy of magistrates' judgment; draft letter from Cook to G.J. Holyoake (1856) and 5 business letters from Holyoake to Cook (1852, 1859, 1861); will of Samuel Quartus Cook, Cook's son, also a Chartist (1891).

47   **DURHAM RECORD OFFICE**

Londonderry Papers
Letters from Sir James Graham to 3rd Marquess of Londonderry, including correspondence about precautions against the Chartists, 1843 *(D/Lo/C80)*. Letters from 3rd Marquess of Londonderry to Lord Adolphus Vane-Tempest, including correspondence about Chartists, 1847-8 *(D/Lo/C 224)*.

48   **DURHAM UNIVERSITY LIBRARY, PALACE GREEN**

Papers of 3rd Earl Grey
3 letters from John Grey, Dilston, to Lord Howick, re Chartist revolutionary plans, the arrest of Dr. John Taylor, and the lack of interest in Chartism by the lead miners of Alston Moor, November-December 1839, with a copy of an intercepted letter to Dr. Taylor from "ML" *(102/4)*.
2 letters from George Binns, Sunderland Chartist, from Durham County Court, May-June 1842, asking Lord Howick for assistance in emigrating to New Zealand *(78/6)*.

49   **GATESHEAD PUBLIC LIBRARY**

Brockie Collection
"Chartism" by William Brockie. Ms. narrative account of events in Newcastle upon Tyne and Gateshead, March to August 1839 written by a local journalist, from an anti-Chartist standpoint. From internal evidence completed after 1842, and not an eyewitness account as Brockie was living in Scotland in 1839 *(Brockie Collection 76/18)*.

50   **GLOUCESTER RECORD OFFICE**

Sotheron-Estcourt Papers
Letters referring to Chartism, 1839 *(D 1571/F 209)*. Letters and papers concerning Chartist riot at Devizes, Wiltshire, 1839 *(D 1571/X 118)*
Chartism in Dursley
Papers concerning Chartist riots, 1840 *(P 124/CW 4/4)*
Chartist Land Company
Snigs End Estate, 1857 *(P 101a MI 2/1-3)*. Sale particulars and plans of Snigs End and Lowbands Estates, 1857-8 (Photocopies 747-8).

51   **HALIFAX: CALDERDALE DISTRICT ARCHIVES**

Chartist Papers
Correspondence and papers re military measures against Chartists, including informers' reports to Halifax magistrates, December 1838-September 1840 *(HAS 1388)*. (These documents are transcribed in G.R. Dalby, 'The Chartist Movement in Halifax and District', *Transactions of the Halifax Antiquarian Society*, 1956, pp.93-111).

52   **HERTFORD RECORD OFFICE**

Chartist Land Company
Plan of settlement at Heronsgate *(Off.Acc.545)*.

53   **HUDDERSFIELD: KIRKLEES DISTRICT ARCHIVES**

Joshua Hobson
Letter from William Cobbett to Hobson, in Wakefield Prison, 1833 *(KC 312/3/1)*.

54   **HULL UNIVERSITY: BRYNMOR JONES LIBRARY**

Papers of General Thomas Marten
1 bundle of letters and papers re Chartist riots at Sheffield, 1839-40, including military orders, May 1839; 10 letters to General Marten, including 6 from General Napier and 1 from Marquis of Normanby, July 1839-April 1840; resolutions of thanks from Sheffield Improvement Commissioners, February 1840 *(DDCV/216/94-98)*. 1 bundle Ashton-under-Lyne and Oldham papers 1842, including 8 letters re Chartist riots, and General Marten's order of thanks to his troops, August-December 1842 *(DDCV/216/99-101)*.

Ernest Jones: Family Papers
Microfilm copy of papers formerly in the possession of the late Thorold Jones, including letters from Major Charles Jones and Mrs. Charlotte M. Jones, parents, 1837-42; letter from Ernest Jones to Jane Jones, wife, 1847; from Jane Jones to Ernest Jones, 1851-4, and other undated family letters; letters from Ernest Jones to his children, 1860s; draft letter, Ernest Jones to M.H. Field, re Reform Bill, May 1867; notes for an article on the Land Question, n.d.; and other miscellaneous items.

Dictionary of Labour Biography Collection
Files on each of the individuals listed in the published volumes of the *DLB* are currently being transferred to the University Library. These files, which contain some material not published in the *DLB*, are not yet (1994) available for consultation, but will become so during the next few years. For further details, contact the Archivist.

55   **IPSWICH: SUFFOLK RECORD OFFICE**

John Goodwyn Barmby: Letters to John Glyde
1 letter with article on marriage by Barmby, in *Educational Circular and Communist Apostle*, November 1841 *(S8 Bar)*.
1 letter re recruitment to the Communist Covenant, n.d., c.1845-7 *(HD 494/33)*

The two letters illustrate the Utopian Socialist period of Barmby, who was an active Chartist only until 1841.

56   LEEDS DISTRICT ARCHIVES

Harewood Papers
Correspondence and papers of Earl Harewood, Lord Lieutenant of Yorkshire, 1819-1856: includes 113 items relating to disturbances, mostly in Bradford and Huddersfield, 1839.

Baines Papers
Letter from J. Bower, Perth, to Edward Baines senior, about Chartism, enclosing silk print of article in *Leeds Mercury*, August 1839 *(Baines 52/5)*.

57   LEEDS UNIVERSITY LIBRARY

A)   BROTHERTON LIBRARY

Marshall Letters
6 letters by James Garth Marshall, Leeds linen manufacturer, to Charles and Thomas Spring-Rice, and to Sir Henry Taylor, about Chartist activity in Leeds, August-September 1842. *(MS. 739)*.

B)   BROTHERTON COLLECTION

Ebenezer Elliott
Small collection of letters and other material by and relating to Elliott, including 6 letters to Richard Otley, Sheffield Chartist, 1832-48.

John Francis Bray
Collection of papers relating to Bray, who was a radical reformer until c.1837, later a socialist. Largely family letters and written before Bray's departure for USA in 1842.

58   LEICESTER RECORD OFFICE

William Jones Papers
The papers of a Leicester Chartist poet, 1843-55, include 8 letters from Thomas Cooper to Jones (1844-53), largely about their writings; two papers probably by Jones, critical of O'Connor's Land Plan; and poems and personal papers of Jones, some relating to Chartist activities *(DE 2964)*.

"Battle of Mowmacre Hill"
Single letter from a Mr. Heathcote to M. Watfield, mentioning fight between Chartists, and police and yeomanry who dispersed meeting, August 1842 *(DE 2180/1)*.

59   LINCOLN: LINCOLNSHIRE ARCHIVES

Thomas Cooper Papers
Miscellaneous collection from the Thomas Cooper (Baptist) Memorial Church, Lincoln, including papers re Cooper's trial and imprisonment at Stafford, 1842 (20 items); ms. sermons and lectures by Cooper, c.1854-8 (14 items); 6 letters

from Cooper and Susanna Cooper (wife) to Mr. Whitwell, 1872-8; 70 letters
between Thomas and Susanna Cooper, Oct.-Dec. 1879; correspondence
between Robert J. Conklin, Cooper's first biographer and Cecil Radford of
Lincoln, 1929-35, with typewritten copies of some of Cooper's poems, and of
a letter and notebook written in gaol. *(2 Baptist)*
5 letters from Cooper to Rev. Arthur O'Neill, 1875, 1887 (mentioning death of
Joseph Linney), 1890. This small group of letters illustrates links continuing
into old age between the former Chartist prisoners in Stafford Gaol, 1842.
(Misc. Don. 282).

60   **LINCOLN PUBLIC LIBRARY**

Thomas Cooper
Ms. of Cooper's long prison poem "The Purgatory of Suicides"; also bound
"Ms. Notebook" with Cooper's proposed literary plans, written in prison.

61   **MANCHESTER PUBLIC LIBRARY, LOCAL STUDIES UNIT**

Anti-Corn Law League Letter Books
These include valuable reports of clashes with Chartists, e.g. letter books 4 and
5 for the experiences of Anti-Corn Law League Lecturer Walter Griffiths in
Chartist strongholds in Wales.

Ernest Jones Mss.
Diary 1839-47, 2 vols.; Legal Memorandum Book, 1860-62; Notes on law cases,
1860-66, 2 vols.; Ms. poems on the French Revolution; ms. poems and notes;
scrapbook of cuttings on Jones; broadsheets and songs re Manchester
election, 1868; cuttings re death and funeral of Jones. (Together with the
library's printed holdings, this collection is the most representative of the
several archives containing material on the life and writings of Jones.)

Frederick Leary
Ms. History of the Manchester Periodical Press.

R.J. Richardson
"Richardson's Works": scrapbook of cuttings, etc., relating to Reginald John
Richardson, Manchester and Salford Chartist, c.1841-2.

Smith Mss.
Papers of J.B. Smith, Anti-Corn Law League Chairman, 5 vols., include some
discussion of Chartist interruptions of League meetings.

Wilson Mss.
Papers of George Wilson, Anti-Corn Law League President, also including
discussion of Chartist interruptions of League meetings.

62   **MANCHESTER: CHETHAM'S LIBRARY**

Ernest Jones Mss.
Prison letters, 1848-50, mainly from his wife, Jane Jones; letters written to
Jones in answer to an appeal for funds, 1859; miscellaneous letters and bills.

63   **MANCHESTER: CO-OPERATIVE UNION LIBRARY**

G.J. Holyoake Collection
4,400 letters and other documents, 1835-1917, of which over 1,000 are from
the years 1838-58. The collection holds many letters from Chartist or ex-
Chartist correspondents to Holyoake, though a large number of these are not
on Chartist topics, and a number of Holyoake's own letters.
These include: 3 letters from W.E. Adams (1898); 1 letter from John Arnott
(1850); 7 letters from Joseph Barker (1848-54); 4 letters from Goodwyn
Barmby (1845-50); 1 anonymous letter from "A Chartist" to Ernest Jones
(1858); 1 manifesto from John Collins, "The Foreign Policy Agitation versus
the People's Charter", (1840?); 54 letters from Thomas Cooper, and 12 letters
from Holyoake to Cooper (1847-92); 78 letters from Joseph Cowen, and 1
letter from Holyoake to Cowen (1851-91); 2 letters from Thomas Duncombe
and 1 from Holyoake to Duncombe (1844, 1852); 1 letter from Ebenezer
Elliott (1842); 18 letters from G.J. Harney (1852-61, 1891); 1 letter from
Richard Hart (1848); 3 letters from Henry Hetherington (1845); 1 letter,
among others, from Austin Holyoake, on O'Connor's funeral (1855); 6 items
of G.J. Holyoake's notes on splits in the Chartist Executive(1850-1); 3 letters
from Joseph Hume (1844); 51 letters from Thornton Hunt, and 3 from
Holyoake to Hunt, (1849-72); 9 letters from Isaac Ironside, 4 to him from
various correspondents (1842-68); 2 letters from Ebenezer Jones (1859); 5
letters from Ernest Jones (1851-60); 4 letters from J. Baxter Langley (1857-77);
10 letters from Robert Le Blond, 1 from Holyoake to Le Blond (1849-61); 5
letters from Eliza Lynne Linton (1873-6); 19 letters from W.J. Linton, 2 letters
from Holyoake to Linton (1846-75); 2 letters from William Lovett (1844, 1846);
1 letter from John McAdam (1860); 2 letters from Gerald Massey (1852, 1903);
1 letter from J.J. Merriman, 1 letter from Holyoake to Merriman (1855, 1868);
2 letters from Richard Moore (1857, 1874); National Charter Association
Constitution and Rules and voting figures for Chartist Executive, printed (1851);
1 letter from William Nixon (1852); 1 letter from James Bronterre O'Brien to
James Watson (1846); 1 letter from Francis Place to M.Q. Ryall (1842), 3 letters
from Place to Holyoake (1848-50); 2 letters from G.W.M. Reynolds (1848,
1850); 1 letter from William Shirrefs (1849); 11 letters from James Watson, 7
to Watson by various correspondents, including Willie Thom (1846-72); 4
letters from George White, of which 3 to Holyoake (1842, 1849) and 1 to Isaac
Ironside (1868).

Robert Owen Collection
Nearly 3,000 letters to Robert Owen, 1821-1858, of which about 2,000 are from
the years 1838-58. They include: 1 letter, among others from Thomas Allsop,
soliciting support for Ernest Jones (1854); 1 letter from Joseph Barker (1854);
1 letter from Henry Hetherington (1847); 2 letters from Joshua Hobson (1837,
1840); 18 letters from G.J. Holyoake (1847-58); 6 letters from Isaac Ironside
(1839-47); 6 letters from Ernest Jones (1851-8); 1 letter from William Lovett
(1836); 3 letters from Richard Oastler (1833, 1836); 1 letter from James
Bronterre O'Brien (1832); 5 letters from Lawrence Pitkethly (1833-8); 3 letters
from Francis Place (1831-8); 1 letter from Edmund Stallwood (1850); 1 letter
from Henry Vincent (1854); 3 letters from Benjamin Warden (1831, 1837); 3
letters from James Watson (1830, 1850, 1854).

64   MANCHESTER: JOHN RYLANDS UNIVERSITY LIBRARY

John Fielden Papers
Political and family correspondence and papers, 1831-49.

Mark Hovell Collection
Papers of Mark Hovell, used in writing his book, *The Chartist Movement*, 1918.
Unlisted.

65   MANCHESTER: NATIONAL MUSEUM OF LABOUR HISTORY

John Minikin/Henry Vincent Papers
51 letters from Vincent to Minikin, 1837-42; 15 items including draft or copy
letters, Minikin to Vincent, and to newspapers; 5 drafts of trial speeches by
Vincent; 4 letters from Lucy Vincent (wife) to Vincent, 1841-2; 8
miscellaneous letters, including 1 from Francis Place to Vincent, 1839; 5
handbills, and posters c.1850-60; 50 issues of the *Western Vindicator* and
National Vindicator, 1839-42; 42 miscellaneous cuttings, 1834-51.

Bronterre O'Brien Mss.
9 letters, O'Brien to "Mathews", 1856-8; 2 printed cards of Eclectic Institute
and National Reform League; ms. draft of National Reform League appeal on
behalf of O'Brien; accounts of the O'Brien Fund, 1865; some of O'Brien's
printed works; "Chartist Bible" by John Finch, with dedication from Finch to
O'Brien, 1853. (This collection was not used by Alfred Plummer for his
biography, *Bronterre*, 1971).

John Frost
1 letter from John Frost, Stapleton, December 1873, promising to write his
memoirs and outlining their intended scope, to an unnamed recipient,
probably W.E. Adams (Cf. *Memoirs of A Social Atom*, Vol.1, pp.201-202).

Frederick Pickles Papers
Anti-Socialist letter from Thomas Cooper to Pickles, 1885 (facsimile in *Among
Our Souvenirs,* folder of documents edited by Asa Briggs for the Labour Party,
1975).

Feargus O'Connor Medal
Commemorating O'Connor's release from York prison, 1841.

Special Constable's Truncheon
Used at Chartist rallies in London.

66   MATLOCK: DERBYSHIRE RECORD OFFICE

Catton Collection
Includes papers of Sir Robert Wilmot-Horton (1784-1841), with some
references to Chartism.

67   NEWCASTLE UPON TYNE: NORTHUMBERLAND RECORD OFFICE

Various Chartist References include:

Letters re Chartist agitation in Northumberland and Carlisle, 1838
(ZM1/577/12)
Papers re miners' strike referring to Chartists, 1839 *(ZR1 27/12)*
Copy of letter from Lord Normanby to Duke of Northumberland re Chartist
agitation, 1839 *(ZSW 620)*
Letter re Bothal parishioners' loyal address opposing attempts to disturb
public peace, May 1848 *(EP.164/43)*.

68   **NEWCASTLE UPON TYNE: TYNE AND WEAR ARCHIVES**

John Brown Papers
Clerk to Newcastle Magistrates. Many letters re Chartist activity in Newcastle
1839-40, especially in August 1839. Also references to Chartist activity in
Carlisle.

Joseph Cowen Papers
Over 4,000 letters, notes, pamphlets and cuttings 1833-1937. Includes circulars
of Peoples' International League, 1847; correspondence and minute books of
Newcastle Foreign Affairs Committee, 1855-6; correspondence of Northern
Reform Union, 1858-62; and Joseph Cowen's personal correspondence.
Letters to Cowen in 1858 include 1 from J. Baxter Langley *(C102)*, 1 from
Ernest Jones *(C197)*, 1 from Joseph Sturge *(C211)*, 1 from Joseph Hedley
(C243), 1 from Frank Garrett *(C282)*. The major part of this large collection
relates to the post-Chartist years, but nevertheless there is much to interest
historians of Chartism, e.g. Cowen's correspondence with Samuel Kydd (1852,
1860).

Hodgeson Family Papers
Includes reports sent to the Mayor of Newcastle of a Chartist meeting, in April
1842 *(13/13/35-8)*.

W.J. Linton Letters
118 letters from Linton to W.E. Adams, 1855-97 (Microfilm. Original in
Houghton Library, Harvard, USA).

69   **NORTHALLERTON: NORTH YORKSHIRE RECORD OFFICE**

Chartist Prisoners
Correspondence re Chartist prisoners in Northallerton Gaol, 1840, including
intercepted letter from Lawrence Pitkethly to Duffy *(QAG, M/C 2388/782-
817)*.

70   **NORTHAMPTON PUBLIC LIBRARY**

Gilbert Flesher of Towcester, Letters
A few references, including letter to J. Nichols, mentioning letter to Sir James
Graham re danger of Queen travelling through Northampton because of
Chartist activity, November 1838 *(2118-LXXXI)*; letter to W. Flesher,
mentioning coach journey with a Chartist, June 1841 *(2.910)*.

71   **NORTHAMPTON RECORD OFFICE**

Gotch Collection
Collection of papers re local politics in Kettering. Includes exchange of letters
between R. Vernon Smith and J.C. Gotch re Chartist election strategy in
Northampton, June 1841 *(639)*, and possibly other relevant but not indexed
material.

72   **NORWICH: NORFOLK RECORD OFFICE**

D.H. Lee Warner
Letter from Walsingham Abbey, mentioning Chartist activity in Norwich at
Protestant Association meeting, October 1841 *(BUL 718, 615x1)*.

73   **NOTTINGHAM ARCHIVES**

Clerk of the Peace Records
About 20 items: circulars, magistrates' letters etc., re Chartist disturbances in
Mansfield, 1839 *(QA/CP5/4/739-762)*.

John Walter Papers
Nottingham Parliamentary elections, 1841-2 (Microfilm *Z17*. Original in
Berkshire Record Office, Reading, q.v. below).

Joseph Sturge
Statement of election expenses, 1842 *(NC/Q325/46)*.

Letters on Chartism in 1842
1 letter re Yeomanry in Mansfield, Chartists and Anti-Corn Law League
(M19,797). 1 letter re Anti-Corn Law League, and O'Connor's address to
Chartist meeting in Birmingham *(M19,801)*.

74   **OLDHAM LOCAL STUDIES LIBRARY**

Edwin Butterworth Collection
Registers of Oldham News, 1829-43. A mass of ms. material, including a day-
by-day account of life and politics in Oldham, by a local journalist who used
this material as a basis for his reports in the Manchester press. (Ref. D-BUT).

75   **OXFORD: BODLEIAN LIBRARY**

Clarendon Collection
Papers of George William Frederick Villiers, 4th Earl of Clarendon, Liberal
politician and minister 1839-41, 1846-58, and later. An important source for
1848, when Clarendon was Viceroy of Ireland. Includes Out-Letter Books with
copies of all Clarendon's letters; correspondence with Sir George Grey (Box
12), and correspondence with Lord John Russell (Box 43) are particularly useful
for 1848. See also correspondence with Lord Normanby (Box 20), Sir Robert
Peel (Box 42), Duke of Wellington (Box 45), and scattered material on
informers and agents (including Boxes 22 and 53). (The collection has been
used extensively by John Saville, *1848: The British State and the Chartist
Movement*, Cambridge, 1987, and may also throw light on other periods of
Chartist activity.)

Disraeli Papers
Very large collection. Includes, in General Correspondence, 12 letters from
David Urquhart (1839-48), 5 letters from T.S. Duncombe (1839-59), 10 letters
from Thomas Cooper (1845-6, 1863), 16 reviews of Disraeli's novel *Sybil*
(1845), 31 letters relating to *Sybil.*

Napier Papers
Correspondence and other family papers, including those of General Sir
Charles James Napier, and Sir William Napier.

Thornton Hunt
A small collection of letters to Hunt 1851-1871 (48 sheets)

76   **OXFORD: BALLIOL COLLEGE LIBRARY**

David Urquhart Papers
Box 8, Chartism includes: 1839-40, ms. letters, reports from anonymous
Urquhart missionary trying to convert Chartists into Urquhartites, in
Birmingham, Manchester, the Potteries, Sept 1839-Sept. 1840, (1E1-2);
Chartism 1853-9, further correspondence, including 7 letters from William
Peplow, Stafford Chartist, August-November 1853 (1E3). About 100 items in
all.

77   **OXFORD: NUFFIELD COLLEGE LIBRARY**

Ernest Jones
Small collection including Jones Memorial Committee leaflets 1891-2, cuttings,
and ms. letters from Atherley Jones, Ella Twynam, A.B. Wakefield about
Ernest Jones, c.1921-31. Unpublished ms. typescript biography of Ernest
Jones by Ella Twynam, c.1930. (Cole Special collection CD.37).

Prints
Fine contemporary prints of John Frost, Richard Oastler, Joseph Rayner
Stephens.

78   **OXFORD: OXFORDSHIRE ARCHIVES**

Charterville
Charterville, Minster Lovell: collection of deeds and rent charges re plots in
Charterville allotments, 1857-1956. (Welch *XXIX/1-2, XXX/1-8).*

79   **PRESTON: LANCASHIRE RECORD OFFICE**

Egerton Papers
Correspondence between Lord Francis Egerton of Worsley and James Loch
MP re Chartism, 1838-9 (DP 378).

1842 Riots in Preston
Material in Depositions *(QJD1/145-153)* and in Earl of Derby Records (DDK
1686).

80   **READING: BERKSHIRE RECORD OFFICE**

John Walter II Papers
Papers relating to the Nottingham elections of 1841-2, and associated
correspondence and papers 1841-7. Includes letter from Richard Oastler,
1841 (in *02/2*), account of "riot" led by Feargus O'Connor (in 02/5, *Bundle B*)
and copies of depositions alleging riotous assemblies organized by O'Connor
and other Chartists on behalf of Joseph Sturge in 1842 by-election *(02/6)*,
letter from National Charter Association (in *02/17*), and much other interesting
information relating to John Walter and the elections. *(D/Ecb 02/1-19)*.

81   **ROCHDALE PUBLIC LIBRARY**

Petition
Ms. petition to Chief Constable of Rochdale, asking him to call a public
meeting on February 10 to call upon the Queen to pardon Frost, Williams and
Jones, now in Monmouth Jail. Signed by 26 householders, including leading
local radicals. (n.d., January 1840).

82   **ROTHERHAM PUBLIC LIBRARY**

Ebenezer Elliott
Small collection of ms. poems, letters and business records.

83   **SALFORD: WORKING CLASS MOVEMENT LIBRARY**

Chartism: Miscellaneous Items
Paper with autographs of 22 delegates to the National Convention, 1839, listing
places represented, including Feargus O'Connor, William Lovett, John Frost,
George Julian Harney, Henry Hetherington and 17 others.
Section of a petition, on several parchment sheets, with up to 1,000 names,
without preamble or addresses, but probably from the North-West, and
possibly part of one of the Chartist petitions.

84   **SHEFFIELD ARCHIVES**

Samuel Holberry Letters
15 letters to Holberry while a prisoner in York Castle, September 1841-May
1842 *(HS 1-15)*.
3 letters to Holberry while a prisoner in York Castle; 1 letter from W.Wells,
February 1842; 2 letters from Mary Holberry, his wife, June 1842.
Photocopies of originals held in private hands. *(Ph.C. 494/1-3)*.

Miscellaneous Documents
Two letters from Michael Ellison, Duke of Norfolk's Sheffield agent, to the
Duke, mentioning Chartist meetings in Sheffield, July-August 1839 *(ACM
S478/17)*.
Letter from John Gibson, Liverpool, to Michael Ellison junior, inquiring re
Chartist activity in Sheffield, August 1839 *(ACM X14)*.
Address, signed by Thomas Briggs, from Sheffield Council of Chartists, to T.S.
Duncombe MP, re Sheffield trades and rejection of Master and Servant Bill,
July 1844 *(MD 6519)*.

Printed sheet of correspondence between Rev. Thomas Kerns and Chartists of Sheffield, re Sunday meetings: 3 letters, April-May 1848 *(MD 1102/4)*.

Letter from Wilson Overend to Earl Fitzwilliam, mentioning death of Briggs in Sheffield Workhouse Lunatic Asylum, June 1848 *(WWM G83/440)*.

Cutting: letter from *Sheffield Daily Telegraph* re fate of those involved in 1840 rising (1872?) (JC 1312 p.80).

85   **SHEFFIELD UNIVERSITY LIBRARY**

A.J. Mundella Papers
Letters, Thomas Cooper to Mundella: 3 letters re Tyneside engineers' strike, 1871; 8 letters, 1880-6, commenting on Liberal politics.

86   **SHREWSBURY: SHROPSHIRE RECORD OFFICE**

Powis Papers
Letters re Chartist riots in Montgomeryshire, 1838-42 *(SRO. 631/3/1312179-191)*. Letter from Lord Hill mentioning Chartism in Birmingham, n.d. *(SRO 1913/28)*. Letter to Lord Powis re national situation, 1848 *(SRO 2183/13)*.

87   **SOUTHAMPTON: UNIVERSITY LIBRARY**

Duke of Wellington Papers
Material on Birmingham Bull Ring riots, 1839; plan and illustration of Westgate Hotel, Newport *(WP 2/64)*.

Material on strikes and riots in North of England, 1842 *(WP 2/90)*.

Material on disturbances in manufacturing districts, Birmingham and the Potteries *(WP 2/91)*. Lord Lieutenancy of Hampshire; correspondence between Wellington and Lord Normanby with enclosures from Colonel Pringle Taylor, including copies of two Birmingham Chartist letters, report of interview re Chartist activity in Liverpool, and reports of a series of interviews between David Urquhart and some Chartists, December 1839 *(WP 4/1/10/65-6)*.

88   **STAFFORD: COUNTY RECORD OFFICE**

Talbot Letter-Book
Letter-book of Lord Lieutenant, Lord Talbot, 1822-1842: not a continuous record, but includes 4 letters from Talbot to Lord John Russell, September 1838; over 30 letters on Chartism and its repercussions in North and South Staffordshire, January-May, August-November 1842. *(D649/10)*.

Alcock Letter-Book
Letter-Book of Samuel Alcock, manufacturer and Chief Constable of Burslem, c. 1835-43. Includes miscellaneous notes and letters relevant to the Potteries riots of 1842, especially 2 letters to Alcock from his former employee, William Ellis, September 1842. Microfilm; original in Foxwell Collection, Kress Room, Baker Library, Harvard University Business School *(MF.49)*.

Staffordshire Special Assizes
Calendar of Prisoners for trial, October 1842 (printed). Includes details of 259 from the 276 prisoners tried.

Hatherton Papers
Papers of Lord Hatherton, Lord Lieutenant, include letters re disturbances in 1850s, especially re Chartism near West Bromwich, mentioning George White, in 1856; miners' strikes 1857 and 1858 *(D260/M/F/5/6/1-3)*.

89   **STOCKPORT PUBLIC LIBRARY**

Chartist Papers, 1842
Letters and minutes of magistrates' meetings, June-September 1842, with 13 posters.

90   **STOKE-ON-TRENT: HANLEY PUBLIC LIBRARY**

Thomas Cooper Mss.
1 bound notebook, including miscellaneous lecture notes, and a ms. story "Mr. Peregrine" set in London in 1851 at the time of the Great Exhibition; 3 bundles containing notes for lectures delivered in London, most at the Hall of Science, City Road, at the John Street Institution, also Finsbury Chapel, South Place, 1847-55. (The range of topics covered, mainly historical and biographical, but also including natural history, architecture, music and philosophy, provides a useful and impressive guide to Cooper's activities as an autodidact lecturer during the years between his retreat from Chartism and his return to religion.)

91   **UXBRIDGE: BRUNEL UNIVERSITY LIBRARY**

Working Class Autobiographies Collection
Ms. autobiographies of Emanuel Lovekin (1820-1905), Shropshire Chartist in 1842, and Joseph Terry (1816-1889), Yorkshire Chartist. (Extracts from these autobiographies are printed in, respectively, J. Burnett (ed.), *Useful Toil*, 1974, and *Destiny Obscure*, 1982).

92   **UXBRIDGE PUBLIC LIBRARY**

J.B. Leno and Gerald Massey
The Attempt, ms. journal produced by Leno and Massey for Uxbridge Young Men's Improvement Society: No.1 1846, No.6 1847, 1848, new series No.1 Feb. 1853, No.3 April 1853.
Ms. poem by Leno, "The Bells of Uxbridge", n.d.

93   **WINDSOR : ROYAL ARCHIVES, WINDSOR CASTLE**

Queen Victoria's Papers
File C56 - "Chartists and the Working Classes, 1848". Also relevant letters in volumes A14, B5, B10, C8, C16, J67, J68.

Melbourne Papers
Papers of Lord Melbourne in 115 boxes, mostly post-1830. Of most interest, correspondence with Lord John Russell (vol.15, Panshanger Papers) and Sir Robert Peel.

Photographic Collection
2 daguerreotypes of Chartist meeting, Kennington Common, 10 April 1848.

94   **WOLVERHAMPTON PUBLIC LIBRARY**

5 letters from George Mitcheson, colliery agent, to W.H. Sparrow, colliery lessee, re colliers' unrest and rioting at Lane End (Longton) in the Potteries, June-August 1842. Useful for the context of Potteries Chartism and the riots of August 1842. *(DX/84/18)*.

95   **YORK: CASTLE MUSEUM**

O'Connor Letters
2 letters from Feargus O'Connor, York Castle, May 1840, to Serjeant Talfourd, MP, Chancery Lane, asking for help re O'Connor's conditions in prison. (Box 4, York Castle prison archive).

96   **YORK PUBLIC LIBRARY**

Anne Knight Letters
To Mrs. Rooke, 1851, re Sheffield female Chartists and women's suffrage, and O'Connor's Land Company *(Y329.942)*.

Thomas Rooke Letters
To Richard Hawkin, 1901-2, re organisation of Chartism in Sheffield in Rooke's youth. Bound with reports of memorial meetings to Ernest Jones in 1879 *(Y 342.42)*.

97   **YORK: DR. ALFRED PEACOCK**

Holberry Letters
Small collection of letters to Samuel Holberry in York Castle, c. 1842. In Dr. Peacock's private possession.

WALES

98   **ABERYSTWYTH: NATIONAL LIBRARY OF WALES**

Aston Hall Papers
Letters re Chartist riots in Shropshire, 1839-42 (878-80, 907-8, 924, 5467-8). Account of Shropshire Yeomanry's stay in Newtown and capture of Chartist leaders, 1839 (5427-8). Letters re Chartism in Montgomeryshire, 1839 (7542-3).
William Chambers Papers
Including correspondence, resolutions, depositions etc., 1843-7, re Rebecca Riots.

Marianne, Lady Frankland Lewis
Diary, containing account of journey through South Wales with Rebecca Riots Commission, 1843.

Glansevern Collection
Papers of A.C.Humphreys-Owen: they include letters re procuring release of Thomas Powell, 1840 (3893-4); letter from Thomas Powell, 1841, thanks for his release and promising to assist in agitation at Newtown and Llanidloes (7702); letter describing visit to London to see the Chartist demonstration, 1848 (4701).

Llangibby Castle Collection
Includes papers relevant to the Newport rising of 1839, among them:
prosecution brief in trial of Samuel Etheridge for conspiracy and riot (C830);
depositions of witnesses in trial of William Jones (C831); thanksgiving after the
failure of the rising (C840); statement re location and size of works in
Pontypool area drawn up for commission of inquiry into Chartism, 1839
(C841).

Ormathwaite Papers
Diary of Sir John Benn Walsh, MP for Radnorshire: entries in April 1848 re
Kennington demonstration, swearing in special constables, discovery of
Chartist arms, and discussions with Feargus O'Connor *(FG 1/16* pp.212-4, 225-
31).

Ernest Jones Mss.
Draft letters and memoranda, 1849 (NLW MS 10581B); file of documents re
Jones (NLW MS 11046E).

Powis Papers
Calendar of letters and documents re Chartist riots in Montgomeryshire (281
items); calendar of correspondence re Montgomeryshire Yeomanry Cavalry,
1809-41 (39 items); 2 calendars of letters and documents re Chartism in
Shropshire (38 items July-November 1842, 55 items August 1842).

St. Asaph Papers
Account of Chartist riots at Newtown and Llanidloes, 1839 by J. Edwards,
Rector of Newtown *(SA/Misc. 481).*

Tredegar Park Mss.
The most important collection of papers held in the National Library
concerning the Newport rising, especially Box 40, which includes about 60
items on the rising, 1839-41. Of especial interest are: *40/1:* copies of letters
from John Frost on the "Mandarin" at sea, near the Cape of Good Hope, 4 May
1840, to Feargus O'Connor, and to Morgan Williams of Merthyr; *40/2:* copy of
a letter from Zephaniah Williams, on the "Mandarin". May 25 1840, to Dr. A.
McKechnie, ship's doctor, outlining Chartist plans for a republican
government. Box 40 also contains material on Chartism in 1842 (19 items), and
1 item each from 1846 and 1848.
There is also relevant material in Box 57(including items 138, 148, 221, 272 and
282) re Monmouthshire Chartism, 1839-42, and in Boxes 71 and 157.

Miscellaneous Twentieth Century Manuscripts
Typescript notes on Chartism in Wales (NLW Ms. 12852E); copy of an essay
on Chartism in Wales, 181 pp. (NLW MS. 12780C); paper by Sir John
Ballinger, NLW Librarian 1909-32, on "Chartism and John Frost" (NLW MS.
9928D); "Chartism in Montgomeryshire", unfinished rough draft by E.R.
Horsfall Turner, 1936 (NLW MS. 12888E); "Chartism in Wales" - D.E. Jenkins
50 (NLW MS. 12780C).

99   **CARDIFF: GLAMORGAN RECORD OFFICE**

Dowlais Iron Company
Letter Books1782-1860: contain letters re Chartism.
Chief Constable of Glamorgan, and Clerk of Peace
Reports and letters, with some relevant items.

100   **CARDIFF: SOUTH GLAMORGAN COUNTY LIBRARY**

Bute Papers
Correspondence of Marquis of Bute, Lord Lieutenant of Glamorgan. Especially
valuable is Bute Mss.XX: 166 documents, mainly letters, re Chartism in
Monmouthshire and Glamorgan, 1839. See also vol. XXII for some material on
Chartism in 1842, and Letter Books 13 and 14 for out letters.

Chartist Prosecutions
Solicitors' accounts and papers, Montgomeryshire prosecutions, 1839 (Cardiff
Ms. 3.71).

101   **CWMBRAN: GWENT COUNTY RECORD OFFICE**

The Record Office holds material, scattered in various categories of record,
concerning the Newport rising of 1839. (There is a very full and helpful listing
of this material in *Chartism, A Guide to Documentary and Printed Sources*,
Gwent CRO, 1993, available from the Record Office, price 30p.).

Quarter Sessions Records
These include some of the most interesting material, especially depositions
against Richard Rorke for riot and conspiracy, January 1840 *(QS/D32/0015-6)*;
despositions against Wright Beatty for riot and conspiracy, September 1840
(QS/D 34/0028).

Miscellaneous Documents on the Rising
These include: letter from W.W. Phillips to J. Maughan with eye-witness
account of march on Newport *(D124.227)*; typed transcript of letter from
Charles Walters, Monmouth Gaol, 1840 *(Misc. Mss. 234)*; Chaplain's Journal,
1838-1842, with record of Chaplain's visits to John Frost, Zephaniah Williams
and other Chartists. *(Q/MG 2 and 17)*.

The Chartist Background
Various documents concerning John Frost's involvement in Newport
municipal politics, notably Newport Improvement Commissioners' minute
book, 1826-50 *(A.1101.M-1)* and Newport Council Minutes 1836-43. *(A.1101 M-
Z)*; Zephaniah Williams' and William Shellard's industrial and commercial
activities (full details in guide mentioned above).

Prints
Various prints and lithographs of Frost, Williams and Jones, the attack on the
Westgate Hotel, Newport, and the ensuing trial at Monmouth.

102   **NEWPORT BOROUGH LIBRARY**

Chartist Trials 1839-40
The fullest and most important source for the Newport rising: 24 volumes of
papers formerly in the possession of W.T.H. Phelps, solicitor of magistrates
conducting preliminary examination of Chartist prisoners. Includes Solicitor-
General's prosecution brief; notes for the use of the Attorney-General;
examinations of prisoners and depositions of witnesses; lists of accused,
witnesses, juries and special constables; various prosecution notes; details of
rewards offered for capture of Chartists, and pensions granted for services;
letters to Phelps, December 1839-January 1840, and other miscellaneous
letters re arrest, trial and reprieve of Frost, Williams and Jones.

103   **SWANSEA: ROYAL INSTITUTION**

Address of Swansea Working Men's Association
One of the few surviving addresses of a South Wales WMA. Dated March 1839.

SCOTLAND

104   **EDINBURGH: SCOTTISH RECORD OFFICE**

Lords Advocates' Papers (AD)
The main source of information on Chartist disturbances and ensuing trials,
e.g. indictments of John Grant, Henry Ranken, Robert Hamilton and James
Cumming, for conspiracy and sedition in Edinburgh, March-July, 1848, with
lists of witnesses etc. *(AD 2/19).*
Precognitions *(AD14)* hold pre-trial statements of evidence, arranged by year
and by name of accused. They include: Petitions by procurator fiscal of
Forfarshire to Sheriff for the arrest of Peter Bennet, John Duncan, James
Graham, John Penny, Hugh Ross, John Scott for breach of the peace, riot and
intimidating workmen, with precognitions by witnesses and declarations by
the accused, August-September 1842 *(AD 14/42/354).*
Indictment against Duncan, Penny, Ross, Scott and 5 others for riot in Dundee,
with lists of witnesses etc., August 1842 *(AD 14/44/81).*
There is also a series of miscellaneous papers *(AD 58)*, including various files
on Riots and Civil Disorder, 1840-50: including letter from Lord Provost of
Dundee to Lord Advocate re public peace at Dundee, June 1848 *(AD 58/67)*;
letters re Chartist activities in Dundee, Glasgow, Greenock and Stirling, March-
June 1848 *(AD 58/71)*; letters re stationing of troops in Midlothian, January
1848 *(AD 58/72)*; letters re Chartist meetings and riots in Glasgow, February-
March and November 1848 *(AD 58/79).*

Justiciary Court Books of Adjournal
These include notes of trial proceedings, complementing Lords Advocates'
papers, e.g. Trial of John Grant, Robert Hamilton, Henry Ranken for sedition,
November 1848 *(JC4/54).*

Home Office Papers
Photocopies of the correspondence re Chartism in Scotland, originals of
which are in the Public Record Office, London. *(HO102 and 103).*

Dalhousie Muniments (GD 45)
These include: papers of Fox Maule, Under-Secretary at the Home Office, re
measures against Chartists in England and Wales, 1838-40 *(GD 45/9/24-35);*
letters concerning relations between Edinburgh Whigs and Chartists, 1839
(GD 45/14/628 and 642). (On this latter topic, see also Rutherfurd *Mss. 9697-8).*

It is likely that the Scottish Record Office contains other collections which
include Chartist material.

105   **EDINBURGH: NATIONAL LIBRARY OF SCOTLAND**

Greenock Chartism
Letter from Greenock Christian Chartist Congregation, 1841 *(Mss. 2281, f.53).*

Rebecca Riots
Correspondence re Rebecca Riots in Wales, 1843-4 *(Mss. 2843, ff.89-386; 2844,
ff.5-78; 2877, f2).*

Radicalism - Letters Concerning
The Library's *Catalogue of Manuscripts Acquired Since 1925, Vol.VIII,* (1992),
includes a number of references under the above heading, most or all re the
period 1837-48, with detailed references to particular folios, *Mss. 9693-4, 9697-
8, 9701, 9705, 9708, 9714.* These references, and perhaps other manuscripts in
the Library's holdings, may well prove to be of interest in relation to
Chartism.

106   **EDINBURGH: UNIVERSITY LIBRARY**

1848 Riots
Letter from T. Cunninghame re Chartist riots in Edinburgh and Glasgow,
March 1848 *(EUL DK.7 46/62).*

107   **EDINBURGH: HUNTLY HOUSE MUSEUM**

Chartist Memorabilia
Blue silk sash, inscribed "Reform", worn in Edinburgh Chartist
demonstrations; also other sashes, banners, bludgeon, clarinet - relics of
Edinburgh demonstration, 1848.

108   **FORFAR PUBLIC LIBRARY**

Lowson Notebook
Note-book of Alexander Lowson, "Ms. notes on Old Forfar", 1858, including
second-hand account of Chartist march from Dundee to Forfar.

109   **GLASGOW: MITCHELL LIBRARY**

James Moir Collection
Private papers of James Moir (1806-1880), Glasgow Chartist, later councillor,
Bailie of Glasgow, and President of Scottish National Reform League. Useful
for details of his life, Complete Suffrage Union, Reform League and Glasgow
local politics.

110   **GLASGOW: McADAM PAPERS**

John McAdam Papers
Ms. autobiography, letters and papers of John McAdam (1806-1883), Glasgow
Chartist and Mazzinian internationalist. Papers are in the private possession of
the McAdam family at Bedlay Castle, Chryston, Glasgow.

111   **HAWICK MUSEUM**

Chartist Minute Book
One mss. volume, containing records of the Chartist Total Abstinence Border
Union, instituted January 1841, and minutes of the Hawick National Association
for Promoting the Political and Social Improvement of the People, January
1842-August 1843. Bound with cuttings, most from the *Kelso Chronicle*,
written by Alex. A. Hogg, Secretary of the Association, including reports of
the Total Abstinence Society's meetings and soirées, lectures by Ernest Jones
and Dr. F.R. Lees, and lectures and articles by Hogg on "The Acquisition of
Wealth" (Hawick Literary and Scientific Institute, January 1849), the evils of
drink, reminiscences of Sir Walter Scott, and Burns Centenary speeches.

112   **KIRKINTILLOCH: STRATHKELVIN DISTRICT ARCHIVES, WILLIAM PATRICK
LIBRARY**

Peter Mackenzie Papers
Minute of Kirkintilloch Interim Committee of Universal Suffrage, convening a
meeting to form a Chartist Association, February 1839. *(T20/11)*.

113   **PAISLEY PUBLIC LIBRARY**

Chartist Minute Book
Paisley Chartist Society Minute Book, September 1842-January 1843. (Usually
on loan to Paisley Museum).

Newspaper Cuttings
Files on Chartist movement, and on Rev. Patrick Brewster.

NORTHERN IRELAND

114   **BELFAST: PUBLIC RECORD OFFICE OF NORTHERN IRELAND**

Downshire Papers
Letter describing the "barbarism of Chartism", November 1839 *(D.671/C/12)*.

Sharman Crawford Papers
Letter from Joseph Hume to W.S. Crawford expressing hope that Chartists
would agitate peacefully, September 1842 *(D. 856/D)*.

IRELAND

115   DUBLIN: NATIONAL ARCHIVES

Chief Secretary's Office: Registered Papers
Metropolitan Police report on Chartism in Dublin, June 1841 *(1841/9/9445)*;
Metropolitan Police report on Ribbonism, Chartism and elections, and the
Chartist activities of Patrick O'Higgins, August 1842 *(1842/9/16973)*; copy of
letter from T. Moxon, Leicester, re purchase of gunstocks by Patrick
O'Higgins, August 1848 *(1848/9/350)*. See also corresponding Out-Letter
Books.

116   DUBLIN: NATIONAL LIBRARY OF IRELAND

Daniel O'Connell Papers
Accounts and papers of the Loyal National Repeal Association: about 200
letters, August-September 1841, some of which contain references to
Chartism *(Ms. 13622/6-48)*. It is probable that there are also other Chartist
references elsewhere in the O'Connell papers.

FRANCE

117   CHATEAU BIGNON, DEPARTEMENT DU LOIRET

Arthur O'Connor Papers
These include a few letters to Arthur O'Connor, living in exile in France, from
his nephew, Feargus O'Connor, written during the Chartist period. (For
Arthur O'Connor, see Marianne Elliott, *Partners in Revolution*, 1982). Papers
in private possession of Arthur O'Connor's descendant, the Marquis de la
Tour du Pin.

ITALY

118   MILAN: FONDAZIONE GIANGIACOMO FELTRINELLI

W.J. Linton Papers
The bulk of Linton's political correspondence for the 1840s and 1850s, and
some important family letters of the 1850s. Includes minutes of Peoples'
International League (1846-8) and 5 letters from Thomas Cooper to Linton,
1853-4.

NETHERLANDS

119   AMSTERDAM: INTERNATIONAL INSTITUTE OF SOCIAL HISTORY

Thomas Cooper Letters
13 letters, Cooper to Charles Kingsley, 1856-7; 4 letters, W.J. Fox to Cooper,
1847-8, 1853.
Ernest Jones
Letters to and from Jones, 1840-67; letters about Ernest Jones, 1892-7; 1 letter
from Major E.C. Jones, father of Ernest Jones, 1813.

W.J. Linton
1 letter, Peoples' International League, 1847.

Marx-Engels Collection
Includes 112 letters from G.J. Harney to Engels, 1846-95; 1 letter from Marie
Harney to Engels, 1888; 3 letters from Isaac Ironside to Karl Marx, 1 letter
from Marx to Ironside, 1856; 52 letters from Ernest Jones to Marx, 1851 and
undated. The Institute also holds full lists of the Marx-Engels collection in
Moscow. See item 120.

RUSSIA

120 MOSCOW: RUSSIAN CENTRE FOR THE PRESERVATION AND STUDY OF MODERN HISTORICAL DOCUMENTS

Letters of Harney and Jones to Marx and Engels
1 letter from Harney to Marx and Engels, 1846; 1 letter from Harney to Marx,
1847; 3 letters from Harney to Engels, 1846-53; 1 letter from Harney to Jenny
Marx, 1847.
44 letters from Ernest Jones to Karl Marx, 1851-1868; 5 letters from Jones to
Engels, 1852-4. There may be other relevant letters in the Moscow Archives.

USA

121 BOSTON: HARVARD UNIVERSITY LIBRARY

Adams-Linton Letters
See above, under Newcastle upon Tyne: Tyne and Wear Archives; item 68

Alcock Letter Book
See above, under Stafford: County Record Office; item 88

121.A EUGENE, OREGON: KNIGHT LIBRARY, UNIVERSITY OF OREGON

Letters to G.J. Harney
The family collection used in *The Harney Papers* (1969), including letters from
Feargus O'Connor (1845-50), William Thom (1846-8) and George White (1849),
as well as other well-known correspondents including Victor Hugo and
Giuseppe Mazzini. One reel of microfilm: Special Collections, *MF.125*.
Originals in the private possession of Mrs Catherine Black Cohen

122 LINCOLN, NEBRASKA: STATE HISTORICAL SOCIETY

Diary of Joseph Barker
1865-75. Contains reminiscences of Barker's life in England, including some
material on hardships of his early life. Much of the diary is scarcely legible.

123 NASHVILLE, TENNESSEE: VANDERBILT UNIVERSITY LIBRARY

Métivier Collection: Library of G.J. Harney
A collection of printed books formerly belonging to Harney with important
and interesting ms. inscriptions and annotations. (For further information see

David Goodway "The Métivier Collection and the books of George Julian Harney", *Bulletin of the Society for the Study of Labour History*, No.49, Autumn 1984, pp.57-60; Margaret Hambrick, *A Chartist's Library*, 1986).

124   **NEW HAVEN, CONNECTICUT : YALE UNIVERSITY: BEINECKE LIBRARY**

Ernest Jones Mss.
Correspondence of William Harrison Riley, File J 1838-72, includes 4 letters from Ernest Jones to W.H. Riley 1848-59, and printed appeal for funds for the *People's Paper*, January 1855, with marginal notes by Jones.

W.J. Linton Papers
Diaries and letters re Linton's life at Miteside and Brantwood, Lake District, 1849-66; letters and mss. re Linton's life in USA 1866-97.

125   **NEW YORK: COLUMBIA UNIVERSITY LIBRARY**

Seligman Collection
Ernest Jones letters family and business papers, 1819-69, 7 boxes. Especially interesting are letters to Jones c.1868 in connection with Reform League, from old Chartists.

126   **NEW YORK: PUBLIC LIBRARY**

Stoddard Papers
Includes some letters from Linton to R.H. Stoddard, poet.

127   **SAN MARINO, CALIFORNIA: HUNTINGTON LIBRARY**

Richard Carlile Papers
A patchy collection, of greater interest for "the infidel tradition" than for Chartism, which Carlile did not support, but contains some letters from the later 1830s which are of interest.

CANADA

128   **REGINA: SASKATCHEWAN ARCHIVES OFFICE**

William Loveless Letters
Letters from William Loveless, Pymore, near Bridport to George Loveless, in Essex and then in Canada, 1842-7. The letters contain evidence of the Tolpuddle brothers' interest in and support for Chartism. Copies; originals in private possession of Miss M.E. Loveless, Regina.

AUSTRALIA

129   **CANBERRA: NATIONAL LIBRARY OF AUSTRALIA**

W.J. Linton Papers
Family correspondence, 1840s and 1850s; later letters to Linton's son, Willie, from USA. Part of the Kashnor Collection.

130   **HOBART: ARCHIVES OFFICE OF TASMANIA**

Convict Records
Conduct registers are of particular interest. See, especially, *CON 33/1-2* for the Chartist transportees of 1839-40; *CON 33/38* for the Staffordshire rioters of 1842; *CON 14/36* for the London Chartists transported in 1848. (Further references may be found in George Rudé, *Protest and Punishment*, Oxford, 1978).

NEW ZEALAND

131   **WELLINGTON: NATIONAL LIBRARY OF NEW ZEALAND, ALEXANDER TURNBULL LIBRARY**

Journal of Thomas Parkinson
1842-3 journal of an emigrant to New Zealand. Contains material about his fellow-passenger, George Binns, Sunderland Chartist, and some of Binns' poems. Photocopy; original in private hands.

Contemporary Printed Sources

BOOKS AND PAMPHLETS

132   Adams, W.E. *Tyrannicide: Is it Justifiable?*, London, 1858. (Copy in Newcastle upon Tyne Public Library. Written in defence of Felice Orsini, who attempted to assassinate Napoleon III)

133   Adams, W.E. *Our American Cousins: Being Personal Impressions of the People and Institutions of the United States*, London, 1883. Reptd. with Introduction by Owen R. Ashton and Alun Munslow, Edwin Mellen, New York, 1992 (Includes information on ex-Chartists living in America, notably W.J. Linton)

134   Aitonn John   *A Tribute to the Memory of the Poor Man's Champion: Being the Funeral Sermon of the late Rev. Patrick Brewster*, Glasgow, 1859

135   Anfryn, Ap Id   *The Late Dr. Price (of Llantrisant). The Famous Arch-Druid*, Cardiff, 1896

136   Anon   *A Second Letter to the Inhabitants of Whitby: Calling Upon Them, in the Name of Justice and for the Sake of Humanity, to Act with Common Sense, and Release the Town from the Tyranny of Toryism*, Whitby, 1838.

137   Anon   *A Third Letter to the Inhabitants of Whitby; Being 'The Conclusion of the Whole Matter'*, Whitby, 1838 (Copies of both pamphlets in Staffordshire University Library. They call for establishment of Chartist Association; possibly written by John Watkins)

138   Anon   *Report of the Proceedings of the Great Anti-Chartist Meeting, Held at Coalbrook Vale, Monmouthshire, on Monday April 29th 1839*, Monmouth, 1839

139   Anon   *The Chartist: Or the Life and Death of James Arnold, Shewing the Progress and Results of Insubordination*, London, 1841 (Copy in Bodleian Library. Anti-Chartist tract in form of fictional moral tale)

140   Anon   *A Letter to Mr. William Lovett, Sometime Resident in Warwick Gaol*, London, 1841

141   Anon   *The Political Jugglers: A New Comic Drama*, Leicester, 1841 (Copy in Leicester Public Library. Satirizes the Chartists' financial dealings with the Tories)

142   *Anon   *Dialogue between John and Thomas. The Corn Laws, the Charter, Teetotalism and the Probable Remedy for the Present Distress*, Paisley, 1842

143   Anon   *The Bonny Bird: A Radical Rhyme. Respectfully Dedicated to the Unenfranchised by One of Their Number*, Dundee, 1848 (Copy in Dundee Public Library. Sixty-seven glorious stanzas!)

144   Anon *The People's Charter and a Letter Written Thereon*, London, n.d.

145   Anon *The Real Chartist*, Norwich, n.d. (Copy in Norwich Public Library)

146   *Anon *What Can the Chartists Do? What Have They Done? What Ought They To Do? By One of the Council of the Birmingham Political Union in 1831-1832*, London, n.d. (Copy in PRO, HO 45/54 fols. 21-26)

147   Applegarth, Augustus *A Letter on Chartism; Addressed to the Operatives of Dartford and its Environs*, Dartford, 1848 (Copy in Dartford Public Library. An anti-Chartist diatribe by a local businessman, described in *NS*, 1 July 1848, as 'garbage')

148   *Baines, Edward *The Designs of the Chartists and their Probable Consequences*, Leeds, 1839. Reptd. Thompson, (ed.) *Chartism*, 1986, see item 350

149   *Barker, Joseph *Aristocracy and Democracy. The Speech of Mr. Barker at the Bolton Tea Party ... September 28, 1848*, Wortley, 1848 (Reptd. with the *People*, Greenwood, Westport, Connecticut, 1968)

150   Barker, Joseph *A Full Account of the Arrest, Imprisonment & Liberation on Bail of Joseph Barker*, Wortley, 1848 (Reptd. with *The People*, Greenwood, Westport, Connecticut, 1968)

151   *Barker, Joseph *The Triumph of Right Over Might; or a Full Account of the Attempt Made by the Manchester Magistrates and the Whig Government to Rob J. Barker of his Liberty...*, Wortley, 1848. (Reptd. with *The People*, Greenwood, Westport, Connecticut, 1968)

152   *Barker, Joseph *Reformer's Almanac and Reformer's Companion to the Almanacs*, Wortley, 1848. Reptd. Thompson, (ed.)*Chartism*, 1986, see item 350 (Some original copies for 1848-50 in Dr. Williams' Library, London)

153   Barmby, Catherine *The Demand for the Emancipation of Women, Politically and Socially*, London, 1842 (Presses case for addition of female suffrage to People's Charter; No.3 in series called *New Tracts for the Times*)

154   *Bates, John *John Bates of Queensbury, the Veteran Reformer*, Queensbury, 1865. Reptd. Thompson, (ed.)*Chartism*, 1986, see item 350

155   *Bezer, John James 'The Autobiography of One of the Chartist Rebels of 1848' Original in *Christian Socialist* 6 Sept. - 13 Dec. 1851. Reptd. Vincent, (ed.) *Testaments of Radicalism*, pp.147-87, see item 354

156   *Binns, George *The Doom of Toil: A Poem by an Ambassador in Bonds*, Sunderland, 1841. (Copy in Sunderland Public Library; long extract in *NS*, 26 February 1848)

157   Blakey, Robert   *An Exposure of the Cruelty and Inhumanity of the New Poor Law Bill; as Exhibited in the Treatment of the Helpless Poor by the Board of Guardians of the Morpeth Union; in a Letter Addressed to the Mechanics and Labouring Men of the North of England,* Newcastle, 1837

158   Blakey, Robert   *Cottage Politics: Letters on the New Poor Law Bill,* Newcastle, 1837

159   Bolton, John   *Bolton's Personal Narrative of a Twenty Four Years' Residence in the Borough of Barnsley,* Ulverston, 1871   (Includes reflections on physical force Chartism)

160   Bradford Sanitary Committee   *Report of the Bradford Sanitary Committee,*160 Bradford, 1845. Reptd. with Introduction by J.A. Jowitt as *Mechanization and Misery,* Ryburn Publishing, Halifax, 1991   (A very detailed account of the living and working conditions of the Bradford woolcombers, compiled by the combers themselves and overseen by George White)

161   Brewster, Patrick   *The Perils and Duties of War,* Paisley, 1854

162   Brewster, Patrick   *The Indian Revolt: Its Duties and Dangers,* Paisley, 1857

163   Brooke, James Williamson   *The Democrats of Marylebone,* London, 1839 (Copy in Marylebone Public Library)

164   *Brough, Barnabas   *A Night with the Chartists, Frost, Williams and Jones. A Narrative of Adventures in Monmouthshire.* Reptd. Thompson, (ed.)*Chartism,* 1986, see item 350

165   Buckley, John   *A Village Politician: The Life Story of John Buckley,* London, 1897. Reptd. with Introduction by John Burnett, Caliban, Horsham, 1982 (Author's actual name was John Buckmaster and, though a member of the Anti-Corn Law League, he provides much information on southern rural and small town Chartism eg. in Calne and Tiverton)

166   Burnett, John (ed.)   *Useful Toil: Autobiographies of Working People From the 1820s to the 1920s,* Allen Lane, London, 1974, pp.364. Reissued Penguin, Harmondsworth, 1984

167   *Burnley, James   *Looking for the Dawn: A Tale of the West Riding,* London, 1874. Reptd. Thompson, (ed.) *Chartism,* 1986, see item 350   (Novel based on interviews with former Chartists)

168   *Bussey, Peter   *Address to the Working Men of England,* Bradford, 1848. Reptd. Thompson, (ed.) *Chartism,* 1986, see item 350

169   Campbell, J.   *Recollections of Radical Times; Descriptive of the Last Hour of Baird and Hardie and the Riots in Glasgow 1848,* Glasgow, 1880   (Copy in Mitchell Library, Glasgow)

170   *Campbell, John   *An Examination of the Corn and Provision Laws, from their First Enactment to the Present Period,* Manchester, 1841. Reptd. Thompson, (ed.) *Chartism,* 1986, see item 350

171   Campbell, John   *Negro-mania: Being an Examination of the Falsely Assumed Equality of the Various Races of Men*, Philadelphia, 1851

172   Candelet, George   *A Letter Addressed to Oddfellows, Foresters, Druids etc; Calling their Attention to the National Land and Labour Bank etc.*, London, 1848

173   *Carlile, Richard   *An Address to that Portion of the People of Great Britain and Ireland Calling Themselves Reformers on the Political Excitement of the Present Time*, Manchester, 1839 (Copy in PRO HO 40/43 fol.443)

174   Charlton, Barbara   *Recollections of a Northumbrian Lady 1815-1866*, Jonathan Cape, London, 1949; pp.183. Reptd. Spredden Press, Stocksfield, 1989 and edited by L.E.O. Charlton, pp.288 (Useful for references to Chartist demonstrations in 1848 and John Frost's daughter, Mrs. Fry)

175   Chatterton, Dan   *Biography of Dan Chatterton: Atheist and Communist*, London, 1891. (Published using pseudonym 'Chat'; active in London Chartism in 1848)

176   Christian Chartist Church   *Constitution Adopted at a Large Meeting of Members*, Glasgow, 1840 (Known to have survived, but location not traced)

177   Clarke, Charles   *War*, Birmingham, 1854 (Copy in Birmingham Public Library; ex-Wiltshire Chartist endorses Crimean War)

178   *Close, Francis   *The Chartists' Visit to the Parish Church: A Sermon Addressed to the Chartists of Cheltenham, Sunday, August 18 1839, on the Occasion of their Attending the Parish Church in a Body*, London, 1839

179   *Close, Francis   *The Female Chartists' Visit to the Parish Church: A Sermon Addressed to the Female Chartists of Cheltenham, Sunday August 25 1839, on the Occasion of their Attending the Parish Church in a Body*, London, 1839. Reptd. Thompson, (ed.)*Chartism*, 1986, see item 350 (Copies of both pamphlets in Gloucester Public Library)

180   Collet, C.D.   *History of the Taxes on Knowledge*, London, 1899 (First vol. has chapter on People's Charter Union, also reptd. in much abbreviated 1933 edn.)

181   Complete Suffrage Union   *Reconciliation between the Middle and Working Classes*, London, 1842

182   ----   *The Suffrage: An Appeal to the Middle Classes by One of Themselves*, London, 1842

183   ----   *The Rise and Complete Progress of the Complete Suffrage Movement*, London, 1842

184   ----   *Abstract of a Bill Amended and Passed by the Conference of the Complete Suffrage Delegates at Birmingham, December 1842*, London, 1843

185   ----   *Report of the Council of the National Complete Suffrage Union, for the year ending April 30 1843*, London, 1843

186   ----   *Report of the Proceedings at the Conference of the Middle and Working Classes Held at Birmingham, April 5 1842 and Three Following Days*, London, 1842

187   ----   *Minutes of the Proceedings at the Conference of the Middle and Working Classes of Great Britain Held First at the Waterloo Rooms and Afterwards at the Town Hall, Birmingham, April 5 1842 and Three Following Days*, London, 1842

188   Cook, Samuel   *To the Magistrates of the County of Worcester...*, Dudley, 1840 (Copy in Dudley Archives)

189   Cooper, Thomas   *The Wesleyan Chiefs, and Other Poems*, London, 1833

190   *Cooper, Thomas   *The Shakespearean Chartist Hymn Book*, Leicester, 1843 (No copy known to have survived)

191   Cooper, Thomas   *Address to the Jury ... at the Stafford Special Assizes, on Wednesday October 11 1842, on a Charge of Arson, Followed by an Acquittal*, Leicester, 1843 (Copy in Bodleian Library)

192   Cooper, Thomas   *A Letter to the Working Men of Leicester*, Leicester, 1845 (Copy in Staffordshire University Library; explains Cooper's opposition to O'Connor)

193   Cooper, Thomas   *The Baron's Yule Feast: A Christmas Rhyme*, London, 1846

194   *Cooper, Thomas   *Land for the Labourers and the Fraternity of Nations*, London, 1848 (Copy in Staffordshire University Library)

195   *Crossley, J.   *Ernest Jones, What Is He? What Has He Done?*, Manchester, 1868

196   *Crowe, Robert   *The Reminiscences of Robert Crowe, the Octogenarian Tailor*, New York, 1902(?). Reptd. Thompson, (ed.) *Chartism*, 1986, see item 350

197   Dartford National Charter Association   *A Reply to a Letter on Chartism*, Dartford, 1848 (Copy in Dartford Public Library; see Applegarth entry)

198   Davenport, Allen   *The Life and Literary Pursuits of Allen Davenport*, London, 1845. Reptd. in Thompson, *Chartism*, 1986, see item 350. Also reptd. with Afterword by Malcolm Chase, Scolar Press, Aldershot, 1994, pp.150 (Copy in Vanderbilt University Library)

199   Davenport, Allen   *The English Institutions: An Educational Poem*, London, 1845 (Copy in Vanderbilt University Library)

200   *Devyr, Thomas Ainge   *The Odd Book of the Nineteenth Century*, New York, 1882. Reptd. Thompson, (ed.) *Chartism*, 1986, see item 350

4

201   *Dorling, William   *Henry Vincent: A Biographical Sketch,* London, 1879. Reptd. Thompson, (ed.)*Chartism*, 1986, see item 350 (Dorling was a friend of Vincent's and the book includes a foreword by Lucy Vincent)

202   Doubleday, Thomas   *Political Pilgrim's Progress,* London, 1839 (A novel; author published other fiction and also poetry)

203   *Doubleday, Thomas   *The True Law of Population Shown to be Connected with the Food of the People,* London, 1842. Reptd. Augustus Kelley, New York, 1967

204   Doubleday, Thomas   *A Financial, Monetary and Statistical History of England,* London, 1847 (Calls for a repudiation of the National Debt and massive cut in taxation)

205   Doubleday, Thomas   *The Crimes of the Whigs; Or a Radical's Reasons for Supporting the Tory Party at the Next General Election,* Edinburgh and London, 1864

206   *Dunning, Thomas   'The Reminiscences of Thomas Dunning'. Reptd. Vincent, (ed.)*Testaments of Radicalism*, 1977, pp.115-46, see item 354

207   *Dyott, W.H.   *Reasons for Seceding from the Seceders; By An Ex-Member of the Irish Confederation,* Dublin, 1847. Reptd. Thompson, (ed.)*Chartism*, 1986, see item 350

208   Edwards, John Passmore   *A Few Footprints,* London, 1905 (Active in both the Chartist movement and the Anti-Corn Law League. Lived in Truro, Manchester and London in the 1840s)

209   Farish, William   *The Autobiography of William Farish. The Struggles of a Handloom Weaver,* n.p. 1889 (Carlisle Chartist; fascinating references to local events, including meetings addressed by George Julian Harney and Robert Peddie)

210   Ferrand, William Busfield   *An Historical Sketch of Baron Munchausen of Farden Grange,* n.p., 1849 (Copy in Bradford Archives. For an account of Chartist meeting on Harden Moor, broken up by Ferrand, who owned the land)

211   *Finsbury Tract Society   *The Question 'What is a Chartist?' Answered,* London, 1839. Reptd. Thompson, (ed.)*Chartism,*1986, see item 354 (Copy in Bodleian Library, John Johnson Collection)

212   Fletcher, Matthew   *Migration of Agricultural Labourers,* Bury, 1837

213   *Frost, John   *Trial of John Frost for High Treason under a Special Commission held at Monmouth in December 1839 and January 1840 ,* London, 1840. Reptd. Thompson, (ed.)*Chartism* ,1986, see item 350 (Copy in Nuffield College Library, Oxford)

214   Frost, Thomas   *Emma Mayfield,* London, 1848 (Novel; author was a Croydon Chartist and wrote other works of fiction)

215   *Frost, Thomas   *Forty Years Recollections: Literary and Political*, London, 1880. Reptd. Thompson, (ed.)*Chartism*, 1986, see item 350

216   *Gammage, R.G.   *The Charter; What It Is and Why We Want It; A Dialogue between John Trueman, a Working Man, and Samuel Timorous, a Shopkeeper*, Stoke-on-Trent, 1854 (Copy in Kashnor Collection, Australian National Library, Canberra; *People's Paper* 11 Nov. 1854 identifies Gammage as author)

217   Gammage, R.G.   *Reminiscences of a Chartist.* Originally in *Newcastle Weekly Chronicle*, 24 Nov. 1883 - 10 Jan.1885; reptd. by Society for the Study of Labour History, 1983, pp.75 (Includes a valuable Introduction and editorial annotation by W.H. Maehl)

218   *General Convention of the Industrious Classes   *Rules and Regulations of the General Convention of the Industrious Classes*, London, 1839

219   ----   *Manifesto of the General Convention of the Industrious Classes*, Birmingham, 1839. Both reptd. Thompson, (ed.)*Chartism*, 1986, see item 350

220   Glasgow Charter Association,   *Principles, Rules and Regulations*, Glasgow, 1840 (Known to have survived, but location not traced)

221   Goding, John   *Norman's History of Cheltenham*, Cheltenham, 1863 (Cheltenham Chartist; reflects on local agitation)

222   Grant, Brewin   *The Life of Joseph Barker, the Infidel; Done From His Own Words*, Sheffield, 1860 (Copy in Staffordshire University Library)

223   *Hamer, Edward   *A Brief Account of the Chartist Outbreak at Llanidloes*, Llanidloes, 1867. Reptd. Thompson, (ed.) *Chartism*, 1986, see item 350

224   Hammond, William   *Recollections of William Hammond, a Glasgow Handloom Weaver*, Glasgow (Includes eyewitness account of Glasgow Chartist disturbances in 1848)

225   Heavisides, Edward Marsh   *Poetical and Prose Remains*, Stockton-on-Tees, 1850 (Refers to local Chartism; edited by father)

226   Henderson, Robert   *Incidents in the Life of Robert Henderson; or Extracts from the Autobiography of 'Newcassel' Bob (A Tyneside Rake)*, Carlisle, 1869 (Brief reference to association with Chartism. Text put together by Rev. J. Martin)

227   Hick, William   *Chartist Songs and Other Pieces*, Leeds, 1840 (Copy in British Library)

228   Higham, R.   *Stella the Factory Master's Daughter: Or Conrad the Chartist. A Story of the Local History of Hyde and Neighbourhood*, n.p., 1890 (A novel. Copy in Tameside Local Studies Library, Stalybridge)

229   Hillocks, James Inches   *Life Story. A Prize Autobiography*, Glasgow, 1860

230   Hillocks, James Inches   *Hard Battles for Life and Usefulness: An Autobiographical Record*, London, 1884 (Secretary of Lochee, Dundee, branch of NCA)

231   Holyoake, G.J.   *Life and Labours of Ernest Jones, Esq. Poet, Politician and Patriot*, London, 1869

232   *Holyoake, G.J.   *Life of Joseph Rayner Stephens*, London, 1881. Reptd. Thompson, (ed.) *Chartism*, 1986, see item 350

233   *Holyoake, G.J.   *Sixty Years of an Agitator's Life*, London, 1892. Reptd. Garland, New York, 1984

234   Hood, Edwin Paxton   *The Peerage of Poverty*, London, 1870 (A survey of self-taught writers, including Chartists)

235   *Irish Universal Suffrage Association   *Civil and Religious Liberty: Address to the Most Reverend and Right Reverend the Roman Catholic Archbishops and Bishops of Ireland*, Dublin, 1843. Reptd. Thompson, (ed.) *Chartism*, 1986, see item 350

236   Jenkinson, John   *The Church and its Exactions. A Poem*, Kettering, Leicester and London, 1840

237   Jenkinson, John   *More Work for Italics. A Letter to the Rev. Corrie, Rector of Kettering*, Kettering, 1840 (Both in Northampton Public Library. Jenkinson was a Baptist minister and Chartist speaker)

238   Johnson, William Harrall   *Autobiography. Agnostic Journal* 1892-3 (Useful Chartist references include account of great meeting on Blackstone Edge to celebrate return of exiled John Frost)

239   Johnston, David   *Autobiographical Reminiscences*, Chicago, 1885 (Moderate London Chartist; emigrated to America and died there)

240   *Jones, Ernest   *Evenings with the People*, London, 1855. Reptd. Thompson, (ed.) *Chartism*, 1986, see item 350

241   *Jones, Ernest   *Trial of Mr. Ernest Jones and Others at the Central Criminal Court, London*, Hulme, 1868

242   *Jones, Ernest   *The Right of Public Meeting. A Letter ... to Lord Chief Justice Wilde*, Hipperholme, 1887. Reptd. Thompson, (ed.)*Chartism*, 1986, see item 350 (Copy in Bodleian Library, John Johnson Collection)

243   Jones, William   *Poems; Descriptive, Progressive and Humorous*, Leicester, 1853 (Prolific Leicester Chartist poet)

244   *Jones, William   *A Funeral Oration Delivered Over the Grave of Mr. Feargus O'Connor*, London, 1855. Reptd. Thompson, (ed.)*Chartism*, 1986, see item 350 (Liverpool Chartist)

245   Kirby, Mary   *Leaflets from My Life. A Narrative Autobiography*, London, 1887
(Has chapter on Thomas Cooper and the 1842 Potteries outbreak)

246   *Kirkdale Chartist Prisoners   *Chartist Tracts for the Times*, Wortley, 1849
(Written by James Leach, John West and George White. Pamphlets nos. 2,4,5
and 6 can be found in the Internationaal Instituut voor Sociale Geschiedenis,
Amsterdam)

247   Kydd, Samuel   *A Letter to the Hon. Secret Committee of the House of
Commons upon Joint Stock Banks*, York, 1837 (Signed by 'Alfred'. Copy in
British Library is second, extended edition and has Kydd's name appended to
it. Banking was a favourite subject of Kydd's during his Chartist years)

248   Kydd, Samuel   *A Sketch of the Growth of Public Opinion*, London, 1888

249   Lanarkshire Universal Suffrage Association, *Principles, Rules and Regulations*,
Glasgow, 1840 (Known to have survived, but location not traced)

250   Lang, John Dunmore   *Letter on the People's Charter*, Bradford, 1848

251   Leach, James   *Stubborn Facts from the Factories by a Manchester Operative*,
London, 1844. Reptd. Thompson, (ed.)*Chartism*, 1986, see item 350 (Long *NS*
review, 17 August 1844)

252   Leach, James   *An Address to the People of Great Britain on the Protection of
Native Industry*, Manchester, 1846

253   Leeds National Charter Association   *The Chartist Almanac for 1841*, Leeds,
1841 (Copy in Kirklees Archives)

254   *Leno, John Bedford   *Herne's Oak; and Other Miscellaneous Poems*, London,
1853

255   Leno, John Bedford   *An Essay on the Nine Hours Movement*, London, 1861
(Copy in Staffordshire University Library)

256   Leno, John Bedford   *King Labour's Songbook*, London, 1861

257   Leno, John Bedford   *Female Labour*, London, 1863 (Copy in Staffordshire
University Library)

258   Leno, John Bedford   *Muscular Poetry, or Songs for the People*, London, 1864

259   *Leno, John Bedford   *Kimburton: A Story of Village Life*, London, 1875-6

260   *Leno, John Bedford   *The Last Idler and Other Poems*, London, 1875-6

261   Leno, John Bedford   *The Aftermath*, London, 1892. Reptd. Thompson, (ed.)
Chartism, 1986, see item 350 (An interesting autobiography, with information
on 1848, physical force Chartism, Chartist journalism and O'Connor's death.
Reprint does not include poetry from original)

262   Lindsay, William *Some Notes; Personal and Public*, Aberdeen, 1898 (Lindsay was a prominent Aberdeen Chartist)

263   Linton, William James *Secretary's Report to the First Public Meeting of the Peoples' International League at the Crown and Anchor Tavern, 15 November 1847*, London, 1847 (Copy in Bishopsgate Library)

264   Linton, William James *Republican Tracts*, London, 1855. Reprints from the *English Republic*

265   Linton, William James *The Cause of Poland*, London, 1863

266   Linton, William James *Claribel and Other Poems*, London, 1865

267   Linton, William James *Ireland for the Irish: Rhymes and Reasons Against Landlordism*, New York, 1867

268   *Linton, William James *James Watson: A Memoir*, New Haven, 1879. Reptd. Augustus Kelley, New York, 1971

269   *Linton, William James *Memories*, London, 1895. Reptd. Augustus Kelley, New York, 1970

270   Linton, William James *Poems*, London, 1895

271   Litchfield, Francis *The Church and its Exactions. A Poem by John Jenkinson, Baptist and Chartist Minister, Kettering, Thoroughly Revers'd and Refuted, Truly Reprov'd and Corrected*, Northampton, 1840 (Copy in Northampton Public Library; see Jenkinson item 236)

272   London Democratic Association *Constitution of the London Democratic Association*, London, 1838 (Copy in PRO HO 44/55)

273   London Trades Committee *An Address from the London Trades Committee Appointed to Watch the Parliamentary Inquiry into Combinations to the Working Class*, London, 1838. Reptd. Thompson, (ed.) *Chartism*, 1986, see item 350

274   *London Working Men's Association *Address and Rules of the London Working Men's Association*, London, 1836. Reptd. Thompson, (ed.) *Chartism*, 1986, see item 350 (Copy in Nuffield College Library, Oxford)

275   ---- *Address to the People of Canada and Their Reply to the London Working Men's Association* , London, 1836

276   ---- *Address of the London Working Men's Association to the Working Classes of Europe and especially to the Polish People*, London, 1837

277   ---- *Address of the London Working Men's Association to the Working Classes on the Subject of National Education*, London, 1837

278   ---- *The People's Charter; Being the Outline of an Act to Provide for the Just Representation of the People of Great Britain in the Commons House of*

Parliament; Embracing the Principles of Universal Suffrage, No Property Qualification, Annual Parliaments, Equal Representation, Payment of Members and Vote by Ballot, London, 1838

279   ---   *Address of the Radical Reformers of England, Scotland and Wales to the Irish People*, London, 1838   (All the London Working Men's Association sources listed here are reptd. Thompson, (ed.) *Chartism*, 1986), see item 350

280   Lovekin, Emanuel   'Some Notes of My Life'. Reptd. Burnett, (ed.) *Useful Toil*,1974, pp.289-96, see item 166   (About half 7000 word autobiography is reptd.;   Lovekin makes brief observations on Chartism in Shropshire in 1842)

281   *Lovett, William   *Letter from Mr. Lovett to Messrs. Donaldson and Mason; Containing his reasons for Refusing to be Nominated Secretary of the National Charter Association*, London, 1843. Reptd. Thompson (ed.) *Chartism*, 1986, see item 350

282   *Lovett, William   *Trial of William Lovett*, London, 1839. Reptd. Thompson (ed.) *Chartism*, 1986, see item 350

283   *Lovett, William   *Life and Struggles of William Lovett in His Pursuit of Bread, Knowledge and Freedom*, London, 1876. Reptd. Thompson, (ed.) *Chartism*, 1986, see item 350

284   Lowery, Robert   *State Churches Destructive of Christianity and Subversive to the Liberties of Man*, London, 1837

285   Lowery, Robert   'Passages in the Life of a Temperance Lecturer, Connected with the Public Movements of the Working Classes for the Last Twenty Years'. Originally in the *Weekly Record of the Temperance Movement*, 15 April 1856-23 May 1857. Reptd. in *Robert Lowery, Radical and Chartist*, with introduction by Brian Harrison and Patricia Hollis, Europa, London, 1979

286   McAdam, John   *Autobiography of John McAdam (1806-1883), with Selected Letters*, Scottish Historical Society, Clark Constable, Edinburgh, 1980   (With introduction by Janet Fyfe;   McAdam was involved in Glasgow Chartism)

287   *McCarthy, Charles Henberry   *Chartist Recollections: A Bradfordian's Reminiscences*, Bradford, 1883. Reptd. Thompson, (ed.) *Chartism*, 1986, see item 350

288   *McDouall, Peter Murray   *Letters to the Manchester Chartists*, Manchester, 1842/43 (?). Reptd. Thompson, (ed.) *Chartism*, 1986, see item 350

289   Mackay, Charles   *Forty Years Recollections of Life, Literature and Public Affairs from 1830 to 1870*, London, 1870   (Vol.2 includes long autobiographical letter from Ernest Jones and hostile account of Kennington Common demonstration)

290   Marx, Karl   *Political Writings of Karl Marx*, London, 1973. 3 vols. edited by David Fernbach   (Amongst Chartist-related items are an article entitled 'The Chartists' in II, pp.262-71, an article discussing the agitation against the Sunday Trading Bill in 1855 and the involvement of James Finlen and other Chartists in

II, pp.288-94 and a speech at the 1856 anniversary of the *People's Paper*, in II, pp.299-300)

291   *Mason, J.W.   *Mr. Ernest Jones and his Candidature: A Reply to 'Ernest Jones: Who is he? What has he Done?'*, Hulme, 1868

292   Massey, Gerald   *Original Poems and Chansons*, London, 1847 (?)

293   Massey, Gerald   *War Waits*, London, 1855

294   Massey, Gerald   *Poetical Works*, Boston, 1857

295   Massey, Gerald   *Robert Burns: A Centenary Song and Other Lyrics*, London, 1859

296   Massey, Gerald   *Havelock March and Other Poems*, London, 1861

297   Mills, John   *Threads from the Life of John Mills, Banker*, Manchester, 1899 (Briefly discusses Chartism in Ashton-under-Lyne in 1848)

298   *Mudie, George   *The Rebels' Route; Or the Chartist Invasion of Forfar, 1842: A Poem in Four Cantos*, Dundee, 1864 (Copy in Lamb Collection, Dundee Public Library. This collection also includes newspaper cuttings re. ex-Chartists, James McPherson and George Whytock)

299   National Assembly   *Address to the French People*, London, 1848

300   ----   *Plan of Organisation for the National Charter Association of Great Britain and Ireland, Adopted by the National Assembly, May 1848 to Obtain the Speedy Enactment of the People's Charter*, London, 1848

301   *National Association of the United Kingdom for Promoting the Political and Social Improvement of the People   *Rules and Objects of the National Association ...* London, 1841. Reptd. Thompson, (ed.) *Chartism*, 1986, see item 350

302   National Reform League   *To All Who Desire A Thorough Reform, by Safe and Legal Means, of Our Political and Social Institutions*, London, 1851 (Known to have survived, but location not traced)

303   ----   *To the Democrats of Great Britain*, London, 1856 (Known to have survived, but location not traced)

304   *Newbould, T. Palmer   *Pages From A Life of Strife, Being Some Recollections of William Henry Chadwick, the Last of the Manchester Chartists.* Reptd. in Thompson, (ed.) *Chartism*, 1986, see item 350 (Includes prefatory note by Liberal politician, Sir Robert A. Hudson; Newbould is author not editor of this booklet. There is also a shorter version, *In Memoriam, William Henry Chadwick, The Old Chartist*, Luton. n.d. pp.16)

305   Newport Working Men's Association   *Address and Rules of the Working Men's Association for Benefiting Politically Socially and Morally the Useful Classes*, Newport, 1838

306   O'Brien, Bronterre, *Land Usurpers and Money Changers*, London, 1848
(Known to have survived, but location not traced)

307   O'Brien, Bronterre *State Socialism*, London, 1850

308   O'Brien, Bronterre *Sermons on the Day of the Public Fast and Humiliation for England's Disasters in the Crimea*, London, 1856

309   *O'Connor, Feargus *A Series of Letters from Feargus O'Connor Esq., Barrister-at-Law, to Daniel O'Connell ... Containing a Review of Mr. O'Connell's Conduct during the Agitation of the Question of Catholic Emancipation etc.*, London, 1836

310   *O'Connor, Feargus *A Practical Work on the Management of Small Farms*, London, 1843

311   *O'Connor, Feargus *The Trial of Feargus O'Connor and Fifty Eight Others on a Charge of Sedition, Conspiracy, Tumult & Riot*, Manchester, 1843. Reptd. Augustus Kelley, New York, 1970

312   *O'Connor, Feargus *The Employer and the Employed; the Chambers' Philosophy Refuted*, London, 1844

313   *O'Connor, Feargus *Reply of Feargus O'Connor Esq. M.P. to the Charges against his Land and Labour Scheme*, London, 1847
(All the above by O'Connor are reptd. Thompson, (ed.) *Chartism* 1986, see item 350)

314   O'Higgins, Patrick *Chartism and Repeal*, London, 1842. Reptd. Thompson, (ed.) *Chartism*, 1986, see item 350

315   Parrott, John *Twenty Years of Chartist Life*, London, 1867 (Copy in Bradford Public Library)

316   *Peddie, Robert *The Dungeon Harp; Being a Number of Poetical Pieces Written During a Cruel Imprisonment of Three Years; Also a Full Proof of the Perjury Perpetrated Against the Author by Some of the Hired Agents of the Authorities*, Edinburgh, 1844 (Copy in Manchester Metropolitan University Library; interesting verse, never reptd.)

317   The People's Charter Text of parliamentary bill. Two copies, one with introduction and dated 1840 (Copy in Bodleian Library. John Johnson Collection)

318   People's Charter Union *Address*, London, 1848 (Copy in Staffordshire University Library)

319   *Peoples' International League *Address of the Council of the Peoples' International League*, London, 1847 (Copies in Newcastle-upon-Tyne Public Library; Cambridge University Library; Staffordshire University Library)

320   Peoples' International League *Report of a Public Meeting ... to Explain the Principles and Objects of the Peoples' International League*, London, 1847

(Copies in Newcastle-upon-Tyne Public Library; Staffordshire University Library)

321   People's League   *The People's League for Obtaining Manhood Suffrage*, London, 1848

322   Pierson, T.   *Roseberry Topping, A Poem*, Stockton-on-Tees, 1847 (For Stockton Chartism)

323   *Price, Rev. Humphrey   *An Address on the People's Charter to His Fellow Townsmen, the Operatives of Kidderminster*, London, 1838 (?)

324   *Price, Rev. Humphrey   *A Glance at the Present Times, Chiefly with Reference to the Working Men*, London, 1838. Both reptd. Thompson, (ed.) *Chartism*, 1986, see item 350

325   Pringle Taylor, Lt. Col.   *Letters Relative to the Chartists, 1839-40* (Copy in Bodleian Library. Associate of David Urquhart; includes text of intercepted Chartist letter. Extracts in Richard Brown and Christopher Daniels (eds.) *The Chartists*, Macmillan, London, 1984, pp. 52-4)

326   Quinn, Roger   *The Heather Lintie*, Dumfries, 1861 (Includes Chartist verse. Copy in Dumfries Public Library)

327   *Rawlings, Job   *Animadversions upon a Sermon by Mr. John Warburton at Zion Chapel, Trowbridge ... upon the Doctrine of Non-Resistance to a Higher Power*, Bath, 1842. Reptd. Thompson, (ed.) *Chartism*, 1986, see item 350

328   *Richardson, R.J.   *The Rights of Woman; Exhibiting Her Natural Civil and Political Claims to a Share in the Legislative and Executive Power of the State*, Edinburgh, London and Manchester, 1840. Reptd. Thompson, (ed.)*Chartism*, 1986, see item 350; also reptd. with Introduction by E. & R. Frow, Working Class Movement Library, Manchester, 1986

328.A   Schofield, John *Peter Bussey, Bradford Chartist*, Bradford, 1895 (Biography. Copy in Bradford District Archives)

329   Shaw, Charles   *When I Was A Child*, London, 1903. Reptd. Caliban, Llanybydder, 1993

330   *Solly, Henry   *What Says Christianity to the Present Distress* London, 1842. Reptd. Thompson, (ed.) *Chartism*, 1986, see item 350

331   *Solly, Henry   *James Woodford, Carpenter and Chartist*, London, 1881 (Lovett was the inspiration for the hero of the book)

332   *Somerville, Alexander   *Dissuasive Warnings to the People on Street Warfare*, London, 1839. Reptd. Thompson, (ed.)*Chartism*, 1986, see item 350

333   Somerville, Alexander   *The O'Connor Land Scheme Examined*, London, 1847

334   Sprigge, S. Squire   *Life and Times of Thomas Wakley*, London, 1897. Reptd.
      Robert E. Krieger Publishing Co., New York, 1974 with Introduction by
      Charles G. Roland

335   Stafford, John   *Songs Comic and Sentimental*, Ashton-under-Lyne, 1840(?)
      (Copy in Tameside Local Studies Library, Stalybridge; little known Chartist
      poet)

336   Stanley, Edward, Bishop of Norwich (1837-50)   *A Sermon Preached in
      Norwich Cathedral on Sunday August 18 1839 by the Right Reverend the Lord
      Bishop of Norwich before an Assemblage of a Body of Mechanics Termed
      Chartists*, London, 1839 (Copy in Norwich Public Library)

337   Stephens, Joseph Rayner   *Copies of the True Bills Found Against the Rev. J.R.
      Stephens at Liverpool and Chester*, Manchester, Liverpool and London, n.d.
      (Copy in Manchester Public Library)

338   *Stephens, Joseph Rayner   *The Political Preacher: An Appeal from the Pulpit
      on Behalf of the Poor...*, London, Manchester, Ashton-under-Lyne, 1839.
      Reptd. Thompson, (ed.) *Chartism*, 1986, see item 350 (Copies in Tameside
      Local Studies Library, Stalybridge; Manchester Public Library)

339   *Stephens, Joseph Rayner   *The Political Pulpit*, n.p., 1839 (Copies in Tameside
      Local Studies Library, Stalybridge; Manchester Public Library; consists of
      fourteen sermons delivered Feb.-June 1839)

340   *Stephens, Joseph Rayner   *Sermon Preached by the Rev. Mr. Stephens ...
      January 6 1839; Being the First Sabbath after his Release from the New Bailey at
      Manchester*, Manchester, 1839 (Copies in Tameside Local Studies Library,
      Stalybridge; Manchester Public Library)

341   Stephens, Joseph Rayner   *The Farewell Sermon of the Rev. J.R. Stephens
      delivered to a Crowded Congregation in Ashton-under-Lyne on Sunday 3
      August 1839*, London, 1839 (Copies in Tameside Local Studies Library,
      Stalybridge; Manchester Public Library)

342   Stephens, Joseph Rayner   *The Trial of the Rev. Mr. Stephens for Uttering
      Seditious Language before Mr. Justice Patterson at the Assizes held at Chester
      on Thursday 15 August 1839*, n.p., 1839 (Copy in Tameside Local Studies
      Library, Stalybridge)

343   Stevens, William   *A Memoir of Thomas Martin Wheeler*, London, 1862. Reptd.
      Thompson, (ed.) *Chartism*, 1986, see item 350

344   Sweet, James   *Address to the Working Classes on the System of Exclusive
      Dealing*, Nottingham, 1840

345   Talbot, Charles John Chetwynd   *Meliora: Or Better Times to Come*, London,
      1853. Reptd. Frank Cass, London, 1971 (Includes 'Statement of a Working
      Man', a Chartist critical of O'Connor)

346   *Taylor, John *The Coming Revolution,* Carlisle, 1840 (Copy in PRO HO 40/57)

347   Teasdale, Harvey *The Life and Adventures of Harvey Teasdale, the Converted Clown and Man Monkey, with his Remarkable Conversion in Wakefield Prison,* Sheffield, 1870(?) (Has references to Chartist demonstrations)

348   Templeton, T.B.   *Report of the Trial of the Rev. J.R. Stephens at the Chester Assizes on Monday August 15 1839 with a Verbatim Report of the Rev. Gentleman's Defence Delivered on the Occasion,* Leeds, 1839 (Copy in Tameside Local Studies Library, Stalybridge)

349   Thomas, George *History of the Chartists and the Bloodless War of Montgomeryshire,* Welshpool, 1840

350   Thompson, Dorothy (ed.)   *Chartism: Working Class Politics in the Industrial Revolution,* Garland, New York, 1986 (A 22 volume facsimile series reproducing contemporary documents of the Chartist movement, 1838-1848)

351   Thompson, John *Memoir of Mr. John Thompson, 87 New Brandling Street, Monkwearmouth, in his 76th Year: What I Have Seen and Gone Through, From the Cradle to the Verge of the Grave,* Sunderland, 1893 (Lived in Harwich and Chatham and active Chartist)

352   Trant, Thomas   *1848: A Reply to Father Fitzgerald's Pamphlet,* Dublin, 1862

353   Universal Suffrage Association, *Principles and Regulations,* London, 1838 (Known to have survived, but location not traced)

354   *Vincent, David (ed.)   *Testaments of Radicalism. Memoirs of Working Class Politicians 1790-1885,* Europa, London, 1977, pp.246

355   Wallis, Thomas Wilkinson *Autobiography of Thomas Wilkinson Wallis, Sculptor in Wood, and Extracts from his Sixty Years' Journal,* Louth, 1899 (Active Chartist in Hull 1839-41)

356   Wardrop, Andrew *Peeps Through the Curtain, at the Manner in which the Affairs of the Burgh of Dumfries are Mismanaged and 'The Way the Public Money Goes',* Dumfries, 1846 (Copy in Dumfries Public Library; a local chemist active in Chartism)

357   Watkin, E.W.   *Alderman Cobden of Manchester,* London, 1891 (Includes extracts from Watkin's diary about Anti-Corn Law League attacks on Chartist meetings; reptd., F.C. Mather (ed.) *Chartism and Society,* Bell and Hyman, London, 1980, pp.214-19)

358   *Watkins, John *John Watkins to the People in Answer of Feargus O'Connor,* London, 1844. Reptd. Thompson, (ed.) *Chartism,* 1986, see item 350

359   Watson, James Autobiographical Speech, *Reasoner,* 16, 5 Feb. 1854, pp.107-11. Reptd. Vincent, (ed.) *Testaments of Radicalism,* 1977 pp.103-114 see item 354; E. Royle, (ed.) *The Radical Tradition from Paine to Bradlaugh,* Macmillan, London, 1976, p.99-106

360   White, George   *Drunkenness: Its Causes and Remedy: A Rhyme Descriptive of Allurement, Tap-Room Politics, Curtain Lectures, Home Miseries, Remorse and Ruin*, Bradford Pt.1, Keighley Pt.2, 1860 (Copies in Bradford Archives; Staffordshire University Library)

361   *Whittaker, John William   *Dr. Whittaker's Sermon to the Chartists. A Sermon Preached at the Parish Church, Blackburn, on Sunday August 4 1839*, Blackburn, 1839 (Copy in Blackburn Public Library)

362   Wilks, Washington   *The Half Century: Its History, Political and Social*, London, 1852 (Includes account of main events of Chartism; particularly unsympathetic on 1848)

363   Willey, Thomas   *A Song for the Times; Illustrative of Passing Events. Liberty or Bondage!* Cheltenham, 1848 (Copies in PRO HO45/OS 2410 AE, Part Five, 1848, Miscellaneous Bundle; Staffordshire University Library)

364   Wilson, Joseph   *Joseph Wilson: His Life and Work*, London, n.d. (A Chartist in Great Horton, near Manchester, in 1848)

365   Wood, Thomas   *Autobiography*, n.p., 1956. Partly reptd. Burnett, *Useful Toil*, 1974, pp.304-12, see item 166 (Touches on Chartism; lived in Bingley and Oldham)

BROADSHEETS AND HANDBILLS

366   **BODLEIAN LIBRARY, OXFORD**
Poster advertising meeting on Chartism of National Association, London, 10 November 1847. John Johnson Collection

367   **BRADFORD PUBLIC LIBRARY**
Poster addressed to middle and working classes on subject of People's Charter, n.d.

368   **CLEVELAND ARCHIVES**
Handbill issued by Stockton Corporation concerning Chartist meeting. Pargeter Papers (Acc 1250)

369   **DUDLEY ARCHIVES**
Samuel Cook Collection. 51 posters, 1823-61; only a small number relate specifically to Chartism

370   **GOLDSMITHS' LIBRARY, UNIVERSITY OF LONDON**
Handbill comprising of a Chartist prayer, delivered by John Taylor, Dalston, 8 December 1839

371   **LAMBETH PALACE LIBRARY**
Handbill entitled 'A Chartist Proclamation', 1841(?) and signed by Arthur O'Neill

372   **NEWCASTLE UPON TYNE PUBLIC LIBRARY**
'The Charter and No Surrender! To the Working Men of Newcastle.' Thomas Wilson Collection (Vol.VII for posters and handbills)

373   **NUFFIELD COLLEGE, OXFORD**
Handbill advertising political pamphlets, 1855(?). Cole Collection

374   **OXFORD PUBLIC LIBRARY**
Rusher Collection. Posters and handbills relating to Henry Vincent's Chartist candidacy in Banbury, 1841. Also a number of Chartist posters 1838-9. Access on microfilm. Banbury Public Library also has microfilm

375   **PUBLIC RECORD OFFICE**
There is a good collection of Chartist broadsheets amongst the Home Office papers. This list gives a brief description of the subject matter of some of them

375.1   Poster addressed to the labouring classes, 14 November 1838 HO 52/38 fol.96

375.2   Poster advertising torchlight meeting to elect delegates to National Convention, Bolton, 30 October 1838 HO 40/38 fol.241

375.3   Poster addressed to the working class and relating to the Poor Law, 14 November 1838 HO 52/38 fol.122

375.4   Poster advertising torchlight meeting to be addressed by F. O'Connor and J.R. Stephens, Bury, 8 December 1838 HO 40/38 fol.472

375.5   Letter from Stephens declining invitation to attend demonstration at Newcastle-upon-Tyne, 25 December 1838 HO 40/38 fol.634 (same at HO 52/37 fol.111)

375.6   Poster advertising meeting occasioned by arrest of J.R. Stephens to be addressed by Richard Oastler, Huddersfield, 22 January 1839 HO 40/51 fol.9

375.7   Poster advertising meeting to be addressed by W.V. Jackson, Pendlebury, 1 April 1839 HO 40/37 fol.136

375.8   Poster advertising meeting to be addressed by W.V. Jackson, 9 May 1839 HO 40/41 fol.68

375.9   Poster advertising demonstration to be addressed by J. Collins and H. Vincent, Northamptonshire, 20 May 1839 HO 40/46 fol.522

375.10 Poster advertising demonstration on Kersal Moor, 25 May 1839 HO 40/43 fol.233

375.11 Poster advertising meeting to be addressed by F. O'Connor and members of the National Convention, Whit-Wednesday 1839, HO 40/47 fol.156

375.12 Poster advertising meetings to be addressed by John Skevington, John Markham and others, Earl Shilton and Hinckley, 17 June 1839 HO 40/44 fol.345

375.13 Poster advertising a meeting regarding the National Holyday, Manchester, 3 August 1839 HO 40/43 fol.463

375.14 Poster advertising church demonstration, Barnsley, 1839 HO 40/51. fol.361

375.15 Poster advertising sermon to be given by W.V. Jackson, Oldham, 2 January 1840. HO 40/43 fol.855

375.16 Handbill detailing Chartist plan of lecturers for South Lancashire, January-March 1841 HO 45/46 fol.3 (same at fol.4)

375.17 Poster advertising funeral of John Clayton and sermon by Jonathan Bairstow, Sheffield, 21 March 1841 HO 45/45 fol.9

375.18 Poster advertising meeting relating to NCA organisation and to be addressed by George White and Dean Taylor. Birmingham, March 1841 HO 45/52 fol.51

375.19 Poster printed on tricolour paper and advertising public entry of F. O'Connor, Birmingham, 20 September 1841 HO 45/52 fol.52

375.20 Handbill agitating for return of J.Frost et.al. Birmingham, 1841 HO 40/56 fol.329

375.21 Poster warning church demonstrators, Leicester, 9 June 1842 HO 45/250 fol.14

375.22 Poster advertising two camp meetings to be addressed by J. Leach and C. Doyle, Manchester (?) 14 August 1842 HO 45/242 fol.18

375.23 Poster advertising sermons by B. Rushton, Keighley, 25 September 1842 HO 45/264 fol.285

375.24 Poster advertising tea party and ball, Manchester, 21 November 1842 HO 45/249C fol.385

375.25 Letter to Chartists exhorting their continued/renewed support, Manchester, 1842 HO 45/249C fol.218

375.26 Poster advertising camp meeting, Peep Green, West Riding, 12 March 1848 HO 45/241 OAC fol.853

375.27 Poster urging signatures for National Petition, Manchester, 14 March 1848 HO 45/2410A fol.584

375.28 Poster advertising meeting to consider adoption of People's Charter, Coventry, 3 April 1848 HO 45/241OP fol.675

375.29 Poster advertising camp meeting at Attercliffe, Sheffield, 16 April 1848 HO 45/2410AC fol.755

375.30 Poster advertising meeting to report on National Convention, Derby, Good Friday 1848 HO 45/2410J fol.220

375.31 Poster advertising demonstration to be addressed by S. Kydd, Birmingham, 11 June 1848 HO 45/241OP fol.599

375.32 Handbill advertising meeting and new edition of Chartist hymn book edited by W. Jones, Leicester, 14 June 1848 HO 45/241OR fol.870

375.33 Poster advertising camp meeting to be addressed by F. O'Connor and J. Mitchel, Oldham, 1848 HO 45/2410A fol.582

375.34 Poster advertising meeting to consider national strike for the Charter, Dundee 1848 HO 45/266 fol.114

376   **SHEFFIELD ARCHIVES**
Handbill with four hymns, 22 September 1839

377   **STOCKPORT PUBLIC LIBRARY**
Thirteen posters issued by authorities during strikes of 1842; concerned with prohibiting public meetings, enrolling special constables etc.

378   **SUNDERLAND PUBLIC LIBRARY**
Five posters issued by Chartists immediately after Sunderland by-election, September 1841; concerned with Tory election bribery and Whig public tea.

379   **WAKEFIELD PUBLIC LIBRARY**
Poster issued by Wakefield Working Men's Association, 1838. John Goodchild
Loan Collection

380   **WORKING CLASS MOVEMENT LIBRARY, SALFORD**
Poster relating to National Petition, n.d.; poster issued by Northern Political
Union calling for a general strike, 1839

CHARTIST AND NEAR-CHARTIST PERIODICALS

381 *The Aberdeen Review* 1843 - Dec. 1844 (British Library, nos. 39-91)

382 *Advocate and Merthyr Free Press* July 1840-April 1841 (PRO HO 41/15 and HO 45/54; National Library of Wales and Merthyr Tydfil Public Library have photocopies of these eight issues)

383 *Ashton Chronicle* March 1848-October 1849 (Tameside Local Studies Library, Stalybridge)

384 *Ayrshire Examiner* July 1838-Nov. 1839 (No copies known to have survived)

385 *The Birmingham Journal* June 1825-Feb. 1869 (British Library; Birmingham Public Library has microfilm)

386 *The Brighton Patriot and Lewes Free Press* Feb.1835-Aug.1839 (British Library; Brighton Public Library)

387 *The British Statesman* March 1842-Jan. 1843 (British Library)

388 *Bronterre's National Reformer* Jan.-March 1837 (Manchester Public Library; British Library has microfilm; reptd. Thompson, (ed.) *Chartism*, 1986, see item 350)

389 *The Cabinet Newspaper* Nov. 1858-Feb. 1860 (British Library; Harvester Press Microform Publication)

390 *The Carlisle Patriot* May 1831-June 1910 (British Library. 1848 and some other years on microfilm)

391 *The Cause of the People* May-July 1848 (Bishopsgate Public Library)

392 *The Champion* Sept. 1836-April 1840 (British Library; Nuffield College Library, Oxford; Bodleian Library, no.1 in John Johnson Collection; Harvester Press Microform Publication)

393 *The Champion of What is True and Right* Nov. 1849-Oct.1850 (Tameside Local Studies Library, Stalybridge. Edited during this period by J.R. Stephens)

394 *The Charter* Jan. 1839-March 1840 (British Library)

395 *The Chartist* Feb.-July 1839 (British Library)

396 *The Chartist Circular* Sept.1839-July 1842 (British Library, nos. 1-104; National Library of Scotland; Dundee Public Library; Bodleian Library, John Johnson Collection; reptd. Augustus Kelley, New York, 1968)

397 *The Chartist Pilot* Nov.1843-Jan.1844 (Albany State Library, New York; Cambridge University Library and Goldsmiths' Library, University of London, have photocopies)

398   *The Chartist Rushlight* June 1841 (No copies known to have survived)

399   *The Cheltenham Free Press* Nov. 1834-June 1908 (British Library; 1837 and some other years on microfilm)

400   *Cleave's London Satirist and Gazette of Variety* Oct.1837-Jan.1844 (British Library; known as *Cleave's Penny Gazette of Variety* after Dec. 1837)

401   *The Commonwealth: Journal of Rights* May 1848 (No copies known to have survived)

402   *The Commonwealth: A Monthly Record of Democratic, Social and Industrial Progress* 1849(?) (No copies known to have survived)

403   *The Commonwealthsman or Chartist Advocate* Dec. 1841-June 1842 (PRO HO 45/260, issues for 2 April, 18 June 1842)

404   *Cooper's Chartist Pioneer* Jan.-July 1842 (No copies known to have survived)

405   *Cooper's Journal* Jan.-Oct. 1850 (Nuffield College Library, Oxford; reptd. Greenwood, Westport, Connecticut, 1968; and Augustus Kelley, New York, 1970)

406   *The Democrat and Labour Advocate* Nov. 1855-Dec. 1855 (British Library; reptd. Thompson, (ed.) *Chartism*, 1986, see item 350; Harvester Press Microform Publication)

407   *The Democratic Review* June 1849-Sept. 1850 (Nuffield College Library, Oxford; reptd. Barnes & Noble, New York, 1968)

408   *Douglas Jerrold's Weekly Newspaper* July 1846-May 1851 (British Library only has microfilm; also Birmingham Public Library)

409   *Dundee Chronicle* Oct. 1832-Nov. 1840 (Original in Dundee Public Library)

410   *Edinburgh Weekly Register* 1843-50 (No copies known to have survived)

411   *The English Chartist Circular* Jan. 1841-Jan. 1843 (Nuffield College Library, Oxford; Sheffield Public Library has nos. 1-90, 92; British Library only has microfilm; reptd. Augustus Kelley, New York, 1968; Harvester Press Microform Publication)

412   *The English Patriot and Irish Repealer* 1848 (20 nos.; Goldsmiths' Library, University of London.   George White was not an editor)

413   *The English Republic* 1851-55 (Birmingham Public Library; Bishopsgate Library; Cambridge University Library has vol.1 and others on microfilm; Nuffield College Library, Oxford has vol.1 only)

414   *The Evening Star* July 1842-Feb. 1843 (British Library)

415   *The Executive Journal of the National Charter Association Oct.-Nov. 1841
       (British Library, Place Newspaper Collection, Set 56; no.1 pp.195-202;
       Birmingham Public Library has microfilm)

416   *The Extinguisher July-Nov. 1841 (No copies known to have survived)

417   *The Free Press Oct. 1855-May 1866 (British Library)

418   The Freeholder 1850-52 (British Library; Birmingham Public Library; useful
       for Land Plan)

419   *The Friend of the People Dec. 1850-July 1851, Feb.-April 1852 (Bradford
       Archives; reptd. Merlin, London, 1966)

420   *The Glasgow Examiner 1844-63 (Mitchell Library, Glasgow)

421   The Glasgow Saturday Post 1828-75 (Mitchell Library, Glasgow)

422   *The Glasgow Sentinel Oct. 1850-Dec. 1877 (Mitchell Library, Glasgow)

423   *The Halifax Reformer April 1847-July 1848 (British Library; Halifax Public
       Library)

424   *Hetherington's Twopenny Dispatch July-Sept. 1836 (British Library)

425   *The Labourer 1847-48 (Bodleian Library; Manchester Public Library; reptd.
       Greenwood, Westport, Connecticut, 1968)

426   *The Leicestershire Movement Feb.-June 1850 (Leicestershire Archives;
       British Library only has microfilm; also Birmingham Public Library)

427   The Lever: Or the Power of the Press Jan.-Oct. 1851 (Horace Barks Reference
       Library, Hanley)

428   *The Liberator 1832-6 (No copies known to have survived)

429   *The Lifeboat Dec.1843-Jan. 1844 (Reptd. Thompson, (ed.) Chartism, 1986,
       see item 350)

430   *Lloyd's Illustrated London Newspaper Nov. 1842-Jan.1843 (British Library;
       continued as Lloyd's Weekly Newspaper, 1843-1918)

431   *The London Chartist Monthly Magazine 1843 (Odd copies in Columbia
       University Library)

432   *The London Democrat April-June 1839 (British Library)

433   *The London Dispatch Sept. 1836-Oct. 1839 (British Library; Nuffield College
       Library, Oxford)

434   *The London Mercury Sept. 1836-Sept. 1839 (British Library)

435   *The London News*   May-Nov. 1858 (British Library)

436   *McDouall's Chartist and Republican Journal*   April-Oct. 1841 (Nuffield College Library, Oxford;   reptd. Greenwood, Westport, Connecticut, 1968)

437   *The Midland Progressionist*   1848 (No copies known to have survived)

438   *The Midlands Counties Illuminator*   Feb.-May 1841 (British Library;   Leicester Public Library has microfilm)

439   *The Monthly Liberator*   June 1838-April 1839 (Single issue, no.11, April 1839, in Mitchell Library, Glasgow)

440   *The Monthly Report of the National Association of United Trades*, Dec. 1847-June 1848 (Bishopsgate Institute; evolves into *The Labour League* 1848-9)

441   *The Movement: Anti-Persecution Gazette and Register of Progress*   Dec. 1843-April 1845 (Mitchell Library, Glasgow;   reptd. Augustus Kelley, New York, 1970)

442   *The National: A Library for the People*   Jan.-June 1839 (Manchester Public Library;   reptd. Greenwood, Westport, Connecticut, 1968)

443   *National Association Gazette*   (1-8 Jan., 21 May-2 July 1842 in National Museum of Labour History, Manchester)

444   *The National Guard*   April-July 1848 (National Library of Ireland; edited by James McCormick, an Irish Chartist)

445   *The National Instructor*   May 1850-May 1851 (Nuffield College Library, Oxford;   reptd. Thompson, (ed.) *Chartism*, 1986, see item 350)

446   *The National Liberator*   March-June 1842 (No copies known to have survived)

447   *The National Reformer*   Nov. 1844-May 1847   Copies have survived from Oct. 1846 on at L.S.E.; microfilm at Warwick University)

448   *The National Union*   May-Dec 1858 (No copies known to have survived)

449   *The National Vindicator*   Jan 1841-April 1842   (Newport Public Library;   13 Nov. 1841-29 Jan. 1842 in National Museum of Labour History, Manchester)

450   *The New Liberator*   1836-38 (No copies known to have survived)

451   *North British Express*   1847-49 (No copies known to have survived)

452   *The Northern Liberator*   Oct. 1837-Dec.1840 (British Library;   Newcastle Public Library has microfilm)

453   *The Northern Star*   Nov. 1837-Nov.1852 (British Library, Jan. 1838-Nov.1852; Leeds Public Library, 1840-50)

454   *The Northern Tribune* Jan 1854-March 1855 (Original in Manchester Public Library; Newcastle Public Library; reptd. by Greenwood, Westport, Connecticut, 1968)

455   *Notes to the People* May 1851-May 1852 (Manchester Public Library; reptd. Merlin, London, 1967)

456   *The Oddfellow* Jan. 1839-December 1842 (British Library; Harvester Press Microfilm Publication)

457   *The Operative* Nov.1838-June 1839 (British Library)

458   *The Penny Times* 1860 (British Library, Feb. and March 1860)

459   *The People* April 1857-May 1858 (British Library; Harvester Press Microfilm Publication. Thomas Cooper wrote editorials, 23 Jan.-20 Feb. 1858, in addition to his series of articles from Oct. 1857 on)

460   *The People: Their Rights and Liberties: Their Duties and Their Interests* May 1848-Sept. 1852 (Mitchell Library, Glasgow; Nuffield College Library, Oxford; Leeds Public Library; reptd. Greenwood,Westport, Connecticut, 1968)

461   *The People's Magazine* Jan.-Dec. 1841 (Butler Library, Columbia University Library)

462   *The People's Paper* May 1852-Sept. 1858 (British Library; Harvester Press Microform Publication)

463   *The People's Police Gazette* Nov.-Dec. 1841 (Original in British Library; Harvester Press Microform Publication)

464   *The People's Press* Jan.-Dec. 1848 (Manchester Public Library)

465   *Perthshire Chronicle* 1836-42 (Odd issues in Perth Public Library 28 Sept. 1837; British Library, 24 Oct. 1839; National Library of Scotland, 28 Nov. 1839)

466   *The Plain Speaker* Jan.-Dec. 1849 (Manchester Public Library; Warwick University Library has microfilm)

467   *Politics for the People* Nos. 1-17, 6 May-July, 1848 (Original in British Library; reptd. Augustus Kelley, New York, 1971. Useful for Christian Socialist commentaries on Chartism)

468   *The Poor Man's Guardian and Repealer's Friend* 1843 (Bodleian Library; reptd. in Thompson (ed.) *Chartism*, 1986, see item 350)

469   *The Potter's Examiner* Dec.1843-1850 (Horace Barks Reference Library, Hanley, 2 Dec. 1843-24 May 1845, microfilm for 31 May 1845-3 July 1847, odd copies for later years 1849-50; odd copies for later years 1847-50 also in William Salt Library, Stafford; Library of Congress, Washington. Useful for Land Plan)

470   *The Potter's Press and Miner's Advocate*   Jan-March 1851 (William Salt Library, Stafford. Includes Chartist contributions)

471   **The Power of the Pence*   1848-49 (Nuffield College Library, Oxford)

472   *The Protector*   April-May 1859 (British Library)

473   **The Reasoner*   June 1846-June 1861 (Manchester Public Library; vol.16, 1854, missing)

474   **The Red Republican*   June-Nov.1850 (British Library; reptd. Merlin, London, 1966)

475   **The Reformer*   Jan.-May 1850 (Norwich Public Library)

476   **The Regenerator*   1839-40 (Odd copies in London University Library, vol.1 nos. 1&2)

477   **The Republican: A Magazine Advocating the Sovereignty of the People* 1848 (Bodleian Library; reptd. Thompson, (ed.) *Chartism*, 1986, see item 350)

478   **Reynolds's Political Instructor* Nov. 1849-May 1850 (British Library; Birmingham Public Library; Manchester Public Library;   reptd. Greenwood, Westport, Connecticut, 1968)

479   **Reynolds's Weekly Newspaper*   Aug. 1850-Feb. 1851 (British Library; continues under different titles, including *Reynolds's Newspaper*, 1851-1923)

480   **Scotch Reformers' Gazette*   1837-54 (Odd copies, nos. 29-31, 19 Aug.-2 Sept. 1837, in National Library of Scotland)

481   **Scots Times*   1825-41 (Mitchell Library, Glasgow, but incomplete; National Library of Scotland for 1830, 1832-33;   British Library has microfilm for 1832-3, 1838-39)

482   **Scottish Patriot*   July 1839-Dec.1841 (Mitchell Library, Glasgow)

483   **Scottish Radical*   Dec.1840-Feb.1841 (No copies known to have survived)

484   **Scottish Vindicator*   1839 (No copies known to have survived)

485   **Sheffield Iris*   1794-1848 (Sheffield Public Library, 1836-39, 1843-48, incomplete)

486   **Sheffield Working Man's Advocate*   March-April 1841 (Sheffield Public Library)

487   **The Social Reformer*   Aug.-Oct. 1849   (London University Library)

488   **The Southern Star*   Jan.-July 1840 (British Library)

489   **The Spirit of Freedom*   1850-54 (No copies known to have survived)

490   *Stephens's Monthly Magazine* Jan.-Oct. 1840 (Tameside Local Studies Library, Stalybridge)

491   *Stoke Adviser* 1852 (No copies known to have survived)

492   *The True Scotsman* Oct. 1838-July 1841 (Paisley Public Library; British Library only has microfilm)

493   *The Truth Teller* 1848 (No copies known to have survived)

494   *Udgorn Cymru* March 1840-Oct.1842 (British Library, April-Oct. 1842)

495   *The United Irishman* Feb.-May 1848 (British Library; Trinity College Library, Dublin)

496   *Uxbridge Pioneer* 1849 (Uxbridge Public Library, nos. 1&2 Feb. and March 1849, Gerald Massey was one of the editors)

497   *The Uxbridge Spirit of Freedom* 1849 (Microfilm & photographs for 1849 in Uxbridge Public Library)

498   *The Vanguard* Jan.-March 1853 (Manchester Public Library; Bodleian Library, John Johnson Collection; National Library of Scotland has single issue)

499   *The Weekly Telegraph* 1860 (Odd copies, 25 Feb., 3 March 1860, in British Library)

500   *Weekly True Sun* Feb. 1833-Dec. 1839 (British Library)

501   *The Western Star* Oct. - Dec. 1840 (Odd copies, 3 Oct., 10 Oct. 1840 in National Museum of Labour History, Manchester)

502   *The Western Vindicator* Feb. 1839-Jan. 1841 (Cardiff Public Library; 2 March 1839-14 Dec. 1839 in National Museum of Labour History, Manchester)

503   *Working Man's Journal and Free Enquirer* 1850 (No copies known to have survived)

504   *The Yorkshire Tribune* July 1855-Sept.1856 (Leeds Public Library)

ARTICLES IN OTHER PERIODICALS BEFORE 1914

505   Burland, John Hugh   Autobiographical article *Barnsley Chronicle*, 10
       September 1902. (Prominent member of Northern Political Union. Also
       reptd. as a pamphlet)

506   Chadwick, W.H.   'Chartist Lecture' *English Labourer's Chronicle*, 18 Jan. 1879

507   Chadwick, W.H.   'Reminiscences' *Bury Times*, 24 Feb. 1884

508   Duigan, W.H.   'A Forgotten Patriot' *Walsall Observer*, 16 April 1887. (A piece
       about Joseph Linney)

509   Frost, Thomas   'Recollections of an Old Croydonian' *Croydon Chronicle*, July-
       Sept. 1877 (Bound set of clippings in Croydon Local Studies Library)

510   Hanson, Abram   Biographical Sketch, *Boot and Shoemaker*, 8 Feb. 1879
       (Hanson was an Elland Chartist)

511   Harney, G.J.   'Chartist Agitators' *Newcastle Weekly Chronicle*, 23 Aug. 1879

512   Hartley, John   'A Memorabilia of the Late John Hartley' *Todmorden and
       District News*, 22 May - 7 Aug. 1903

513   *Lindsay, W. & W.   Series of articles on Aberdeen Chartists, John Mitchell,
       Archibald MacDonald and James McPherson *Aberdeen People's Journal*, 29
       Jan.-26 Feb. 1887

514   McCarrie, John 'Andrew Wardrop. Chemist, Politician and Postman',
       Gallovidian, Autumn 1910 (A leading Dumfries Chartist)

515   Marston, E.   Recollections of a Special Constable in 1848, *Notes and Queries*,
       17 Feb. 1906

516   Maughan, John   'Memoir of Mr. C.H. Neesom' *National Reformer*, 27 July 1861

517   O'Neill, Arthur   Series of letters reflecting on Chartist agitation *Birmingham
       Daily Post*, 17 Jan-16 March 1885

518   Urquhart, David   'Mr. Urquhart's Letters on the International, No.2: Her
       Connection with the Chartist Conspiracy in England' *Diplomatic Review*,
       January 1872

519   Urquhart, David   'Chartism: A Historical Retrospect' *Diplomatic Review*, July
       1873 (This piece is unsigned, but Urquhart was very probably the author)

520   Winter, John Strange   'Mr. W.E. Adams' *Winter's Magazine*, 25 March 1893

Published Secondary Material

BOOKS AND PAMPHLETS

521 Anderson, Olive *A Liberal State at War. English Politics and Economics During the Crimean War*, Macmillan, London, 1967, pp.306. (Both Chapter 3 'The Effect of the Crimean War upon Class-Consciousness' pp.95-128, and Chapter 4 'The War and Radical Ideas of the Ancient Constitution' pp.129-162 include important discussions of late Chartism, Ernest Jones and the Crimean War, and Chartist antipathy to the ideas of David Urquhart)

522 Anderson, Robert *The Potteries Martyrs*, Military Heritage Books, Stoke-on-Trent, 1992, pp.72. Revised and Updated, 1993, pp.46 (A commemorative pamphlet on the 1842 disturbances in the Potteries)

523 Andréas, Bert (ed.) Introduction pp.7-31 in *Gründungsdokumente des Bundes Kommunisten (Juni bis September 1847)*, Dr. Ernest Hauswedell and Co., Hamburg, 1969, pp.79. ('Founding Documents of the League of Communists, June to September 1847'. The Introduction, in German, includes a consideration pp.10-18 of the relationship between the League of Communists, exiled refugees in England, and the Chartist inspired groups, the Democratic Friends of All Nations and the Society of Fraternal Democrats)

524 Armstrong, Isobel *Victorian Poetry. Poetry, Poetics and Politics*, Routledge, London, 1993, ʼ,p.545. (See pp.191-198 and pp.214-217 for a useful discussion of the Chartist poets, Thomas Cooper, J.B. Leno, W.J. Linton and Ernest Jones)

525 Armytage, W.H.G. *A.J. Mundella 1825-1897: The Liberal Background to the Labour Movement*, Ernest Benn Ltd., London, 1951, pp.386 (Chapter 1, pp.13-24 'The Successful Stockinger, 1824-1860' includes an examination of Mundella's life as a Chartist, c.1840-1848, in Leicester and his connections with Thomas Cooper then and later)

526 Arzhanov, E.M. 'Veitlingiantsy protiv chartistov', *Istoriya sotsialisticheskikh uchenii* ('The Weitlingians versus the Chartists', *The History of Socialist Teachings)*, Moscow, 1988, pp.76-84 (In Russian)

527 Ashraf, Phyllis Mary *Introduction to Working Class Literature in Great Britain, Part 1 : Poetry*, East Berlin, 1978, pp.250 (Explores the poetry associated with the rise of the modern proletariat. Includes much on the Chartist poetry of J.B. Leno, P. McDouall, Ernest Jones, Ebenezer Jones, R. Peddie, G. Massey, Thomas Cooper and W. Thom)

528 Ashraf, Phyllis Mary *Introduction to Working Class Literature in Great Britain, Part II: Prose*, East Berlin, 1979, pp.251 (includes pp.62-82 a consideration of the works of Chartist novelists Ernest Jones, G.W.M. Reynolds, Thomas Frost and T.M. Wheeler)

529 Ashraf, Phyllis Mary *Englische Arbeiterliteratur vom 18 Jahrundert bis zum ersten Weltkrieg. Entwicklungstendenzen im Uberlick*, Berlin und Weimar, 1980, pp.919. (In German. Includes a discussion of the writings of Thomas

Cooper, Ernest Jones, Ebenezer Jones, Thomas Frost, J.B. Leno and T.M. Wheeler)

530   Ashton, Owen R. *W.E. Adams : Chartist, Radical and Journalist (1832-1906)*, Bewick Press, Whitley Bay, Tyne and Wear, 1991, pp.200 (Biographical study of the Cheltenham Chartist leader)

531   Ashton, Owen R. and Munslow, Alun 'Transatlantic Radical Liberalism: A Comparative Analysis of H.D. Lloyd and W.E. Adams' pp.35-54 in David K. Adams and Cornelis A. van Minnen (eds.) *Reflections on American Exceptionalism,* Ryburn Publishing, Keele University Press, Keele, 1994, pp.255 (Explores the common concerns of two radical liberal journalists, W.E. Adams, the ex-Chartist, and the American, Henry Demarest Lloyd)

532   Ashton Rosemary *Little Germany. Exile and Asylum in Victorian England,* Oxford University Press, Oxford, 1986, pp.304. (See particularly Chapter 1 'The Road from Germany to England' pp.25-55 and Chapter 2 'Three Communist Clerks: Engels, Weerth and Freiligrath in Manchester, Bradford and London' pp.56-110 for both the role played by German exiles in Chartism and their extensive contacts with G.J. Harney and Ernest Jones)

533   *Barnsby, George J. *The Dudley Working Class Movement 1832 to 1860,* Dudley, 1967. Reptd. in *The Dudley Working Class Movement 1750 to 1860,* Dudley Leisure Services, Dudley, 1986, pp.63 (For Chartism in Dudley see pp.27-62)

534   Barnsby, George J. *Dictatorship of the Bourgeoisie : Social Control in the Black Country,* Communist Party of Great Britain Historians Group, 'Our History' series, No.55, Summer, 1972, pp.12 (An outline history of how the working class were controlled 1750-1880 and the Chartists' challenge of 1842)

535   Barnsby, George J. *Chartism in the Black Country,* Wolverhampton Integrated Publishing Services, Wolverhampton, 1980, pp.71

536   Barnsby, George J. *Birmingham Working People: A History of the Labour Movement in Birmingham 1650-1914,* Wolverhampton Integrated Publishing Services, Wolverhampton, 1989, pp.514. Second impression 1990 (See Chapter 4 'Chartism', covers 1836-60 in Birmingham, pp.68-124)

537   Baxter, John L. *Armed Resistance and Insurrection: The Early Chartist Experience,* Communist Party of Great Britain. Historians Group, Our History Series, No.76, London, 1984, pp.38 (Argues that all Chartist speakers who implied the case for physical force were *bona fide* insurrectionists)

538   Baxter, John L. *We'll Be Masters Now. The Story of the 1844 Miners' Strike and Its Impact on the Working Class Movement in Sheffield and the South Yorkshire Region.* Holberry Society Publications, Sheffield, 1986, pp.22.

539   Bebb, Einiona *Y Siartwyr,* Aberystwyth, 1989, pp.41 (Paratowyd y llyfr hon gan Broject Defnyddiau ac Adnoddau y Swyddfa Gymreig, ac fe'i cynhyrchwyd fel un o gyhoeddiadau'r Swyddfa Gymreig gan y Ganolfan Adnoddau Y Gyfadran Addysg, Coleg Prifysgol Cymru, Aberystwyth, 1989). In Welsh. 'The

Chartists'. (Prepared by the Welsh Office: Project on Resources and Materials as one of its publications in association with the Resource Centre of the Faculty of Education, University College of Wales, Aberystwyth, 1989. Looks at Chartist activities both in Mid-Wales and Gwent, with the aid of primary source materials)

540   Behagg, Clive   'Secrecy, Ritual and Folk Violence: The Opacity of the Workplace in the First Half of the Nineteenth Century, pp.154-179 in Robert D. Storch (ed.) *Popular Culture and Custom in Nineteenth Century England*, Croom Helm, London and New York, 1982, pp.213 (Explores some of the intricacies and experiences of the work place organization and culture which lay behind the formulation of the Chartist six points)

541   Behagg, Clive   'An Alliance with the Middle Class: the Birmingham Political Union and Early Chartism' pp.59-86 in James Epstein and Dorothy Thompson (eds.) *The Chartist Experience: Studies in Working-Class Radicalism and Culture, 1830-60*, Macmillan, London, 1982, pp.392

542   Behagg, Clive   *Politics and Production in the Early Nineteenth-Century*, Routledge, London, 1990, pp.273 (Chapter 5 'The Early Chartist Experience' pp.184-226 places Chartist demands in the context of changing structures of industrial and class relations in Birmingham. Valuable re-appraisal, too, of the Bull Ring Riots, July 1839)

543   Behagg, Clive   *Labour and Reform: Working Class Movements 1815-1914* Hodder and Stoughton, London, 1991, pp.154 (Specially written for 'A' level and first year undergraduates, the Chartist section pp.38-73, combines solid narrative and analysis, and also sets Chartism in a wider perspective)

544   Belchem, John   '1848: Feargus O'Connor and the Collapse of the Mass Platform' pp.269-310 in James Epstein and Dorothy Thompson (eds.) *The Chartist Experience: Studies in Working-Class Radicalism and Culture, 1830-1860*, Macmillan, London, 1982, pp.392

545   Belchem, John   *'Orator Hunt': Henry Hunt and English Working Class Radicalism*, Clarendon Press, Oxford, 1985, pp.304 (Looks at the bedrock of support on which the Chartist movement was built, and the importance of Hunt to the Chartists)

546   Belchem, John   'English Working-Class Radicalism and the Irish, 1815-50' pp.85-97 in Roger E. Swift and Sheridan J. Gilley (eds.) *The Irish in the Victorian City*, Croom Helm, London, 1985, pp.312 (Looks at the extent of the Irish presence in English popular radicalism and the distinctive Irish contribution to the last phase of Chartism. Argues that the failure of Chartism had the effect of increasingly isolating the Irish, socially and politically, in mid-century Britain)

547   Belchem, John   *Industrialization and the Working Class: The English Experience 1750-1900*, Scolar Press, Aldershot, 1990, pp.287 (Includes a valuable 40 page section on Chartism, pp.104-144)

548   Belchem, John   'Beyond *Chartist Studies*: Class, Community and Party in
       Early-Victorian Populist Politics', pp.105-126 in Derek Fraser (ed.) *Cities, Class
       and Communication: Essays in Honour of Asa Briggs*, Harvester Wheatsheaf,
       London, 1990, pp.264. (Valuable synopsis, in the light of recent research, of
       the nature, appeal and strategies of Chartism, the responses of the authorities
       and reasons for Chartist decline)

549   Belchem, John   'Liverpool in the Year of Revolution: The Political and
       Associational Culture of the Irish Immigrant Community in 1848' pp. 68-97 in
       John Belchem (ed.) *Popular Politics, Riot and Labour: Essays in Liverpool
       History, 1790-1940*, Liverpool University Press, Liverpool, 1992, pp.257
       (Indicates that Liverpool Chartism enjoyed only a minor revival in 1848,
       overshadowed by the potentially insurrectionary activities of the Liverpool
       Irish Confederates)

550   Bennett, Jennifer   'The London Democratic Association 1837-41: A Study in
       London Radicalism' *The Chartist Experience: Studies in Working-Class
       Radicalism and Culture, 1830-60*, Macmillan, London, 1982, pp.392.

551   Benson, George   *A History of English Socialism*, The New Leader Ltd.,
       London, n.d. circa 1928, pp.132 (See Chapter VI 'Chartism' pp.55-86 stressing
       the movement's left-wing credentials)

552   Berridge, Virginia   'Popular Sunday Papers and Mid-Victorian Society' pp.247-
       264 in George Boyce, James Curran, Pauline Wingate (eds.) *Newspaper
       History from the Seventeenth Century to the Present Day*, Constable, London,
       1978, pp.423 (For the Chartist G.W.M. Reynolds and the importance of his
       Reynolds's Newspaper in the 1850s)

553   Biagini, Eugenio F.   *Liberty, Retrenchment and Reform: Popular Liberalism in
       the Age of Gladstone, 1860-1880*, Cambridge University Press, Cambridge,
       1992, pp.476 (Includes detailed accounts of the activities of ex-Chartists: W.E.
       Adams; Joseph Cowen jr; Thomas Frost; J.B. Leno; William Lovett; and
       Henry Vincent)

554   Biagini, Eugenio F. and Reid, Alastair J.   'Currents of Radicalism 1850-1914'
       pp.1-19 in Eugenio F. Biagini and Alastair J. Reid (eds.) *Currents of Radicalism.
       Popular radicalism, organized labour and party politics in Britain 1850-1914*.
       Cambridge University Press, Cambridge, 1991, pp.305 (For late Chartism and
       the links with mid Victorian radical-liberal politics)

555   Billy, George J. *Palmerston's Foreign Policy: 1848*, Peter Lang, New York, 1993,
       pp.256 (See Chapter IV 'Chartism and Irish Nationalism' pp.55-84)

556   Blaszak, Barbara J.   *George Jacob Holyoake (1817-1906) and the Development
       of the British Co-operative Movement*, Edwin Mellen, New York, 1988, pp.116
       (Sets Holyoake, the Chartist, in a wider, radical context)

557   Bond, Winifred L.   *From Hamlet to Parish, The Story of Dodford,
       Worcestershire*, published by the author, Dodford, 1972, pp.51 (The Chartist
       Land Settlement is discussed pp.23-29)

558   Brook, Charles *Battling Surgeon,* The Strickland Press, Glasgow, 1945, pp.176 (Biography of Thomas Wakley. See Chapter 5 'Parliamentary Militant' pp.97-143 for his associations with Chartism)

559   Brook, Charles *Thomas Wakley,* The Socialist Medical Association, n.d. (c. 1962), pp.33 (The pamphlet includes a chapter on his parliamentary career and covers briefly his support for Chartism)

560   Brooke, Alan J.   'Labour Disputes and Trade Unions in the Industrial Revolution' pp.221-239 in E.A. Hilary Haigh (ed.) *Huddersfield. A Most Handsome Town; Aspects of the History and Culture of a West Yorkshire Town,* Kirklees Cultural Services, Huddersfield, 1992, pp.716 (Includes the political dimensions of trade unions in the Chartist years)

561   Brown, Arthur F.J. *The Chartist Movement in Essex and Suffolk: The Burrows Lecture (February 1979),* Local History Centre, Department of History, University of Essex, 1979, pp.15

562   Brown, Arthur F.J.   *Chartism in Essex and Suffolk* Chelmsford/Ipswich, Essex Record Office and Suffolk Record Office, 1982, pp.138 (A substantial regional study)

563   Brown, Brian R.   'Industrial Capitalism, Conflict and Working Class Contention in Lancashire, 1842' pp.111-141 in Louise A. Tilly and Charles Tilly (eds.) *Class Conflict and Collective Action,* Sage Publications, Beverly Hills and London, 1981, pp.260 (The author engages in a sociological analysis of Lancashire Chartism and the political mass strike of 1842)

564   Brown, W. Henry *Charles Kingsley. The Work and Influence of Parson Lot,* T. Fisher Unwin Ltd., London and The Co-operative Union Ltd., Manchester, 1924,pp.116 (Has short Chapter VIII on the 'Collapse of Chartism' pp.47-50, and numerous references to Kingsley's association with Thomas Cooper, Walter Cooper, G.J. Holyoake and J.B. Leno)

565   Bryson, Anne   'Riotous Liverpool, 1815-60' pp.98-134 in John Belchem (ed.)*Popular Politics, Riot and Labour: Essays in Liverpool History, 1790-1940,* Liverpool University Press, Liverpool, 1992, pp.257 (Includes a consideration of Chartism in Liverpool in 1848 and the authorities' responses)

566   Burt, Thomas *An Autobiography,* T. Fisher Unwin Ltd., London, 1924, pp.319. Reptd. Garland, New York, 1984 (See pp.24-25 for references to Chartism in the North East amongst the pit-men. Several of Burt's relatives are referred to as 'physical force Chartists'. Also has a number of references to the careers of ex-Chartists, W.E. Adams and Joseph Cowen)

567   Calder-Marshall, Arthur *Lewd, Blasphemous and Obscene,* Hutchinson, London, 1972, pp.248 (See Chapter 3 'Holyoake the Righteous' pp.121-161 for an account of G.J. Holyoake's lectures in Cheltenham Spa to assembled Socialists and Chartists in 1842, his subsequent arrest and conviction for blasphemy. Indicates Socialist and Chartist co-operation)

568   Cazamian, Louis   *The Social Novel in England 1830-1850*, Routledge and Kegan
       Paul, London, 1973, pp.369 (Translated with a Foreword by Martin Fido. First
       edition *Le Roman Social en Angleterre*, in French, 1903. See Chapter 6 pp.196-
       198 for Disraeli's attitude to Chartism; and Chapter 8 pp.241-291 for Charles
       Kingsley, *Alton Locke*, Chartism and Christian Socialism circa 1845-50)

569   Chadwick, Stanley   *'The Factory King': The Life and Labours of Richard
       Oastler*, Kirkburton, Yorkshire, 1944. With an Introduction by Reg Groves,
       pp.27 (Centenary pamphlet to commemorate the release of Richard Oastler
       from prison in 1844)

570   Chadwick, Stanley   *'A Bold and Faithful Journalist': Joshua Hobson 1810-1876*,
       Kirklees Metropolitan Council, Huddersfield, 1976, pp.82 (Centenary
       memorial book by Kirklees Libraries and Museum Service. A short
       biography, including Hobson's years as printer and publisher of the *Northern
       Star*)

571   Challinor, Raymond   *A Radical Lawyer in Victorian England: W.P. Roberts and
       The Struggle for Workers' Rights*, I.B. Tauris, London, 1990, pp.302 (The
       Chartist solicitor from Bath, relative of John Frost, friend of Feargus
       O'Connor, and national Miners' Association attorney)

572   *Challinor, Raymond and Ripley, Brian   *The Miners' Association: A Trade
       Union in the Age of the Chartists*, Lawrence and Wishart, London, 1968.
       Second Edition, Bewick Press, Whitley Bay, Tyne and Wear, 1990, pp.266
       (Argues for close links between the miners and the Chartist movement 1842-
       1848)

573   Chancellor, Valerie   *The Political Life of Joseph Hume 1777-1855. The Scot
       Who Was for Thirty Years a Radical Leader in the British House of Commons*,
       published by the author, Bennett Lodge, BCM Box 6067, London, 1986 pp.184
       (Chapter VI pp.121-153 looks at 'Hume and the New Radicalism 1838-1848',
       and covers his association with Chartism)

574   Chase, Malcolm   *The People's Farm. English Agrarianism 1775-1840*,
       Clarendon Press, Oxford, 1988, pp.221 (Important for Thomas Spence's ideas
       on public land ownership and how Spenceans passed their views on to
       Chartist leaders such as Bronterre O'Brien and G.J. Harney. Useful, too, for
       perspectives on land ownership before the Chartist Land Plan)

575   Claeys, Gregory   *Machinery, Money and the Millennium: From Moral
       Economy to Socialism, 1815-1860*, Polity Press in association with Blackwell,
       Cambridge, 1987, pp.245 (See pp.156-159 for the impact of Thomas Spence's
       land nationalization ideas on Bronterre O'Brien, G.J. Harney and Ernest Jones
       alongside the communitarian socialism of Robert Owen and William
       Thompson)

576   Claeys, Gregory   *Citizens and Saints. Politics and Anti-Politics in Early British
       Socialism*, Cambridge University Press, Cambridge, 1989, pp.360 (Chapters 6,7
       and 8, pp.208-309 have a detailed analysis of the relationships between
       Chartism and Owenism 1836-45, the emergence of socialist Chartism 1845-50,
       and Chartist republicanism in the mid 1850s)

577   Clarke, Tony   'Early Chartism: A "Moral Force" Movement?', pp.106-121 in T.
        Devine (ed.) *Conflict and Stability in Scottish Society 1700-1850*, John Donald,
        Edinburgh, 1990, pp.139 (Argues that the traditional view of Chartism in
        Scotland 1839-1840 as a 'moral force' movement is inaccurate. The movement
        was in fact much closer to the mainstream of the movement in Britain than is
        generally acknowledged)

578   Clarke, T. and Dickson, T. 'Class and Class Consciousness in Early Industrial
        Capitalism: Paisley 1770-1850', pp.8-60 in Tony Dickson (ed.) *Capital and Class
        in Scotland*, John Donald, Edinburgh, 1982, pp.286 (For Radicalism, Chartism
        and aspects of class collaboration in Paisley 1833-1850)

579   *Cole, G.D.H.   *Chartist Portraits*, Macmillan, London, 1941. Reptd. London,
        1965; Reptd. Cassell, London, 1989, pp.378

580   Cole, John   *Conflict and Co-operation: Rochdale and the Pioneering Spirit
        1790-1844,*, George Kelsall Publishers, Littleborough, Rochdale, 1994, pp.54
        (Includes a chapter on local Chartism, pp.25-34)

581   Colls, Robert   *The Pitmen of the Northern Coalfield. Work, Culture and
        Protest 1790-1850*, Manchester University Press, Manchester, 1987, pp.386 (See
        pp.267-301 for the reception of Chartism in the pit-villages of
        Northumberland and Durham, in Newcastle and Sunderland, and for the close
        connections with the national Miners' Association)

582   Cooke, G.K. (ed.)   *A History of the Parish of Redmarley D'Abitot*, Redmarley
        D'Abitot Women's Institute, 1959, pp.58 typescript (Includes passing
        references to the Chartist Land Plan with illustration of a Chartist house. Copy
        in Local Studies Department, Gloucester Public Library)

583   Cooter, Roger   *The Cultural Meaning of Popular Science. Phrenology and the
        Organization of Consent in Nineteenth Century Britain*, Cambridge University
        Press, Cambridge, 1984, pp.418 (See pp.168-255 for the Chartists', including
        specifically G.J. Holyoake, Arthur O'Neill and James Williams, interest in and
        involvement with phrenology)

584   Cowherd, Raymond G.   *The Politics of English Dissent. The Religious Aspects
        of Liberal and Humanitarian Reform Movements from 1815 to 1848*, New
        York, 1956, The Epworth Press, London, 1959 pp.242 (See particularly
        Chapter 8 'Christian Chartists and Complete Suffrage' pp.107-116. The
        chapter, however, contains a number of important errors: the author blurs
        the distinction on p.109 between Christian and educational Chartism; and his
        description of the split at the Complete Suffrage Conference of 1842 on p.115
        is inaccurate)

585   Craik, W.W.   *A Short History of the Modern British Working-Class
        Movement*, The Plebs League, London, 1919, third edition, p.123 (See Chapter
        V 'The Chartist Movement and the Anti-Corn Law League' pp.34-46 for an
        early twentieth century interpretation stressing the class character of
        Chartism)

586   Crossick, Geoffrey *An Artisan Elite in Victorian Society: Kentish London,*
        1840-1880, Croom Helm, London, 1978, pp.306 (See Chapter 10 'Political
        Ideology and Action' pp.199-242 for an examination of Chartism in Kentish
        London and its legacy after 1858)

587   Crossick, Geoffrey 'The Petite-Bourgeoisie in Nineteenth Century Britain: the
        Urban and Liberal Case', Chapter 3 pp.62-94 in Geoffrey Crossick and Heinz-
        Gerhard Haupt (eds.) *Shopkeepers and Master Artisans in Nineteenth Century*
        Europe, Methuen, London and New York, 1984, pp.283 (Suggests the
        importance of the petit-bourgeois' radical involvement in Chartist localities)

588   Davies, Brian 'Empire and Identity: the "case" of Dr. William Price' in David
        Smith (ed.) *A People and a Proletariat, Essays in the History of Wales 1780-*
        1980, Pluto Press, London, 1980, pp.239 (Essay on the rebellious life of the
        Pontypridd Chartist who took part in the Newport Rising of 1839, and who
        retreated into Druidism)

589   Davies, Graham *The Irish in Britain 1815-1914,* Gill and Macmillan, Dublin,
        1991, pp.248 (See Chapter 5 'Chartism' pp.159-190 for a summary of the
        debate about the Irish involvement in Chartism 1838-48)

590   Davies, Harold, Daniels, J.C. and Swingler, Stephen *The Potteries and The*
        People's Charter, North Staffordshire May Day Committee, 1939, unpaginated,
        pp.20 (Commemorative pamphlet to celebrate locally the centenary of
        Chartism. Covers the period 1838-1842)

591   Davies, Herbert 'A Shot in the Dark' pp.16-28 in Sylvia A. Harrop and E.A.
        Rose (eds.) *Victorian Ashton,* Tameside Libraries and Arts Committee, 1974,
        pp.116 (For Chartist disturbances in Ashton-under-Lyne in 1848 and the
        subsequent trial of political prisoners at Liverpool Assizes)

592   Davies, James *The Chartist Movement in Monmouthshire,* Newport, 1939.
        Reptd. Starling Press, Newport, 1981 with an Introduction by F.E.A. Yates,
        pp.51 (A useful, illustrated introduction to the movement in Gwent)

593   Derry, J.W. *The Radical Tradition. Tom Paine to Lloyd George,* Macmillan,
        London, 1967 pp.435 (See the 'Chartist interlude' pp.155-181)

594   Dinwiddy, J.R. *Chartism,* Historical Association pamphlet. New
        Appreciations in History 2 Series, London, 1987; Reptd. London, 1990, pp.24
        (An invaluable introduction to students on the nature of the movement.
        Summarizes some of the more recent research)

595   Dinwiddy, J.R. *Radicalism and Reform in Britain, 1780-1850,* Hambledon
        Press, London and Rio Grande, Ohio, 1992, pp.452 (A collection of previously
        published articles, including one on Chartism pp.403-420, prepared for the
        Historical Association New Appreciations in History Series. See immediately
        above, item 594)

596   Driver, Cecil *Tory Radical: The Life of Richard Oastler,* Oxford University
        Press, New York, 1946, pp.597 (See especially Chapter XXIX, 'Chartism')

597   Dunbabin, J.P.D.   'Oliver Cromwell's Popular Image in Nineteenth-Century England' pp.141-163 in J.S. Bromley and E.H. Kossmann (eds.) *Britain and The Netherlands, Vol.V Some Political Mythologies,* Martinus Nijhoff, The Hague, 1975, pp.212 (Papers delivered to the Fifth Anglo-Dutch Historical Conference. Contains a section dealing with changing perceptions of Cromwell amongst some of the Chartists and their leaders, including Feargus O'Connor and Thomas Cooper)

598   Duncan, Robert   *Conflict and Crisis: Monklands' Miners and the General Strike of 1842,* Airdrie Library Services, Airdrie, 1982, pp.30 (Argues that Chartist influence was significant in raising political consciousness within the Monklands mining community around Airdrie and Coatbridge from 1838 and particularly in the 1842 struggle)

599   Duncan, Robert   *Textiles and Toil: The Factory System and the Industrial Working Class in Early Nineteenth Century Aberdeen,* Aberdeen City Libraries, Aberdeen, 1984, pp.56 (For Chartism in Aberdeen see pp.45-56)

600   Duncan, Robert   'Chartism in Aberdeen: Radical Politics and Culture 1838-48' pp.78-91 in Terry Brotherstone (ed.) *Covenant, Charter and Party: Traditions of Revolt and Protest in Modern Scottish History,* Aberdeen University Press, Aberdeen, 1989, pp.131

601   Duncker, Hermann von, Goldschmidt Alfons, Wittfogel, K.A. (eds.) 'Geschichte der internationalen Arbeiterbewegung, 2. Kap. "Die industrielle Unwälzung in England und der Chartismus" in *Marxistische Arbeiterschulung,* Vienna/Berlin, 1930. Reptd. Erlangen 1970 (In German. Part of a course on the history of the international labour movement: Chapter 2, 'The Industrial Upheaval in England and Chartism' in *Marxist Workers' Training)*

602   Dutton, H.I. and King, J.E.   *Ten Per Cent and No Surrender: The Preston Strike, 1853-54,* Cambridge University Press, Cambridge, 1981, pp.274 (For Chartism and the cotton operatives' 7 month strike)

603   Edsall, Nicholas C.   *Richard Cobden, Independent Radical,* Harvard University Press, Cambridge, Massachusetts and London, 1986, pp.465 (For Cobden's attitude to the Chartists, the Chartists' relationships with the Complete Suffrage Union and their confrontations with the Anti-Corn Law League, and the importance of 1848, See part II: 'Agitator, 1838-1846' pp.75-140 and pp.192-209)

604   Edwards, Michael S.   *Purge this Realm: the Life of Rayner Stephens, 1805-79,* Epworth Press, London, 1994, pp.240 (First modern biography of the Chartist leader which deals with all aspects of his life and career)

605   Egan, David   *People, Protest and Politics: Case Studies in Nineteenth Century Wales,* Gomer Press, Llandysul, 1987, pp.117 (Welsh History Teaching Materials for 14-16 year olds which explore case studies. No. III is 'Chartism in Wales' pp.63-88)

606   Egan, David and Stevens, Catrin   *Pobl, protest a gwleidyddiaeth: mudiadau poblogaidd ung Nghymru Bedwaredd Ganrif ar Bymtheg,* Gower Press, Llandysul, 1988 pp.117 (The Welsh edition of *People, Protest and Politics.* See above)

607   Eisenberg, Christiane   'Chartismus und Allgemeiner Deutscher Arbeiterverein. Die Enstehung der politischen Arbeiterbewegung in England und Deutschland' pp.151-170 in Arno Herzig and Günter Trautmann (eds.) *'Der Kühnen Bahn nun folgen wir … 'Enstehung und Wandel der deutschen Arbeiterbewegung,* Vol.1, Reidar, Hamburg, 1989, pp.353 (On Chartism and the General German Workers' Association, particularly the origins in both countries)

608   Elliott, Adrian   'Municipal Government in Bradford in the Mid-Nineteenth Century' pp.112-161 in Derek Fraser (ed.) *Municipal Reform and the Industrial City,* Leicester University Press, Leicester and St. Martin's Press, New York, 1982, pp.165 (Considers the Chartist challenge in municipal politics and to the police between 1848-1855)

609   Epstein, James   *The Lion of Freedom: Feargus O'Connor and the Chartist Movement, 1832-1842.* Croom Helm, London, 1982, pp.327 (An extremely important work, central to our understanding of Chartism and its leadership. Reasssesses O'Connor's contribution)

610   Epstein, James   'Some Organisational and Cultural Aspects of the Chartist Movement in Nottingham, pp.221-268 in James Epstein and Dorothy Thompson (eds.) *The Chartist Experience. Studies in Working-Class Radicalism and Culture, 1830-1860,* Macmillan, London, 1982, pp.392 (Stresses the cultural dimensions of local Chartist activities)

611   Epstein, James   'Some Reflections on National Chartist Leadership, Strategy and Organisation' pp.25-37 in Warren F. Spencer and Louise Salley Parker (eds.) *The Consortium on Revolutionary Europe 1750-1850. Proceedings 1989, Vol.II,* The University of Georgia, Department of History, Athens, Georgia, 1989 pp.679. (Includes a commentary at the close by Peter Mandler pp.38-45. Epstein discusses the political culture in which Chartism flourished and particularly stresses the vision of the movement's leaders)

612   Epstein, James   *Radical Expression. Political Language, Ritual, and Symbol in England 1790-1850,* Oxford University Press, New York, 1994, pp.233 (Important work on the formation of radical ideologies. Includes three chapters which both draw on and enlarge previously published articles. See items 960, 961, 962 in Articles section)

613   Ervine, St. John G.   *Francis Place. The Tailor of Charing Cross,* Fabian Tract No.165, Biographical Series No.1, The Fabian Society, London, 1912; Third Reprint 1935, pp.27 (Section on Chartism attempts to distance Place from the Chartist Movement)

614   Finlayson, Geoffrey B.A.M.   *England in the Eighteen Thirties. Decade of Reform,* Edward Arnold, London, 1969, pp.115 (See pp.90-103 for an assessment of early Chartism)

615   Finn, Margot C. *After Chartism. Class and Nation in English Radical Politics, 1848-1874*, Cambridge University Press, Cambridge, 1993, pp.361 (Charts the course of working and middle class radical politics in England from 1848 to 1874, and emphasizes the persistence of radical agitation after the fall of the Chartist mass platform and before the rise of organised Socialism)

616   Fladeland, Betty 'Our Cause being One and the Same: Abolitionists and Chartism' pp.69-99 in James Walvin (ed.) *Slavery and British Society 1776-1846*, Macmillan, London, 1982 pp.272 (Stresses the links between the two movements)

617   Fladeland, Betty *Abolitionists and Working Class Problems in the Age of Industrialization*, Louisiana State University Press, Baton Rouge, 1984, pp.232 (Looks at the concern of British abolitionists with political and social reform movements at home as well as with black slavery across the Atlantic between the 1770s-1860s. Chapters on Joseph Barker, Patrick Brewster, Henry Solly, Joseph Sturge and Perronet Thompson. Looks at links specifically between Chartism and anti-Slavery)

618   Flick, Carlos *The Birmingham Political Union and the Movement for Reform in Britain 1830-1839*, Archon Books, Hamden, Connecticut and Dawson, Folkestone, 1978, pp.206 (Reappraisal of the Union's significance and provides a narrative history 1830-1837, and an account of its demise with the emergence of Chartism in 1839)

619   Fomichev, V.N. 'Propaganda I.G. Ekkariusom idei marxisma v chartistskoi presse 1850-1852'. *Iz Istoric Marxisma-Leninisma mezhdunarodnogo Rabochego Dvizheniya* ('I.G. Eccarius's propagation of the ideas of Marxism in the Chartist Press 1850-1852'. From *The History of Marxist-Leninism and the International Workers' Movement*. Moscow, 1982, pp.250-269. In Russian)

620   Fraser, W. Hamish 'The Scottish Context of Chartism' pp.63-73 in Terry Brotherstone (ed.), *Covenant, Charter and Party: Traditions of Revolt and Protest in Modern Scottish History*, Aberdeen University Press, Aberdeen, 1989, pp.131 (Looks at the general facets of Scottish Chartism 1838-1848 in the light of recent research)

621   Freer, Walter *My Life and Memories*, Civic Press Limited, Glasgow, 1929, pp.133 (Chapter 1 'Looking Back' pp.9-18 recalls his father's involvement as a handloom weaver in Chartism in Glasgow circa 1846)

622   Frow, Edmund 'Working Class Consciousness in Radical Poetry in Manchester 1790-1850', pp.59-65 in Hanna Behrend (ed.) *Problems of the History and Literature of the Working Class in Britain from the Eighteenth to the Twentieth Century*, Humboldt University, Berlin, 1982 pp.110 (Includes a consideration of some of Ernest Jones's Chartist poetry)

623   Frow, Edmund and Frow, Ruth *Chartism in Manchester, 1838-58*, Manchester, 1980, pp.26, (Includes very brief biographical details of William Benbow, Abel Heywood, W.H. Chadwick, R.J. Richardson and James Wroe)

624   Frow, Edmund and Frow, Ruth   *Radical Salford. Episodes in Labour History,*
       Neil Richardson, Swinton, Manchester, 1984, pp.35 (Includes a short chapter
       on Chartism pp.11-13)

625   Frow, Edmund and Frow, Ruth (eds.)   *Political Women 1800-1850* (with
       Introduction by Julia Swindells), Pluto Press, London, 1989, XIV + pp.220 (See
       Chapter 9, 'The People's Charter' pp.183-204)

626   Frow, Edmund and Frow, Ruth   *Essays on the Irish in Manchester,* Working
       Class Movement Library, Salford, 1991, pp.46 (Includes chapter on 'Chartism
       and the Irish')

627   Fryer, Peter   *Staying Power. The History of Black People in Britain,* London,
       1984, pp.632 (For the contribution of black Chartists, particularly the London
       leader, William Cuffay, see pp.237-246 and pp.407-9)

628   Fyson, Robert   'The Crisis of 1842: Chartism, the Colliers' Strike and the
       Outbreak in the Potteries' pp.221-268 in James Epstein and Dorothy
       Thompson (eds.) *The Chartist Experience. Studies in Working-Class
       Radicalism and Culture, 1830-1860,* Macmillan, London, 1982, pp.392
       (Emphasizes the relations between miners' unionism and Chartism in the
       Potteries and reconstructs the outbreak)

629   Gadian, David   'Class Formation and Class Action in North-West Industrial
       Towns, 1830-1850', pp.24-66 in R.J. Morris (ed.) *Class, Power and Social
       Structure in British Nineteenth Century Towns,* Leicester University Press,
       Leicester, 1986, pp.222 (Provides an overview of the nature of Chartist
       leadership, political ideology, social support and class conflict in Manchester,
       Ashton, Bury, Heywood, Blackburn, Rochdale and Stockport)

630   Galkin, V.V.   'Idei sotsialisma v chartistskom dvizhenii-konets 40-X-nachals
       50-X gg XIX V', *Istoriya Sotsialisticheskitch Uchenii* ('The Ideas of Socialism in
       the Chartist Movement between the late 1840s and early 1850s, *The History of
       Socialist Teachings,* Moscow, 1985, pp.3-28. In Russian)

631   Garrard, J.   *Leadership and Power in Victorian Industrial Towns 1830-1850,*
       Manchester University Press, Manchester, 1983, pp.228 (See pp.109-220 for
       Chartism and the transition to Liberalism in Rochdale, Bolton and Salford.
       Particularly useful for the career of Thomas Livesey, the Rochdale Chartist, and
       his involvement in municipal politics)

632   Goddard, Henry   *Memoirs of a Bow Street Runner,* With an Introduction by
       Patrick Pringle, Museum Press Limited, London, 1956, XXXI + pp.253
       (Memoirs of policing 1824-64. Includes on pp.154-161 an account of some
       early Chartist activity in the manufacturing towns around Manchester, and a
       detailed account of the arrest in December 1838 by Goddard of Rev. J.R.
       Stephens, the 'Chartist and Torchlight Agitator')

633   Godfrey, Christopher   *Chartist Lives. The Anatomy of a Working-Class
       Movement,* Garland Publishing, London and New York, 1987 pp.596
       (Formerly the author's Ph.D thesis, Harvard, 1978. A prosopographic study of
       the Chartist movement through the life experiences of 121 activists)

634   Godfrey, John and Goldie, Ella *Chartism and Paisley,* Jordanhill College of
Education Publications, Glasgow, 1978, pp.32 (Small collection of documents,
illustrations and commentary with a local slant, for students and Scottish VIth
Formers)

635   *Golby, John   'Chartism and Public Order' pp.36-40 in Clive Emsley (and the
Course Team) *Popular Politics 1750-1850* (A.401, Block II, Units 3-6), The
Open University, Milton Keynes, 1974, pp.40.

636   Goodway, David *London Chartism 1838-1848,* Cambridge University Press,
Cambridge, 1982, pp.330 (A major work on the nature of Chartism in the
capital, including a consideration of the events of 1848)

637   Groves, William W. *Chartism in Scotland* (An Individualised Learning Unit),
Jordanhill College of Education, Glasgow, 1989, pp.14 (A very short collection
of primary source materials for 'A' level and undergraduate study)

638   Grugel, Lee *George Jacob Holyoake. A Study in the Evolution of a Victorian
Radical,* Porcupine Press, Philadelphia, 1976, pp.189 (Includes a consideration
of his Chartist career)

639   Guest, Revel and John, Angela V. *Lady Charlotte: A Biography of the
Nineteenth Century,* Weidenfeld and Nicolson, 1989, pp.320 (This life of Lady
Charlotte Guest draws very fully upon her journals, which are not publicly
available. Chapter 3 'The Educator of the People' contains material relating to
Chartism in South Wales)

640   Gurney, Peter 'George Jacob Holyoake: Socialism, Association and Co-
operation in Nineteenth-Century England' pp.52-72 in Stephen Yeo (ed.) *New
Views of Co-operation,* Routledge, London, 1988, pp.276 (History Workshop
Series. Looks at Holyoake and the links between Chartism, 1848-1852, and
early Liberalism)

641   Halévy, Elie *A History of the English People in the Nineteenth Century,* in
French, 1923, English edition 1927; Ernest Benn, London, 1961, Vol.III *The
Triumph of Reform 1830-1841,* pp.364 (See Part II, Chapter II 'Chartists and
Free-Traders' pp.270-351 which deals with the growth of Chartism and the
Rising of 1839. See also Vol.IV *Victorian Years 1841-1895,* London, 1961
pp.507 (This volume incorporates 'The Age of Peel and Cobden 1841-1852.' by
Halévy up to pp.414. See pp.236-250 for April 10 1848 and scattered
references elsewhere. Halévy's work on radicalism and Chartism represents a
major early twentieth century interpretation of working class movements in
Britain)

642   Hall, Frank *A Northern Pioneer. The Study of J. Lancashire,* Leonard Parsons,
London, 1927, pp.206 (Includes 'The Study of Ernest Jones, pp.123-131. Copy
available in Manchester Central Library)

643   Halstead, John *'The Voice of the West Riding:* Promoters and Supporters of a
Provincial Unstamped Newspaper, 1833-34', pp.22-57 in C. Wrigley and J.
Shepherd (eds.) *On the Move: Essays in Labour and Transport History
Presented to Philip Bagwell,* Hambledon Press, London, 1991, pp.256

(Includes the early Chartist careers of Joshua Hobson, John Leech, Lawrence Pitkethley and Christopher Tinker)

644   Hamling, William   *A Short History of the Liverpool Trades' Council, 1848-1948*, Liverpool Trades' Council and Labour Party, Liverpool, 1948, pp.47 (pp.6-15 considers Liverpool radical and Chartist politics 1800-1848)

645   Hammond, Barbara L.   'William Lovett, 1800-1877' (Fabian Tract No.199, Fabian Biographical Series No.8, London, 1922) Reptd. pp.100-126 in Michael Katanka (ed.) *Radicals, Reformers and Socialists*, Charles Knight and Co., London, 1973, pp.270

646   Hanson, T.W.   *The Story of Old Halifax*, F. King and Sons, Halifax, 1920. Reptd. S.R. Publishers, Wakefield, 1968, pp.286 (Chapter XVII, pp.241-257 includes a consideration of the local Chartist movement and the role of the Chartist sympathiser, William Milner, a local grocer and general dealer, who provided working men with cheap editions of radical books)

647   Haraszti, Eva H.   *Chartism*, Akademiai Kiado, Budapest, 1978, pp.276 (In English)

648   Hardy, Dennis   *Alternative Communities in Nineteenth Century England*, Longman, London, 1979, pp.268 (See pp.75-105 for the Chartist Land Plan communities and their place in the history of nineteenth century attempts to create a different political and social order)

649   Hargreaves, John A.   *Factory Kings and Slaves: South Pennine Social Movements, 1780-1840*, Pennine Heritage Network, Hebden Bridge, 1982 pp.20 (A pamphlet briefly explaining the Anti-Poor Law agitation and the early Chartist and trade union activity in the South Pennine textile districts in the conflict-torn 1840s)

650   Hargreaves, John A.   'A Metropolis of Discontent: Popular Protest in Huddersfield c.1780-c.1850' pp.189-220 in E.A. Hilary Haigh (ed.) *Huddersfield. A Most Handsome Town. Aspects of the History and Culture of a West Yorkshire Town*, Kirklees Cultural Services, Huddersfield, 1992, pp.716 (Important for Chartism in Huddersfield)

651   Harker, David   'Introduction to Thomas Allan and George Allan', *Allan's Illustrated Edition of Tyneside Songs*, Newcastle-upon-Tyne, 1862. Reptd., Frank Graham, Newcastle-upon-Tyne, 1972 pp.578 (Introduction vii-xxviii includes a consideration of Newcastle as a radical and Chartist centre in the early nineteenth century)

652   Harrison, Albert   *Joseph Cowen, Orator, Patriot and Englishman. A Paper Read before the Priory Street Wesleyan Young Men's Class, York, April 1st, 1900, The Yorkshire Gazette*, York, 1900, pp.14 (The pamphlet includes Cowen's involvement with Tyneside Chartism in the early 1850s)

653   Harrison, Brian   *Peaceable Kingdom. Stability and Change in Modern Britain*, Oxford University Press, Oxford 1982, pp.493 (For a consideration of Chartist

concepts of respectability and the links with mid Victorian Liberalism, see Chapter IV 'Traditions of Respectability in British Labour History' pp.156-216)

654   Harrison, Brian   'Press and Pressure Groups in Modern Britain' pp.261-295 in Joanne Shattock and Michael Wolff (eds.) *The Victorian Periodical Press: Samplings and Soundings*, Leicester University Press, Leicester and University of Toronto Press, Toronto, 1982, pp.400 (Includes discussion on the vital role of the Chartist press for the Chartist leadership)

655   Harrison, J.F.C. *Learning and Living 1790-1960*, Routledge and Kegan Paul, London, 1961, pp. 404 (A study of adult education, drawing especially on Yorkshire, which provides the background of English artisan autodidact culture. See especially Chapter 3 - 'The Dynamic of Reform')

656   Harrison, J.F.C.   *The Common People. A History from the Norman Conquest to the Present*, Flamingo edition of Fontana Books, London, 1984, pp.445 (See pp.261-271 for Chartism, with scattered references elsewhere in the book)

657   Harrison, J.F.C.   'Early Victorian Radicals and the Medical Fringe' pp.198-215 in W.F. Bynum and Roy Porter (eds.) *Medical Fringe and Medical Orthodoxy 1750-1850*, Croom Helm, London, 1987, pp.274 (Explores the Owenite and Chartist involvement with spiritualism, mesmerism, phrenology, herbalism and homoeopathy, particularly after 1848)

658   Harrison, Stanley   *Poor Men's Guardians. A Record of the Struggles for a Democratic Newspaper Press 1763-1973*, Lawrence and Wishart, London, 1974, pp.256 (See pp.104-141 for the importance of the *Northern Star* and *People's Paper*)

659   Hearn, F. *Domination, Legitimation and Resistance: The Incorporation of the Nineteenth-Century English Working Class*, Greenwood Press, Westport, Connecticut, 1978, pp.309 (Critical theory and working class history; includes two chapters, pp.195-230, on Chartism embracing its narrative history, social basis, links with Methodism and the Irish)

660   Hearnshaw, F.J.C.   *A Survey of Socialism*, Macmillan, London, 1928, pp.473 (See pp.186-189 'The Chartists', viewed as an important stage in the rise of Socialism)

661   Hennock, E.P.   *Fit and Proper Persons*, Edward Arnold, London, 1973, pp.395 (Provides the context of Chartist attempts to enter local government, with especial reference to Birmingham and Leeds)

662   Himmelfarb, Gertrude   *The Idea of Poverty. England in the Early Industrial Age*, Faber and Faber, London and Boston, 1984, pp.595 (See Chapter XI, 'Chartism: The Politicization of the Poor' pp.253-269 for a substantial discussion in the light of more recent research, of the political, social and cultural nature of Chartism, 1838-1848)

663   Hinde, Wendy   *Richard Cobden. A Victorian Outsider*, Yale University Press, New Haven and London, 1987, pp.367 (For Cobden's attitude to the Chartists,

the Chartists' relationships with the Complete Suffrage Union and their confrontations with the Anti-Corn Law League and 1848)

664 Hobsbawm, E.J. and Scott, J. Wallach   'Political Shoemakers' pp.103-130 in E.J. Hobsbawm, *Worlds of Labour: Further Studies in the History of Labour*, Weidenfeld and Nicolson, London 1984, pp.369 (Also in *Past and Present*, No.89, November, 1980. A broad survey which emphasizes that of the persons active in Chartism, whose occupations are known, shoemakers formed much the largest single group, after the weavers and unspecified 'labourers')

665 Hodgkins, J.R.   *Over the Hills to Glory: Radicalism in Banburyshire, 1832-1945*, Clifton Press, Southend, 1978, pp.218 (A study of labour history in Banbury, with an introduction by Barrie Trinder. See pp.15-39 for Chartism including a section on William Bunting, the leading Banbury Chartist and Co-operator)

666 Hollis, Patricia   'Anti-Slavery and British Working-Class Radicalism in the Years of Reform' pp.294-315 in Christine Bolt and Seymour Drescher (eds.) *Anti-Slavery, Religion and Reform: Essays in Memory of Roger Anstey*, Dawson, Folkestone and Archon Books, Hamden, Connecticut, 1980, pp.377 (Argues the case that between 1823-1840, the abolitionist cause attracted little working class support amongst radicals and early Chartists)

667 Hostettler, John   *Thomas Wakley: An Improbable Radical*, Barry Rose Law Publishers, Little London, Chichester, 1993, pp.158

668 *Hovell, Mark   *The Chartist Movement* (ed. and completed with a memoir by T.F. Tout), Manchester University Press, 1966, third edition. Reptd. Gregg Revivals, Aldershot, 1994, pp.368

669 Huch, Ronald and Ziegler, Paul   *Joseph Hume: The People's M.P.*, The American Philosophical Society, Philadelphia, 1985, pp.172 (pp.113-163 are useful for an understanding of Hume's attitude towards and relationship with the Chartists, and the reception of his 'Little Charter')

670 Humpherys, Anne   'G.W.M. Reynolds: Popular Literature and Popular Politics' pp.3-21 in Joel H. Wiener (ed.) *Innovators and Preachers: The Role of the*

Editor in Victorian England, Westport, Connecticut, 1985, pp.332 (The chapter also appears as an article with the same title in *Victorian Periodicals Review*, Vol.16, Part 3/4, Fall, 1983)

671 Humpherys, Anne   'Popular Narrative and Political Discourse in *Reynolds's Weekly Newspaper'* pp.33-47 in Laurel Brake, Aled Jones and Lionel Madden (eds.) *Investigating Victorian Journalism*, Macmillan, London, 1990, pp.210 (Has examples of melodrama shaping radical political thought and the seeming contradiction in the *Weekly* between revolutionary analyses and liberal resolutions)

672 Humphries, Barbara   *Chartism: The First Political Movement of the Working Class*, London, 1978, pp.24 (A West London 'Militant' Supporters' pamphlet with 24 typed pages of text and 6 chapters; no contents page)

673   Hunt, E.H. *British Labour History 1815-1914*, Weidenfeld and Nicolson, London, 1981, pp.428 (See pp.219-249 for 'Chartism, Revolution and the Making of Class')

674   Hutchison, I.G.C. 'Glasgow Working-Class Politics' pp.98-141 in R.A. Cage (ed.) *The Working Class in Glasgow 1750-1914*, London, 1987, pp.203 (Deals with reformers and Chartists in Glasgow)

675   Hyndman, H.M. *The Evolution of Revolution*, Grant Richards Ltd., London, 1920, pp.406 (See Chapter XXVIII 'The Rise and Fall of the Chartist Movement' pp.295-308 for Hyndman's sympathetic interpretation of the nature and place of Chartism in British working class history)

676   James, Leslie *The Struggle for the Charter*, Newport, 1973, pp.5 (A Newport Museum and Art Gallery Information production. Basic information on the Chartist personalities, the Rising, trials and exile of the leaders, with illustrations by Keith Phelpstead. No pagination)

677   James, Louis *Fiction for the Working Man 1830-1850*, Penguin, Harmondsworth, Middlesex, 1973, pp.261 (Useful for the literary activities of the Chartist leaders Thomas Cooper, Thomas Frost and G.W.M. Reynolds)

678   Jenkins, Mick *The General Strike of 1842*, Lawrence & Wishart, London, 1980, pp.300 (Survey of the wave of strikes, focusing mainly on Lancashire. Also has biographical chapters on the local Chartist leaders, Alexander Hutchinson and Richard Pilling)

679   John, Angela V. *By the Sweat of their Brow: Women Workers at Victorian Coal-Mines*, Routledge and Kegan Paul, London, 1980. Reptd. 1984, pp.247 (See pp.47-58 for the Chartists' opposition to the employment of women underground)

680   Johnson, Richard 'Really Useful Knowledge': Radical Education and Working-Class Culture 1790-1848' pp.75-102 in John Clarke, Chas Critcher, Richard Johnson (eds.) *Working Class Culture. Studies in History and Theory*, Hutchinson, London, 1979, pp.301 (Includes a consideration of the Chartists' alternative radical culture, its forms, press, content, shifts and differences)

681   Jones, D.J.V. *The Last Rising: the Newport Insurrection of 1839*, Clarendon Press, Oxford, 1985, pp.273 (A major work of reinterpretation which sets the Rising in the context of the social and economic history of South Wales)

682   Jones, D.J.V. 'Scotch Cattle and Chartism', pp.139-164 in Trevor Herbert and Gareth Elwyn Jones (eds.) *People and Protest: Wales 1815-1880*, University of Wales Press, Cardiff, 1988. Reptd. 1990, pp.215 (Part of a series on 'Welsh History and its Sources' combining documents and interpretation of these two forms of working class protest in early nineteenth century Wales)

683   Jordan, Heather *The 1842 General Strike in South Wales*, Communist Party of Great Britain. Historians Group, Our History Series, No.75, London, 1982, pp.22 (Explores the events surrounding 1842 and underlines the links between Chartist and industrial strategies of the colliers and iron-miners in the South Wales coalfield)

684   Journès, Hugues *Une Litterature Revolutionnaire En Grande-Bretagne: La Poesie Chartiste*, Paris, 1991, pp.430 (In French. A discussion of the Chartist poets and their main writings)

685   Jowett, Frederick William *What Made Me a Socialist*, Independent Labour Party, London, 1925, pp.8 and The Strickland Press, Glasgow, 1941, pp.10 (The pamphlet explains how Jowett's political beliefs were formed by the influence of his parents and their memories of Chartist demonstrations)

686   Joyce, Patrick *Visions of the People: Industrial England and the Question of Class 1848-1914*, Cambridge University Press, Cambridge, 1991, pp.449 (Attacks orthodox views of class and sets up new questions on how social bonds were forged by attending to a wide range of contemporary experiences from politics to work, language and art. Covers the period from the decline of Chartism with particular reference to the Lancashire textile districts and workers. See pp.27-55 for the transition from radicalism to Liberalism)

687   Kidd, Alan *Manchester*, Ryburn Publishing, Keele University Press, Keele, 1993, pp.251 (See Chapter 5 'The Politics of Protest: From Food Riots to Chartism' pp.81-102)

688   Kiernan, Victor 'Labour and the Literate in Nineteenth Century Britain', pp.32-61 in D. Martin and D. Rubinstein (eds.) *Ideology and the Labour Movement. Essays Presented to John Saville*, Croom Helm, London, 1979, pp.276 (Contains material on the 'self-educated' Chartists William Lovett, Thomas Cooper and Robert Gammage, and on Feargus O'Connor, Bronterre O'Brien and Ernest Jones. The piece is also reproduced in V.G. Kiernan *Poets, Politics and the People*, Verso, London, 1989, pp.239. Edited and introduced by Harvey J. Kaye. See Chapter 7, pp.152-177)

689   Kiernan, V.G. *Poets, Politics and the People*, Verso, London, 1989, pp.239 (Edited and introduced by Harvey J. Kaye. See Chapter 1 'Patterns of Protest in English History' pp.18-39 for Chartist attitudes to direct action)

690   King, J.E. *Richard Marsden and the Preston Chartists 1837-1848*, Centre for North-West Regional Studies, University of Lancaster Occasional Paper No.10, 1981, pp.48

691   Kirby, R.G. and Musson, A.E. *The Voice of the People: John Doherty 1798-1854, Trade Unionist, Radical and Factory Reformer*, Manchester University Press, Manchester, 1975, pp.474 (See Chapter XI 'A Political Radical' pp.414-461, although it appears that his connections with Chartism were intermittent)

692   Kirk, Neville *The Growth of Working Class Reformism in Mid-Victorian England*, Croom Helm, London, 1985, pp.369 (Examines the post-Chartist period in the north west cotton districts and their transition to relative political stability and accommodation with the new capitalist order)

693   Kirk, Neville *Labour and Society in Britain and the United States. Volume One: Capitalism, Custom and Protest, 1780-1850*, Scolar Press, Aldershot, 1994, pp.240 (For Chartism see pp.122-143)

694   Kitz, Frank   *Recollections and Reflections*, Freedom Press, London, 1912,
        pp.33. Reptd. Carl Slienger, London, 1976 (Discusses Chartists he knew pp.
        8-9)

695   Klaus, H. Gustav   *The Literature of Labour; Two Hundred Years of Working
        Class Writing*, Harvester Press, Brighton, 1985, pp.210 (Chapter 3 'The
        Historical Bent of the Chartist Novel' pp.46-61 looks at the political novels of
        Thomas Martin Wheeler - 'Sunshine and Shadow', 1849-50 - and Ernest Jones -
        'De Brassier, A Democratic Romance', 1851-52)

696   Knott, John   *Popular Opposition to the 1834 Poor Law*, Croom Helm,
        London, 1986, pp.284 (Discusses the links between the anti-poor law
        campaign and Chartism)

697   Koditschek, Theodore   'The Dynamics of Class Formation in Nineteenth-
        Century Bradford' pp.511-554 in A.L. Beier, David Cannadine and James M.
        Rosenheim (eds.) *The First Modern Society. Essays in English History in
        Honour of Lawrence Stone*, Cambridge University Press. Cambridge, 1989,
        pp.654 (Explores the part played by a series of challenges, including Chartism,
        to the rise of and crises amongst bourgeois liberals in Bradford)

698   Koditschek, Theodore   *Class Formation and Urban-Industrial Society,
        Bradford, 1750-1850*, Cambridge University Press, Cambridge, 1990, pp.611
        (See pp.445-565 for the emergence of working class culture and
        consciousness, the challenge of Chartism, and the foundations of the mid-
        Victorian Liberal consensus)

699   Koga, Hideo   *Chartist Undō* (The Chartist Movement) Kyōiku Sha, Tokyo,
        1980, pp.281 (In Japanese. A concise history of the Chartist movement based
        upon up-to-date information and recent research. At least one copy in
        England in the possession of Dorothy Thompson)

700   Koseki, Takashi   *1848: Chartism to Irish Nationalism*, Mirai-sha, Tokyo, 1993,
        pp.362 (In Japanese. In 1848 an 'official' alliance between the Chartists and
        Irish nationalists, which the former had been advocating for more than a
        decade, finally came into existence. The author considers the meaning of 1848
        in British history by examining the 'defeat' of the alliance)

701   Kovalev, Yuri V.   Politicheskaya livika Vil 'yama Lintona' (The Political Lyrics
        of William Linton), *Iz Istorii demokraticheskai literatury v Anglii XVIII-XX
        Vekov* (The History of Democratic Literature in England from the Eighteenth
        to the Twentieth Centuries, Leningrad, 1955. In Russian)

702   Kuhnigk, Armin M.   *Karl Schapper. Ein Vater der europäischer
        Arbeiterbewegung*, Camberger Verlag, Ulrich Lange, Camberg, Germany,
        1980, pp.250 (Schapper was an initiator, whilst in exile in London, of the
        Chartist Democratic Friends of All Nations and the Society of Fraternal
        Democrats. See pp.107-120 and other scattered references for both his
        relationship with these organisations and with Ernest Jones, G.J. Harney and
        other London Chartists)

703   Kunina, V.E. 'K voprosu ob avtorstue stati ob Ernste Dzhonse v Londonskoi
       gazete *Das Wolk, Teoria Marixisma i rabochego dvizhenia VXIX v* ('The
       Question of the Authorship of the Article on Ernest Jones in the London
       Newspaper *Das Wolk* in *The Theory of Marxism and the Nineteenth Century
       Workers' Movement*, Moscow, 1979, pp.174-181. In Russian)

704   Kunina, W. 'George Julian Harney' pp.421-455 in E.P. Kandel (ed.) *Marx und
       Engels und die ersten proletarischen Revolutionäre*, Berlin, German
       Democratic Republic, 1965 (In German)

705   Kuzcynski, Ingrid (ed.) *Den Kopf tragt hoch trotz allem! Englische
       Arbeiterantobiographien des 19 Jahrhunderts*, Leipzig, 1983, pp.370 (In
       German. Includes pp.259-347 extracts from the autobiographies of Thomas
       Cooper, J.B. Leno and William Lovett)

706   Lancashire Communist Party of Great Britain *Lancashire 1848-1948
       Communist Manifesto Centenary*, London, 1948, unpaginated, but pp.32
       (Includes brief reference to Ernest Jones and a short section on 'Lancashire
       Chartists')

707   Lancaster, W. *Radicalism, Cooperation and Socialism: Leicester Working-
       Class Politics 1860-1906*, Leicester University Press, Leicester, 1987, pp.232
       (See Chapter 6 'Leicester Politics and the Working Class, 1860-85', particularly
       pp.76-84, for the continuing importance of Chartist politics and the careers of
       ex -Chartists in Leicester, George Buckby, John Markham and John Sketchley)

708   Langley, Arthur S. *Birmingham Baptists: Past and Present*, The Kingsgate
       Press, London, 1939, pp.262 (pp.150-152 contain a very useful summary of the
       political career of the Birmingham Christian Chartist leader, Arthur O'Neill)

709   Laqueur, Thomas W. *Religion and Respectability: Sunday Schools and
       Working-Class Culture, 1780-1850*, Yale University Press, New Haven, 1976,
       pp.293 (Argues for the integration of Sunday Schools in working class culture,
       but points to the relative weakness of 'alternative' Sunday Schools organized
       by the Chartists by 1851. See pp.178-186 for Chartist-inspired Sunday
       Schools)

710   Large, David 'London in the Year of Revolutions, 1848' pp.177-211 in John
       Stevenson (ed.) *London in the Age of Reform*, Blackwell, Oxford, 1977, pp.214
       (Concise assessment of the strength of metropolitan Chartism and the
       responses of the authorities throughout 1848)

711   Large, David *Radicalism in Bristol in the Nineteenth Century*, Bristol
       University, Bristol, 1981, pp.20.

712   Lattek, Christine 'Radikalismus im Ausland. Die Entwicklung des deutschen
       Frühsozialismus in London 1840-1852' pp.39-64 in Gregory Claeys and
       Liselotte Glage (eds.) *Radikalismus in Literatur und Gesellschaft des 19
       Jahrhunderts*, Peter Lang, Bern, 1987, pp.316 (Chapter in German. Examines
       the development of early German socialism in London 1840-52; also includes

consideration of G.J. Harney, E. Jones, the Democratic Friends of All Nations and the Society of Fraternal Democrats)

713   Lattek, Christine 'The Beginnings of Socialist Internationalism in the 1840s: The "Democratic Friends of All Nations" in London', pp.259-282 in Frits van Holthoon and Marcel van der Linden (eds.) *Internationalism in the Labour Movement 1830 to 1940*, E.J. Brill, Leiden, 1988, Vol.1, pp.368 (A lengthy and pioneering analysis of the London-based Democratic Friends of All Nations, founded in 1844, in which British Owenites and Chartists and refugees from France, Germany and Poland formed an international workers organization)

714   Laybourn, Keith 'Labour Movements' pp.183-197 in Rex Pope (ed.) *Atlas of British Social and Economic History Since c.1700*, Routledge, London, 1989, pp.250 (pp.185-188 look at Chartism in Britain c.1836-1848, its spatial distribution and the geography of Bradford Chartism)

715   Lees, Lynn Hollen *Exiles of Erin. Irish Migrants in Victorian London*, Manchester University Press, Manchester, 1979, pp.276 (See pp.225-231 and pp.237-239 for the London Irish communities' Chartist affiliations, 1841-1848)

716   Lindsay, Jack 'Ebenezer Jones, 1820-1860 - an English Symbolist' pp.151-175 in Maurice Cornforth (ed.) *Rebels and Their Causes: Essays in Honour of A.L. Morton*, Lawrence and Wishart, London 1978, pp.224 (Literary study of a forgotten Chartist and Owenite poet and friend of W.J. Linton)

717   Little, Alan 'Liverpool Chartists: Subscribers to the National Land Company, 1847-1848' pp.247-251, Appendix, in John Belchem (ed.) *Popular Politics, Riot and Labour. Essays in Liverpool History 1790-1940*, Liverpool University Press, Liverpool 1992, pp.257 (Occupational analysis of the 171 Liverpool subscribers to the National Land Company)

718   Littlewood, Kevin *From Reform to the Charter: Merthyr Tydfil 1832-1838*, Merthyr Tydfil Heritage Trust, Merthyr Tydfil, 1990, pp.31 (For the beginnings of Chartism in Merthyr)

719   Longmate, Norman *The Breadstealers: The Fight against the Corn Laws 1838-1846*, Temple Smith, London, 1984, pp.270 (See Chapter 9 'Upset by Chartists' pp.81-95; the author contrasts the successes of the League with the ineffectualness of Chartism)

720   Lowe, W.J. *The Irish in Mid-Victorian Lancashire: The Shaping of a Working Class Community*, Peter Lang, New York, 1989, pp.227 (See Chapter 7 'Irish Politics in Lancashire', particularly pp.183-189, for Chartism amongst the Lancashire Irish in 1848 in Liverpool, Manchester and Salford)

721   McCabe, Joseph *Life and Letters of George Jacob Holyoake*, Rationalist Press Association, Watts and Co., London, 1908, 2 Vols. (Vol.1 pp.356 covers Chartism and Holyoake's involvement in the movement; see generally)

722   McCalman, Iain *Radical Underworld. Prophets, Revolutionaries and Pornographers in London, 1795-1840*, Cambridge University Press, Cambridge, 1988, pp.338. Reptd. Clarendon Paperbacks, Oxford University

Press, 1993 (For the early history of the London Democratic Association, circa 1838-40, the ultra-radical underworld and the transmission of Spencean ideas into Chartism)

723   McCalman, Iain   'Erin go Bragh': The Irish in British Popular Radicalism c.1790-1840' pp.168-184 in Oliver MacDonagh and W.F. Mandle (eds.) *Irish-Australian Studies: Papers Delivered at the Fifth Irish-Australian Conference*, Australian National University, Canberra, 1989, pp.356 (Underlines the importance of the contribution of Irish revolutionary expatriates and causes in English popular radicalism by 1840, and how these traditions became part of Chartism)

724   *McCord, Norman   *The Anti-Corn Law League*, Allen and Unwin, London, 1958. Reptd. Gregg Revivals, Aldershot, 1993, pp.224

725   McNulty, David   'Bristol Trade Unions in the Chartist Years', pp.220-236 in John Rule (ed.) *British Trade Unionism 1750-1850: The Formative Years*, Longman, London, 1988, pp.275.

726   Machin, Frank   *The Yorkshire Miners. A History*, Vol. I, National Union of Mineworkers, Yorkshire Area, Barnsley, 1958, pp.496 (See Chapter III 'National Organization and the Strike of 1844', pp.42-66 for the links between the Yorkshire miners and Chartism)

727   Malmgreen, Gail   *Neither Bread nor Roses: Utopian Feminists and the English Working Class 1800-1850*, J.L. Noyce, Brighton, 1978, pp.42 (Useful for the involvement of women in both Chartism and Owenism; see generally)

728   Malos, Ellen   'Bristol Women in Action (1839-1919)', pp.97-128 in Ian Bild (ed.) *Bristol's Other History (1840-1940)*, Bristol Broadsides (Co-op) Ltd., Bristol, pp.160 (The chapter begins with a consideration of female Chartists in Bristol and the West Country)

729   Marchant, James   *Dr. John Clifford, C.H. Life, Letters and Reminiscences*, Cassell and Company Ltd., London and New York, 1924, pp.312 (Biography of a noted Baptist leader 1836-1923 which includes scraps of autobiography written by Clifford towards the end of his life. Chapter 1, pp.1-10 provides interesting information on his working class background, life in a Beeston lace mill, sympathy for Chartism and Chartist leaders, particularly Thomas Cooper)

730   Marinicheva, Maria P.   'The Red Republican - Journal of Revolutionary Chartism' pp.522-535 in *Symposium of Studies in the History of Marxism and the International Workers' Movement*, Institute of Marxism-Leninism, Moscow, 1964 (In Russian)

731   Martin, G. Currie   *Poets of the Democracy*, Headley Bros. Publishers, London, 1917, pp.142 (Chapter VIII includes a consideration on pp.73-74 of Thomas Cooper as a Chartist poet)

732   Marxist Study Courses   *History of the Working Class. Course 2, Lesson 2. The English Industrial Revolution and Chartism*, Martin Lawrence, London, 1932,

pp.50 (Pamphlet for trade unionists and socialists activists studying Chartism in the 1930s. Almost certainly written by Theodore Rothstein)

733   Miles, Dudley *Francis Place. The Life of a Remarkable Radical 1771-1854*, Harvester Press, Brighton, 1988, pp.303 (For Place and the early history of Chartism see pp.226-247)

734   Moore, Bill, Holmes, Sam and Baxter John L. *Samuel Holberry 1814-1842: Sheffield's Revolutionary Democrat*, Holberry Society Publications, Sheffield, 1978, pp.26 (For Holberry and Chartism in Sheffield, the Sheffield Rising in 1840 and imprisonment of local leaders, including Holberry)

735   Moore, Kevin   'This Whig and Tory Ridden Town': Popular Politics in Liverpool in the Chartist Era' pp.38-67 in John Belchem (ed.) *Popular Politics, Riot and Labour: Essays in Liverpool History, 1790-194-*, Liverpool University Press, Liverpool, 1992, pp.257. (An interesting chapter arguing that Chartism was strong rather than weak in Liverpool until 1843; thereafter it declined steadily until 1847)

736   Moran, Richard   *Knowing Right From Wrong*, Free Press, New York, 1981, pp.234 (Important for the case of Daniel McNaughten, a Chartist sympathiser, who, in 1843, assassinated Sir Robert Peel's secretary, mistaking him for the Prime Minister)

737   Morris, E. Ronald   *Chartism in Llanidloes 1838-1839*, Llanidloes Chartist Celebration Committee, Llanidloes, 1989, pp.96 (A detailed account of the Chartist riots in April 1839 and a valuable assessment of the careers of the local activists thereafter)

738   Morris, Geoffrey   *The Rise of the Labour Movement*, Wayland Publishers, Hove, East Sussex, 1978, pp.128 (See Chapter 2 'Charter and Chartists' pp.31-46. For schools; with documents and illustrations)

739   Morris, Will   *England Has Risen*, Redflag Fellowship, Fulham, London, n.d. but c.1940, pp.22 (Pamphlet with left-wing slant on Chartism pp.10-12)

740   Morton, A.L.   *A People's History of England*, Victor Gollancz, London, 1938, Left Book Club, pp.544 (See pp.418-426 for 'The Chartists' interpreted in the left-wing traditions of the publisher)

741   *Morton, A.L. & Tate, G.   *The British Labour Movement 1770-1920. A History*, Lawrence and Wishart, London, 1956. Reptd. with new bibliography, Lawrence and Wishart, London, 1979, pp.318. (See Chapter 2 'Chartism' pp.49-99 and pp.100-112 for the aftermath of Chartism)

742   Moss, David J.   *Thomas Attwood: The Biography of a Radical*, McGill-Queen's University Press, Montreal, 1990, pp.377 (Moss attempts to distance Attwood from Chartism. For Attwood's involvement in early Chartism see pp.276-298)

743   Murray, Norman   *The Scottish Handloom Weavers, 1790-1850: A Social History*, John Donald, Edinburgh, 1978, pp.269 (The final chapter is devoted

to a consideration of radical attitudes and activities; see particularly pp.228-233 for the Chartist phase)

744   Musson, A.E. *British Trade Unions 1800-1875,* Macmillan, London, 1972, pp.80. Reptd. pp.1-70 in Leslie Clarkson (ed.) *British Trade Unions and Labour History: A Compendium,* Humanities Press International Inc., Atlantic Highlands, New Jersey, 1990, pp.290 (For the links between Chartism, trade societies and the trade cycle, and a review of writings on Chartism and the trades up to 1970)

745   Neal, Frank *Sectarian Violence. The Liverpool Experience 1819-1914,* Manchester University Press, Manchester, 1988, pp.272 (See pp.115-124 for the activities of and links between Liverpool Chartists and Irish Confederates in the city in 1848)

746   Neale, R.S. *Bath 1680-1850: A Social History, Or a Valley of Pleasure, Yet a Sink of Iniquity,* Routledge and Kegan Paul, London, 1981, pp.466 (For Chartism in Bath, see pp.367-380)

747   Nettlau, Max *Anarchism in England One Hundred Years Ago,* The Oriole Press, Berkeley Heights, New Jersey, 1955, pp.20. Reptd. Carl Slienger, London, 1976 (Shows how anarchism developed in the last years of Chartism; describes items in the *Reasoner,* discusses Thornton Hunt and the *Leader*)

748   Newens, Stanley A. *Chartism and other Antecedents of the Labour Movement in Essex,* Alf Killick Memorial Trust, Southend-on-Sea, 1987, pp.12 (Examines local events from the Peasants' Revolt of 1381 to the Chartist agitation of the 1840s)

749   Newport Museum and Art Gallery *The Monmouthshire Chartists,* Newport, 1958. Reptd. 1968, pp.33 (Signed 'Cefni Barnett'. A brief history and picture book of some of the material and documents connected with the Chartist movement in Monmouthshire and preserved at the Museum and Art Gallery)

750   Newport Museum and Art Gallery *The Chartists 1839-1989, 150th Anniversary, Prints and Broadsheets from the Chartist Period,* Newport Borough Council Leisure Services, Newport, 1989 (Pack comprises booklet of pp.12 by Leslie James; 5 Chartist broadsheets; and 17 contemporary prints connected with the Newport Rising in 1839)

751   Nicholas, T. Islwyn *Four Welsh Rebels,* Foyle's Welsh Co., Ltd., London, 1946, pp.290 (Includes *A Welsh Heretic: Dr. William Price, Llantrisant,* Foyle's Welsh Co., Ltd., London, 1939, pp.48; Reptd. Ffynnon Press, Aberystwyth, 1973, pp.48. Brief biography of the Pontypridd Chartist leader involved in the Newport Rising, a Welsh Druid and pioneer of cremation)

752   Nossiter, T.J. *Influence, Opinion and Political Idioms in Reformed England: Case Studies from the North East 1832-74,* Harvester Press, Hassocks, Brighton, 1975 pp.255 (For Chartism in the North East see pp.149-156)

753   O'Brien, Jo *Women's Liberation in Labour History: A Case Study from Nottingham,* The Bertrand Russell Peace Foundation, Spokesman Pamphlets,

No.24, Nottingham, n.d. (circa 1970), pp.15 (Pamphlet has references to women and Chartism in Nottingham 1838-39)

754   O'Callaghan, Bryn   *The Chartists*, Longman, London, 1974, pp.32 (For schools, in the 'Making of the Modern World' Series)

755   Orlova, T.F.   'Ernst Dzhons i ego borba v zashchitu indeitsev', *Narody Azii i Afriki*, ('Ernest Jones and his struggle in defence of the Indians' *The People of Asia and Africa*, Moscow, 1983, pp.76-81. In Russian)

756   Osmond, David   *The Chartists 150th Anniversary. A Guided Walk through Newport, Scene of the Chartist Uprising of 1839*, Newport Local History Society and Newport Borough Council, Newport, 1989, pp.15 (A brief pamphlet history of the Newport Rising to accompany the walk details of the march to the Westgate Hotel and other relevant sites)

757   Palmer, Roy   *A Touch on the Times. Songs of Social Change 1770-1914*, Penguin, Harmondsworth, 1974, pp.352 (See pp.299-305 for Chartist songs and commentary)

758   Palmer, Roy   *A Ballad History of England. From 1588 to the Present Day*, Batsford, London, 1979, pp.192 (See Section 51, pp.117-119 for the Chartists at Newport and the ballad 'The Last Farewell to England of Frost, Williams and Jones')

759   Palmer, Roy   *The Sound of History. Songs and Social Comment*, Oxford University Press, Oxford, 1988, pp.361. (The Introduction, pp.1-29, deals with Chartist ballad printers Thomas Willey and John Livesey; pp.256-264 explore Chartist ballads and their influence)

760   Palmer, Stanley H.   *Police and Protest in England and Ireland 1780-1850*, Cambridge University Press, Cambridge, 1988, pp.824 (For the extensive military and new police force preparations and responses to Chartism in 1839, 1842 and 1848 in both countries, see Chapters 11 and 12, pp.430-517)

761   Palmer, Stanley H.   'Power, Coercion and Authority: Protest and Repression in 1848 in England and Ireland' pp.274-289 in Warren F. Spencer and Louise Salley Parker (eds.) *The Consortium on Revolutionary Europe 1750-1850. Proceedings 1989, Vol.II*, The University of Georgia, Department of History, Athens, Georgia, 1989, pp.679 (Includes a commentary by Joel Cleland pp.303-307. Examines the nature of popular unrest and the state's handling of it in England and Ireland)

762   Patterson, A. Temple   *A History of Southampton 1700-1914, Vol.Two: The Beginnings of Modern Southampton, 1836-1867*, Southampton University Press, 1971, pp.189 (Has a number of references pp.31-32, pp.37-38, pp.146-148 on Chartism in Southampton in 1839, 1842 and 1848. The only known study of Chartism in the town)

763   Porter, Bernard   *The Refugee Question in mid-Victorian Politics*, Cambridge University Press, Cambridge, 1979, pp.242 (Includes in various parts of the

book a consideration of Chartist attitudes and responses to refugees following the revolutions of 1848, ending with the Orsini affair of 1858)

764   Prest, John   *Lord John Russell*, Macmillan, London, 1972, pp.558 (See pp.139-150 and pp.283-285 for a discussion of Russell in relation to the Chartists)

765   Prest, John   *Politics in the Age of Cobden*, Macmillan, London, 1977, pp.165 (Includes in Chapter 6 'Had the Corn Laws Not Been Repealed So Soon', particularly pp.116-121 an interesting discussion of Chartist attitudes to parliamentary elections and voter registration)

766   Price, Emyr   *Hanes Ennill y Bleidlais*, Gwasg Prifysgol Cymru, Caerdydd, 1982, pp.21 ('The History of Winning the Vote', University of Wales Press, Cardiff, see pp.8-10 for the part played by the Chartists with particular reference to the Welsh Chartist experience. In Welsh; for schools)

767   Prothero, Iorwerth J.   *Artisans and Politics in Early Nineteenth-Century London: John Gast and his Times*, Dawson, Folkestone, 1979, pp.418 (See particularly Part Four: 'From Reform Crisis to Chartism' pp.268-327 for many aspects of early Chartism in London)

768   Pulman, S.   *Forum Echoes. The Substance of More Than Twenty Debates in the ... Manchester County Forum*, Abel Heywood and Son, Manchester, 1910, pp.285 (In verse. Puts into verse some of the speeches heard by the author during twenty years' attendance at the Manchester County Forum. Includes 'The Good Old Times?' and 'Ancient and Modern States', pp.77-88, both from 'An Old Chartist'; and 'Education v. Force' by 'Mr. Chadwick (another Chartist)', pp.131-141)

769   Reay, Barry   *The Last Rising of the Agricultural labourers: Rural Life and Protest in Nineteenth-Century England*, Clarendon Press, Oxford, 1990, pp.226 (Contains interesting passing references to the Chartist support for the so-called 'last rising' of the agricultural labourers, led by a man known locally as 'Sir William Courtenay', at the Battle of Bossenden Wood, May 1838, in Kent)

770   Rendall, Jane   *The Origins of Modern Feminism : Women in Britain, France and the United States, 1780-1860*, Lyceum Books, Chicago and Macmillan, London, 1985, pp.382. (See pp.238-247 for a summary of the role of women in the Chartist movement 1838-1858)

771   Reynolds, Jack   *The Great Paternalist: Titus Salt and the Growth of Nineteenth Century Bradford*, Temple Smith, London, 1983, pp.382 (Contains an account of Bradford Chartism 1837-1858, the sympathies of Salt for certain Chartist ideals, and also charts the fashioning of a political consensus around radical Liberalism by 1870)

772   Ridley, F.A.   *The Revolutionary Tradition in England*, National Labour Press, London, 1947, pp.316 (See Chapter V 'The Chartist Movement' pp.247-267. A substantial chapter written very much in the Mark Hovell tradition of interpretation)

773   Roberts, Robert   *'Of Masters and Men'. The Clarkes of Silkstone and their Colliers*, Barnsley W.E.A., 1981, pp.39 (A study of the power of one family of coal-owners in the South Yorkshire coalfield four miles from Barnsley during the 1840s. See particularly Chapter 3 pp.17-29 for industrial relations, Chartism and the Miners' Strike of 1844)

774   Roberts, Stephen   *Radical Politicians and Poets in Early Victorian Britain: The Voices of Six Chartist Leaders*, Edwin Mellen Press, New York, 1993, pp.149. (Considers the Chartists George White, George Binns, Robert Peddie, Charles Clarke, Thomas Clark and Samuel Kydd; each selected to represent a different strand in the Chartist movement)

775   Rössler, Horst   *Literatur und Arbeiterbewegung. Studien zur Literaturkritik und frühen Prosa des Chartismus*, Peter Lang, Frankfurt/Main-Bern-New York, 1985, pp.272 (In German. *Literature and the Labour Movement. Studies in the Literary Criticism and Early Prose of Chartism*. Deals with the literary prose and criticism of Chartism. The centre-piece is a study of a cycle of ten 'moral fables' by W.J. Linton and two stories by Thomas Doubleday)

776   * Rothstein, Theodore   *Une Epoque du Movement Ouvrier Anglais. Chartisme et Trade-Unionism*, Bibliothèque Marxist, 7, Paris, 1928

777   *Rothstein, Theodore   *From Chartism to Labourism. Historical Sketches of the English Working Class Movement*, London, 1929. Reptd. Lawrence and Wishart, London, 1983, pp.365 with an Introduction by John Saville, XXVI. The 1929 edition was also reptd. by Garland Publishing, London and New York, 1984.

778   Rowe, D.J.   'Tyneside Chartism' pp.62-87 in Norman McCord (ed.), *Essays in Tyneside Labour History*, for the North East Labour History Society, Department of Humanities, Newcastle-upon-Tyne Polytechnic, Newcastle, 1977, pp.197.

779   Rowlands, John   'Physical Force Chartism on Tyneside in 1839' pp.8-16 in M. Callcott and R. Challinor (eds.) *Working Class Politics in North East England*, Essays published on behalf of the North East Labour History Society, Newcastle-upon-Tyne Polytechnic, Newcastle-upon-Tyne, 1983, pp.103.

780   Royle, Edward   *Radical Politics 1790-1900. Religion and Unbelief*, Longman, London, 1971, pp.152 (See Chapter 6 'Liberalism, Chartism and Republicanism' pp.59-69)

781   Royle, Edward   *Chartism*, Longman, London, 1980, pp.142. Second edition, Longman, London, revised, 1986, pp.149 (A key text for all students and sixth-formers beginning their study of Chartism)

782   Royle, Edward   'Chartism', pp.157-169 in A. Digby and C.H. Feinstein (eds.) *New Directions in Economic and Social History*, Macmillan, London, 1989, pp.203 (Intended for teachers, pupils and undergraduates, the piece surveys the changing interpretations of Chartism from the economic to the political, from leaders to followers, and to a rehabilitation of Feargus O'Connor.

Originally published in *ReFresh (Recent Findings of Research in Economic and Social History)*, No.2, Spring 1986)

783   Royle, Edward   'Newspapers and Periodicals in Historical Research' pp.48-59 in Laurel Brake, Aled Jones and Lionel Madden (eds.) *Investigating Victorian Journalism*. Macmillan, London, 1990, pp.210 (For the value of radical newspapers such as the *Northern Star* and *People's Paper* as source material for the historian)

784   Royle, Edward and Walvin, James   *English Radicals and Reformers 1760-1848*, Harvester Press, Brighton and University Press of Kentucky, 1982, pp.233 (See the final chapter 'The Charter and No Surrender' pp.160-180)

785   Rozhkov, B.A.   'Otsenka klassovogo kharactera chartisma v novykh rabotakh angliiskikh burzhuaznykh istorikov' *Problemy Britanskoi Istorii* ('Assessments of Chartism's class character in new works by bourgeois English historians' in *Problems of British History*, Moscow, 1984, pp.198-202. In Russian)

786   *Rudé, George   *The Crowd in History, 1730-1848. A Study of Popular Disturbances in France and England*, London, 1964. Reptd., Lawrence and Wishart, London, 1981, pp.279 (See Chapter 12 'Chartism' pp.179-191)

787   Rudé, George   *Protest and Punishment: The Study of the Social and Political Protesters Transported to Australia 1788-1868*, Clarendon Press, Oxford, 1978, pp.270 (Includes a consideration of the lives of some of the Chartists transported in the 1840s)

788   Rudé, George   'Why Was There No Revolution in England in 1830 or 1848?'. Reptd., pp.148-163 in Harvey Kaye (ed.) *The Face of the Crowd. Studies in Revolution, Ideology and Popular Protest. Selected Essays of George Rudé*, Humanities Press International, Inc. Atlantic Highlands, New Jersey, 1988, pp.271.

789   Rule, John   *The Labouring Classes in Early Industrial England 1750-1850*, Longman, London, 1986, pp.408 (See Chapter 13 'Post 1834: Craft Unionism, Miners and Chartism', pp.310-347, particularly for the nature of Chartist support in London, the 'General Strike' of 1842 and the relationship of Chartism to the rise and fall of the Miners' Association)

790   Rule, John and Wells, Roger   *Crime, Protest and Popular Politics in Southern England, 1740-1850*, Hambledon Press, London, 1994, pp.224 (A collection of essays including revision of former articles on Chartism: 'The Chartist Mission to Cornwall'; Richard Spurr - Small Town Radical'; and 'Southern Chartism'. See also Articles section)

791   Saville, John   *1848, The British State and the Chartist Movement*, Cambridge University Press, Cambridge, 1987, pp.319 (An important contribution to the studies that seek to answer why there was no revolution in Britain during the conflict-torn 1840s)

792   *Schlüter, Hermann *Die Chartisten-Bewegung; Ein Beitrag zur Sozial-
       politischen Geschichte Englands*, New York, 1916, pp.398; another edition,
       Moscow, 1925, pp.398

793   Schmidtgall, Harry *Friedrick Engels' Manchester-Aufenthalt 1842-1844*,
       Schriften aus dem Karl-Marx-Haus, Trier, Germany, 1981, pp.161 (In German.
       About the life of the young Engels in Manchester and his attempts - with some
       success - to exert influence on the Owenite Socialists and Chartists, particularly
       with John Watts, James Leach and G.J. Harney. See particularly pp.60-85.
       Copy available in Working Class Movement Library, Salford)

794   Schwab, Ulrike *The Poetry of the Chartist Movement: A Literary and
       Historical Study*, Kulwer Academic Publishers, Dordrecht, 1993, pp.247.
       (Subjects some of the Chartist poets - Thomas Cooper, Ernest Jones and J.B.
       Leno - to intense theoretical analysis)

795   Schwarzkopf, Jutta *Women in the Chartist Movement*, Macmillan, London,
       1991, pp.337 (Assembles many of the references to Chartist women and their
       activities)

796   Scott, Joan Wallach *Gender and the Politics of History*, Columbia University
       Press, New York, 1988, pp.242 (See Chapter 3 'On Language, Gender and
       Working Class History'. pp.53-67. With particular reference to Gareth
       Stedman Jones' work on Chartism, the author re-reads Chartism and argues
       for a more subtle understanding of both the force of language and dimension
       of gender as a means of uncovering the formation of class. The piece also
       appeared as an article. See Articles section)

797   *Searby, Peter *The Chartists*, Longman 'Then and There' Series, London 1967.
       Second edition, Longman, Harlow, 1989, pp.56 (For schools. Focuses on
       Leicester as an example of Chartist activities)

798   Searby, Peter *The Chartists in Wales*, Longman 'Then and There' Series,
       Longman, Harlow, 1986, pp.64 (For Schools. Important contribution to the
       study of Chartism in Wales as a whole)

799   Seehase, Georg 'Poetry of and for the Working Class in Ernest Charles
       Jones's *Notes to the People*' pp.144-152 in Anselm Schlösser (ed.) *Essays in
       Honour of William Gallacher*, Humboldt University, Berlin, 1966, pp.354

800   Sharratt, Bernard *Reading Relations. Structures of Literary Production. A
       Dialectical Text Book*, Harvester Press, Brighton, 1982, pp.341 (See pp.241-
       319 for a textual and contextual analysis of the autobiographies of Samuel
       Bamford, Alexander Somerville, James Dawson Burn and Thomas Frost)

801   Shestoperova, L.A. 'Pedagogicheskie idei revolyutsionnogo Chartisma 40-50-e
       gg.XIX v.' *Borba progresasivnoi and reaktsionnoi tendentsii v pedagogike
       domonopolisticheskogo Kapitalisma* ('Pedagogical ideas of revolutionary
       Chartism in the 1840s and 1850s', *The Struggle between Progressive and
       Reactionary Pedagogical tendencies in pre-monopoly Capitalism*, Moscow,
       1982, pp.87-94. In Russian)

802   Shikanyan, I.N.   *'Norzern Star* - massovaya gazeta revolyutsionnykh Chartistov', *Formirovanie proletariata* (*'The Northern Star* - mass circulation newspaper of the revolutionary Chartists', *The Formation of the Proletariat,* Moscow, 1980, pp.253-271. In Russian)

803   Shikanyan, I.N.   'F. Engels i Chartistskaya gazeta *Norzern Star', Iz Istorii sotsialnykh dvizhenii i obshchestvennoi mysli* ('F. Engels and the Chartist newspaper *Northern Star', From the History of Social Movements and Social Thought,* Moscow, 1981, pp.3-23. In Russian)

804   Shikanyan, I.N.   'Korrespondentskaya rabota Engelsa v *Norzern Star, Istoriya sotsialisticeskikh idei* ('Engels' writing in correspondence with the *Northern Star. The History of Socialist Ideas,* Moscow, 1984, pp.19-35. In Russian)

805   Shikanyan, I.N.   'E. Dzhons i K. Marx. Iz Istorii ikh politicheskogo sotrudnichestva, po materialam perepiski 1864-1868 gg', *Marxism i rabochee dvizhenie XIX V. Nekotovye aktualnye problemy teorii i istorii* ('History of the political collaboration between E. Jones and K. Marx, based on their correspondence 1864 and 1868'. *Marxism and the Nineteenth Century Workers' Movement. Some Current Problems of Theory and History,* Moscow, 1988, pp.171-197. In Russian)

806   Sims, George R.   *My Life: Sixty Years Recollections of Bohemian London,* Eveleigh Nash Co., London, 1917, pp.351 (See pp.9-12 for the activities of his maternal grandfather, a London Chartist, John Dinmore Stevenson, and his involvement at Kennington Common in April 1848)

807   Smith, Dennis   *Conflict and Compromise. Class Formation in English Society 1830-1914. A Comparative Study of Birmingham and Sheffield,* Routledge and Kegan Paul, London, 1982, pp.338 (Chapter 4 'From Conflict to Equipoise' pp.79-103 explores the political, industrial and religious conflicts in the two cities, circa 1830-1864)

808   Smith, F.B.   'The View from Britain 1: Tumults Abroad, Stability at Home', pp.94-120 in Eugene Kamenka and F.B. Smith (eds.) *Intellectuals and Revolution. Socialism and the Experience of 1848,* Edward Arnold, London, 1979, pp.165. (For Chartism and the reactions of the authorities in Britain during and immediately after 1848. A near identical version appeared in article form. See Articles section)

809   *Smith, F.B. and McBriar, A.M. (eds.) *Historical Studies: Eureka Supplement,* Melbourne, 1965. Reptd., 1972

810   Smith, L.D.   *Carpet Weavers and Carpet Masters: The Hand Loom Carpet Weavers of Kidderminster 1780-1850,* Kenneth Tomkinson, Kidderminster, 1986, pp.316 (See Chapter 7 'Popular Politics and the Chartist Movement' pp.220-251 and Chapter 8 'The Final Struggles, 1840-1852' pp.252-274)

811   Snell, K.D.M. (ed.)   Introduction to Alexander Somerville, *The Whistler at the Plough* London, 1852; Reptd. Merlin Press, London and Augustus Kelley, New York, 1989, pp.438 (The Introduction, xxxi, includes a consideration of Somerville's relationship with Chartism)

812   Spence, Nigel A.   'Joseph Rayner Stephens - "He Hath Done What He Could"
pp.35-47 in Alice Lock (ed.) *Looking Back at Stalybridge*, Librarians and Arts
Committee, Tameside Metropolitan Borough, 1989, pp.150 (A potted
biography with much emphasis on Stephens' political career, particularly in
early Chartism)

813   Stedman Jones, Gareth   'The Language of Chartism' pp.3-58 in James Epstein
and Dorothy Thompson (eds.) *The Chartist Experience: Studies in Working-
Class Radicalism and Culture, 1830-60*, Macmillan, London, 1982, pp.392 (A
provocative and penetrating essay which has generated considerable debate
with its insistence that the Chartist movement was primarily political rather
than economic and social in character)

814   Stedman Jones, Gareth   'Rethinking Chartism' pp.90-178 in Gareth Stedman
Jones, *Languages of Class. Studies in English Working Class History 1832-1982*,
Cambridge University Press, Cambridge, 1983, pp.260 (An extended version
of the contribution to *The Chartist Experience*)

815   Steer, Chris   *Radicals and Protest 1815-50*, Macmillan, London, 1986, pp.56
(History in Depth Series for Schools, with documents and interpretation. See
pp.41-55 for a chapter on the rise and fall of Chartism)

816   Stevenson, John   *Popular Disturbances in England 1700-1870*, Longman,
London, 1979, pp.374 (See Chapter 12 'The Chartist Era' pp.245-274; an
important work of synthesis at undergraduate level)

817   Strauss, E.   *Irish Nationalism and British Democracy*, Methuen, London, 1951,
pp.307. Reptd., Greenwood Press, Westport, Connecticut, 1975 (See pp.125-
131 for an early view in the debate about the degree to which the Irish were
involved in Chartism. Stresses how the Irish provided Feargus O'Connor, the
agitator, and Bronterre O'Brien, the theoretician, and a readiness in general for
revolutionary change)

818   Swift, R.E.   *The Irish in Britain 1815-1914: Perspectives and Sources*, Historical
Association, H.93, London, 1990 pp.40 (See pp.23-24 for a survey of recent
historical scholarship on the extent to which the Irish were involved in
Chartism)

819   Swift, R.E.   'The Historiography of the Irish in Nineteenth-Century Britain'
pp.52-81 in Patrick O'Sullivan (ed.) *The Irish in the New Communities*,
Leicester University Press, Leicester and London, 1992, pp.266 (pp.66-68 looks
at recent historical scholarship over the debate concerning Irish involvement
in Chartism. Reprints virtually the piece on Chartism and the Irish found in
the Historical Association, H.A.93, 1990 pamphlet, see item 818)

820   Sykes, Robert   'Early Chartism and Trade Unionism in South-East Lancashire'
pp.152-193 in James Epstein and Dorothy Thompson (eds.) *The Chartist
Experience: Studies in Working-Class Radicalism and Culture, 1830-60*,
Macmillan, London, 1982, pp.392

821   Taylor, A.J.P. *Revolution and Revolutionaries*, Hamish Hamilton, London,
        1980; Rept., Oxford University Press, Oxford 1981, pp.165 (See Chapter 2
        'Chartism: The Revolution that Never Was' pp.39-59. A general overview)

822   Taylor, Barbara *Eve and the New Jerusalem: Socialism and Feminism in the
        Nineteenth Century*, Virago, New York and London, 1983, pp.402 (See
        pp.264-275 for the links between Owenism, Chartism and Feminism)

823   Taylor, Miles 'The Old Radicalism and the New: David Urquhart and the
        Politics of Opposition, 1832-1867' pp.23-43 in Eugenio F. Biagini and Alastair J.
        Reid (eds.) *Currents of Radicalism. Popular radicalism, organized labour and
        party politics in Britain 1850-1914*, Cambridge University Press, Cambridge,
        1991, pp.305. (For the relationship between Urquhart and Chartism in the
        1850s, particularly the Sheffield Chartist leader, Isaac Ironside, and the
        Newcastle Chartist leader, Joseph Cowen jr.)

824   Taylor, Peter *Class Formation and Popular Politics in Early Industrial Britain:
        Bolton 1825-1850*, Ryburn Publishing, Keele University Press, Keele, 1994,
        pp.256 (For Chartism in Bolton)

825   Thomis, M.I. and Grimmett, J. *Women in Protest, 1800-1850*, Croom Helm,
        London, 1982, pp.166 (See Chapter 6 'Chartist Women' pp.111-137)

826   Thomis, M.I. and Holt, P. *Threats of Revolution in Britain 1789-1848*,
        Macmillan, London, 1977, pp.147 (See Chapter 5 for a narrative account 1838-
        1848 of 'Chartism: the Working Class Threat' pp.100-116)

827   Thompson, Dorothy *Il Cartismo, 1838-1858*, La Pietra, Milan, 1978, pp.315. (In
        Italian. Comprises pp.62 of introduction followed by a selection of
        documents and extracts on the Chartist movement. The volume is part of a
        series by Lelio Basso (ed.) *Il Filo Rosso del movimento Operaio* on the history
        of the European Labour movement)

828   Thompson, Dorothy 'Ireland and the Irish in English Radicalism before 1850'
        pp.120-151 in James Epstein and Dorothy Thompson (eds.) *The Chartist
        Experience: Studies in Working-Class Radicalism and Culture, 1830-1860*,
        Macmillan, London, 1982, pp.392 (Argues that the Irish were not hostile to
        Chartism on the whole and finds that they had a very considerable influence
        within the movement)

829   Thompson, Dorothy *The Chartists, Popular Politics in the Industrial
        Revolution*, Temple Smith, London and Pantheon Books, New York, 1984;
        Japanese edition, 1988, pp.399 (The most important single volume covering
        many aspects of the Chartist movement 1838-1850)

830   Thompson, Dorothy 'Il Movimento Cartista' pp.67-74 in Marco Guidi and
        Nadia Torcellan (eds.) *Europa 1700-1992- Il trionfo della borghesia*, Vol.3,
        Electa, Milan, 1992, pp.687 (In Italian. Part of a wide-ranging history of Europe
        series)

831   Thompson, Dorothy *Outsiders: Class, Gender and Nation*, Verso, London,
        1993, pp.186 (Collection of essays. Focus is on Chartism which is analysed not

simply as a political programme, but as a mass phenomenon of the unskilled, of women and of the Irish. Author responds to recent debates on the reinterpretation of Chartism)

832   Thornes, Robin 'Change and Continuity in the Development of Co-operation, 1827-1844' pp.27-51 in Stephen Yeo (ed.) *New Views of Co-operation*, Routledge, London, 1988, pp.276 (History Workshop Series. Considers the links between Chartism and the Co-operative movement)

833   Thornes, Robin 'The Origins of the Co-operative Movement in Huddersfield: The Life and Times of the First Huddersfield Co-operative Trading Association' pp. 171-188 in E.A. Hilary Haigh (ed.) *Huddersfield: A Most Handsome Town. Aspects of the History and Culture of a West Yorkshire Town.* Kirklees Cultural Services, Huddersfield, 1992, pp.716 (Explores the early links with Chartism)

834   Thornes, Vernon *Chartists and Reformers in Sheffield 1846-1870: Their Impact on Municipal Politics*, Sheffield City Libraries, Sheffield, 1981, pp.20

835   Tiller, Kate 'Late Chartism: Halifax 1847-58' pp.311-44 in James Epstein and Dorothy Thompson (eds.) *The Chartist Experience: Studies in Working-Class Radicalism and Culture, 1830-60*, Macmillan, London, 1982, pp.392 (Explores the basis of Ernest Jones' support and emphasizes the fact that in Halifax, as in so many areas, the local working-class movement was community-based)

836   Todd, Nigel *The Militant Democracy. Joseph Cowen and Victorian Radicalism*, Bewick Press, Whitley Bay, Tyne and Wear, 1991, pp.201 (Important for its consideration and evaluation of Joseph Cowen's involvement with Chartism and Republicanism on Tyneside in the 1850s)

837   Townshend, Charles *Making the Peace. Public Order and Public Security in Modern Britain*, Oxford University Press, Oxford, 1993, pp.264 (A wide-ranging analysis of 150 years of public order in Britain. Includes Chartist disturbances. See particularly Chapter 1 'The English Image of Order')

838   Trinder, Barrie *Victorian Banbury*, Banbury Historical Society, Chichester, 1982, pp.235 (See particularly pp.56-64 for the fullest account to date of Chartism in Banbury)

839   Turley, David *The Culture of English Antislavery, 1780-1860*, Routledge, London, 1991, pp.284 (See Chapter 6 'Antislavery, Radicalism and Patriotism' and particularly pp.182-195 for the links between abolitionists and Chartists. Focuses in part on the shaping of the Complete Suffrage Union in Birmingham)

840   Tyrrell, A. *Joseph Sturge and the Moral Radical Party in Early Victorian Britain*, Christopher Helm, London, 1987, pp.255 (See particularly pp.95-167 for Sturge and Chartism)

841   Vernon, N. James *Politics and the People : A Study in English Political Culture c. 1815-1867*, Cambridge University Press, Cambridge, 1993, pp.429 (Stresses

the importance of 'language' to embrace the forms as well as the content of social communication; plays down 'class' and 'class conflict')

842   Vicinus, Martha *Broadsides of the Industrial North*, Frank Graham, Newcastle-upon-Tyne, 1975, pp.79 (Includes a small number of Chartist ballads relating to Barnsley and Sheffield in 1839 and 1848)

843   Vicinus, Martha 'Chartist Fiction and the Development of a Class-Based Literature' pp.7-25 in H. Gustav Klaus (ed.) *The Socialist Novel in Britain: Towards the Recovery of a Tradition*, Harvester Press, Brighton, 1982, pp.190 (Looks at the fiction of Thomas Cooper, Ernest Jones, T.M. Wheeler and G.W.M. Reynolds)

844   Vincent, David *Bread, Knowledge and Freedom. A Study of Nineteenth Century Working Class Autobiography*, Europa, London, 1981 and Methuen, London, 1982, pp.221 (Looks at many Chartists including W.E. Adams; J. Bezer; James Dawson Burn; Thomas Cooper; James Myles; Henry Hetherington; W. Lovett; J.B. Leno and W. Thom)

845   Vincent, David *Literacy and Popular Culture : England 1750-1914*, Cambridge University Press, Cambridge, 1989 pp.362 (Includes an exploration of the relationship between literacy and Chartist politics)

846   Wallace, Ryland *Organise! Organise! Organise! : A Study of Reform Agitations in Wales 1840-1886*, Cardiff, 1991, pp.267 (A comprehensive account of radical politics, including an informative study of Chartism in nineteenth century Wales)

847   Walton, John K. *Lancashire, A Social History 1558-1939*, Manchester University Press, Manchester, 1987, pp.406 (See Chapter 8 'Radicals and Trade Unions: Popular Protest and Working Class Organization from the Jacobins to the Chartists', pp.141-165, for an overview of Chartism in Lancashire)

848   Ward, J.T. 'Some Aspects of Working-Class Conservatism in the Nineteenth Century', pp.141-157 in John Butt and J.T. Ward (eds.) *Scottish Themes : Essays in Honour of Professor S.G.E. Lythe*, Scottish Academic Press, Edinburgh, 1976, pp.189 (For a consideration of Tory-Chartists, particularly Joshua Hobson and Samuel Kydd who fell under the influence of Richard Oastler)

849   Warren, A.S. *Memoirs of a Countryman,* Castle Cary Press, Somerset, 1972, pp.81 (See pp.8-10 for comments on the Lowbands estate of the Land Plan; also has a sketch of a Chartist house and says his father worked some of the Lowbands land)

850   Watson, Aaron *A Newspaper Man's Memories*, Hutchinson, London, 1925, pp.324 (see Chapter V 'The Brantwood Republicans' pp.51-58 for the Chartist republicanism of W.E. Adams, Joseph Cowen and W.J. Linton)

851   Watson, Ian *Song and Democratic Culture in Britain. An Approach to Popular Culture in Social Movements*, Croom Helm, London, 1983, pp.247

(Explores the nature and significance of working class and popular song and poetry. Includes links with Chartism)

852   *Wearmouth, Robert F. *Methodism and the Working-Class Movements of England*, 1800-1850, London, 1937. Reptd., London, 1947. Reptd., Augustus Kelley, Clifton, New Jersey, 1972, pp.289.

853   Weaver, Stewart Angas *John Fielden and the Politics of Popular Radicalism, 1832-1847*, Clarendon Press, Oxford, 1987, pp.320

854   Weisser, Henry G. *April 10 : Challenge and Response in England in 1848*, University Press of America, Lanham, Maryland, 1983, pp.329 (A detailed account of Chartism in 1848)

855   Wells, Roger A.E. 'Resistance to the New Poor Law in the Rural South' pp.15-53 in Malcolm Chase (ed.) *The New Poor Law*, Middlesbrough Centre Occasional Papers, No.1, University of Leeds, Department of Adult and Continuing Education, 1985, pp.93 (Details the development of southern Chartism from the anti-Poor Law mobilizations of 1834)

856   Wells, Roger A.E. 'Rural Rebels in Southern England in the 1830s' pp.124-165 in Clive Emsley and James Walvin (eds.) *Artisans, Peasants and Proletarians 1760-1860, Essays Presented to Gwyn A. Williams*, Croom Helm, London, 1985, pp.236. (Points to the links of the agricultural proletariat with Chartism, trade unionism and opposition to the New Poor Law of 1834)

857   *West, Julius *A History of the Chartist Movement. With an Introductory Memoir by J.C. Squire*, Constable, London, 1920. Reptd., Augustus Kelley, New York, 1968, pp.316

858   Whitfield, Roy *Frederick Engels in Manchester*, Working Class Movement Library, Salford, 1988 (Gives potted biographies of Engels' Chartist friends and acquaintances during his residence in Manchester, circa 1842-1864)

859   Wiener, Joel H. *Radicalism and Freethought in Nineteenth Century Britain : The Life of Richard Carlile*, Westport, Connecticut, 1983, pp.285 (Carlile, 1790-1843, became anti-Chartist and parted company with popular radicalism)

860   Wiener, Joel H. *William Lovett*, Manchester University Press, Manchester, 1989, pp.153 (In the 'Lives of the Left Series'; a valuable, short biography)

861   Wiles, Eric *Chepstow and the Chartists*, Chepstow, For the Chepstow Society, 1985, pp.12 (Pamphlet on the Newport Rising and details of the nocturnal movement of the Newport Chartist prisoners from Monmouth Gaol February 3 1840 to Chepstow, to board the steamer 'Usk' for Portsmouth)

862   Wilkinson, John *Protest in Victorian England : Chartism*, Network Educational Press, Stafford, 1993, pp.8 (An 'A' Level Study Guide Leaflet directing teachers and students on the study of Chartism)

863   Wilks, Ivor G.H. *South Wales and the Rising of 1839 : Class Struggle as Armed Struggle*, Croom Helm, London, 1984, pp.270. Reptd., Gomer Press,

Llandysul, 1989, pp.270 (An interesting reinterpretation where the emphasis is placed on the Welsh nationalist dimension of the Newport rising)

864   *Williams, David *John Frost : A Study in Chartism,* University of Wales Press, Cardiff, 1939, pp.355. Reptd., Evelyn, Adams and Mackay, 1969. Reptd., Augustus Kelley, New York, 1978, pp.355.

865   Williams, Glanmor (ed.) *Merthyr Politics: The Making of a Working-Class Tradition,* University of Wales Press, Cardiff, 1966, pp.109 (For a number of references to Chartism in Merthyr)

866   *Wilson, Alexander *The Chartist Movement in Scotland,* Manchester University Press, Manchester, 1970, pp.294. Reptd., Augustus Kelley, New York 1970, pp.294

867   Wilson, Gordon M. 'The Strike Policy of the Miners of the West of Scotland 1842-74', pp.29-64 in Ian MacDougall (ed.) *Essays in Scottish Labour History: a Tribute to W.H. Marwick,* John Donald, Edinburgh, 1979, pp.265 (A detailed analysis of the causes, frequency, scale and political nature, including Chartism, of the miners' strikes in the Clyde Valley in 1842, 1844, 1847, 1850, 1855)

868   Wilson, John and Cucksey, Roger *Art and Society in Newport: James Flewitt Mullock and the Victorian Achievement,* Newport Museum and Art Gallery, 1993, pp.69 (Mullock was Newport's most significant Victorian artist. He witnessed Chartist activities and sketched a commemorative lithograph 'The Attack of the Chartists on the Westgate Hotel November 4 1839', in 1840, which is reproduced on p.2. The book also contains on pp.11-12 references to Chartism and other commemorative activity on the Newport Rising)

869   Wilson, Keith '"Whole Hogs" and "Suckling Pigs" - Chartism and the Complete Suffrage Union in Sunderland' pp.17-22 in M. Callcott and R. Challinor (eds.), *Working Class Politics in North East England,* Essays published on behalf of the North East Labour History Society, Newcastle-upon-Tyne Polytechnic, Newcastle-upon-Tyne, 1983, pp.103.

870   Wilson, Keith 'Chartism and the North East Miners : A Reappraisal' pp.81-104 in R.W. Sturgess (ed.) *Pitmen, Viewers and Coalmasters. Essays on North East Coalmining in the Nineteenth Century.* North East Labour History Society, Sunderland Polytechnic, Sunderland, 1986, pp.158 (Demonstrates that the miners' involvement in Chartism was both more complex and long-lived than has previously been regarded)

871   Wilson, Keith 'Local News, National Interest : Patriotism in the Wear Valley', pp.80-83 in B. Ormsby and G. Rigby (eds.), *We are the Valley,* Durham Voices, Durham Community Arts Association, Durham, 1988, pp.96 (A brief account of Chartism in West Auckland, Bishop Auckland, the Wear Valley and South West Durham)

872   Wilson, W. Lawler *The Menace of Socialism,* Grant Richards, London, 1909, pp.520 (See Chapter XXIV 'England : Owenism and Chartism' pp.167-172 and Chapter XI '1832 to 1848' particularly pp.267-269, for the place of Chartism in the author's argument)

873   Working Class Movement Library   *Frederick Engels in Manchester, Two Tours with Maps,* Salford, 1988, pp.8 (A pamphlet offprint, with new cover, from the *Quarterly Bulletin of the Marx Memorial Library,* No.108, Autumn and Winter 1986/87. Includes a short piece on James Leach, the Chartist, whom Engels knew)

874   Working Class Movement Library   *Chartism in Salford,* Salford, 1988, pp.32 (Researched and produced by the staff of the Library to commemorate the anniversary of the Kersal Moor demonstrations in 1838/39. Includes brief biographical details of Chartist leaders in Manchester - M. Fletcher, J.W. Hodgetts and R.J. Richardson)

875   Wright, D.G. *The Chartist Risings in Bradford,* Bradford Libraries and Information Service, 1987, pp.85

876   Wright, D.G. *Popular Radicalism. The Working Class Experience 1780-1880,* London, 1988, pp.211 (Valuable student text which both summarizes recent research on Chartism and places it in a wider context)

877   Wybron, Norman   *The Chartists of Blaenau Gwent: An Account of the Part They Played in the March to Newport on the 3-4 November 1839,* Kerin Publications on behalf of Blaenau Gwent Tourist Association, Starling Press, Newport, 1989, pp.49 (Looks at the attraction of Chartism across Monmouthshire in the late 1830s, the preparations for the march, the rising and the confrontation with the authorities)

878   Yates, Alan   *Jeremiah Yates, Chartist and his descendants,* privately published, Hampstead, London, 1985, pp.77 (Copies in Hull University Library and Hanley Public Library. Account of a Potteries Chartist by his great-grandson)

879   Yeo, Eileen   'Culture and Constraint in Working-Class Movements, 1830-1855', pp.154-186 in Eileen Yeo and Stephen Yeo, (eds.) *Popular Culture and Class Conflict 1590-1914,* Harvester Press, Brighton, 1981, pp.315 (Explores the nature of Owenite, Chartist and Friendly Society culture working people were making for themselves and the struggle to survive against difficult odds, not least a middle class cultural offensive)

880   Yeo, Eileen   'Some Practices and Problems of Chartist Democracy', pp.345-380 in James Epstein and Dorothy Thompson (eds.) *The Chartist Experience: Studies in Working-Class Radicalism and Culture, 1830-60,* Macmillan, London, 1982, pp.392 (Looks at how Chartism and the Chartists tried to organize in a democratic manner in their political and cultural life)

881   Yeo, Eileen   'Chartist Religious Belief and the Theology of Liberation', pp.410-421 in J. Obelkevich, Lyndel Roper and Raphael Samuel (eds.), *Disciplines of Faith: Studies in Religion, Politics and Patriarchy,* Routledge and Kegan Paul, London, 1987, pp.581 (In History Workshop Series. The essay focuses on some of the Chartist beliefs of the Rev. William Hill and Rev. J.R. Stephens in 1839 as exponents of the theology of the liberation of humanity, but with reservations about the position of women)

882   Young, James D. *The Rousing of the Scottish Working Class,* Croom Helm, London and McGill-Queen's University Press, Montreal, 1979, pp.242 (See particularly Chapter 4 on 'Nationalism, Radicalism and Chartism in Sleepy Scotland', pp.72-103. See also pp.88-98 for an overview indicative of the political, industrial and cultural challenges posed by the Scottish Chartists to the authorities between 1838-1848)

ARTICLES

883   Abelove, Henry 'Reading the People', *Berkshire Review* (USA) Vol.19, 1984 (Article on William Lovett and his autobiography)

884   Alexander, Sally 'Women, Class and Sexual Differences in the 1830s and 1840s: Some Reflections on the Writing of a Feminist History', *History Workshop Journal,* Issue 17, Spring 1984 (Includes a section on women and Chartism)

885   Amphlett Micklewright, F.H. 'Joseph Rayner Stephens: A Reassessment', *London Quarterly and Holborn Review,* January 1943

886   Andrews, James R. 'The Passionate Negation: The Chartist Movement in Rhetorical Perspective', *Quarterly Journal of Speech,* Vol. LIX, 1973 (Identifies and clarifies the pressures exerted on the Chartist movement by the physical-moral force conflict)

887   Anon 'A Re-union of Old Chartists', *The Locomotive Engineers' and Firemen's Journal,* Vol.11-12, December 1898 (Refers to a report of a dinner given in honour of old Chartists by the Manchester '95 Club. Cited also in the *Quarterly Bulletin of the Marx Memorial Library,* No.77 January/March 1976)

888   Anon 'The Cry of the Chartists 1839-1939', *Bulletins for Socialists,* No.5, Leeds, May 1939 (Commemorative publication comprising poems by Ebenezer Elliott, Ebenezer Jones, Ernest Jones, Gerald Massey, Thomas Wade. Copy found in Special Collection CD76, Nuffield College Library, Oxford)

889   Anon 'The Fight for the Franchise', *Quarterly Bulletin of the Marx Memorial Library,* No.40, October/December 1966

890   Armbrust, Crys 'Tennyson's Political Readers: W.J. Linton's *The National* and the Chartist Literary Canon', *Victorian Periodicals Review,* Vol XXVI, No 4, Winter, 1993 (Discussion of Linton's inclusion of Tennyson in his *The National: A Library for the People,* 1839, as a poet for the people)

891   Ashcroft, Richard 'Liberal Political Theory and Working-Class Radicalism in Nineteenth Century England', *Political Theory,* Vol.21, No.2, May 1993 (Includes a lengthy discussion of how the Chartists utilized the values and beliefs of liberalism)

892   Ashton, Owen R. 'Clerical Control and Radical Responses in Cheltenham Spa, 1838-1848', *Midland History,* Vol.VIII, 1983 (Considers the wide-ranging challenges of the Chartists to the evangelical controls exercised by the Rev. Francis Close, who was referred to as the 'Pope of Cheltenham')

893   Ashton, Owen R. 'The Mechanics' Institute and Radical Politics in Cheltenham Spa 1834-1840', *Cheltenham Local History Society Journal,* No.2, 1984 (For the Chartists' assault on and control of the local Mechanics' Institute)

894   Ashton, Owen R.   'Chartism in Gloucestershire: the Contribution of the Chartist Land Plan', *Transactions of the Bristol and Gloucestershire Archaeological Society*, Vol.104, 1986

895   Ashton, Owen R.   'Chartism and Popular Culture: An Introduction to the Radical Culture in Cheltenham Spa, 1830-1847', *Journal of Popular Culture*, Vol.20, No.4, Spring 1987 (Examines the dynamic nature of the Chartist cultural challenge to the evangelical forces of the 1830s and 1840s, and its place alongside the surviving remnants of eighteenth century plebeian culture)

896   Ashton, Owen R.   'W.E. Adams and Working Class Opposition to Empire 1878-80: Cyprus and Afghanistan', *North East Labour History Bulletin*, No.27, 1993 (Considers the survival of Chartist internationalist traditions into the beginnings of the era of 'New Imperialism')

897   Barber, Chris   'Mayor Thomas Phillips', *Newport Local History News, Chartist Special*, Local History Society, Newport, 1986 (No pagination; one page profile of the Mayor of Newport who read the Riot Act against the Chartists and was regarded by the authorities as the hero of the hour)

898   Baxter, John   'Chartist Notions of "Labour Aristocracy" in 1839", *Bulletin of the Society for the Study of Labour History*, No.40, Spring 1980 (Scholarly letter to the editor challenging Michael Shepherd's views on the usage of the term, 'labour aristocracy' in the late 1830s in his article found in *Bulletin of the Society for the Study of Labour History*, No.39, Autumn 1978)

899   Behagg, Clive   'Custom, Class and Change: the Trade Societies of Nineteenth Century Birmingham', *Social History*, Vol.4, No.3, October 1979 (Includes an important Chartist dimension in relation to the workplace)

900   Belchem, John   'Henry Hunt and the Evolution of the Mass Platform', *English Historical Review*, Vol.XCIII, No.369, October 1978 (Important perspective provided on the genesis of the Chartist mass platform agitation)

901   Belchem, John   'The Spy-System in 1848: Chartists and Informers - An Australian Connection', *Labour History*, No.39, November 1980 (Looks at the activities of Thomas Powell, an informer-cum-*agent provocateur,* who infiltrated Chartist circles shortly after Kennington Common. He encouraged a Chartist rising for August 16 1848 which the authorities nipped in the bud)

902   Belchem, John   'Republicanism, Popular Constitutionalism and the Radical Platform in Early Nineteenth Century England', *Social History*, Vol.6, No.1, January 1981 (Shows how the post Napoleonic War radical mass platform matured into the Chartist challenge of 1839 and beyond)

903   Belchem, John   'Chartist Informers in Australia: The Nemesis of Thomas Powell', *Labour History*, No.43, 1982.

904   Belchem, John   'English Working-Class Radicalism and the Irish, 1815-1850', *North West Labour History Bulletin*, No.8, 1982/83 (Argues for increasing levels of political cooperation between English radicals and Irish immigrants. Exemplifies this trend by focusing on 1848 in Lancashire))

905   Belchem, John   'Chartism and the Trades, 1848-1850', *English Historical Review*, Vol. XCVIII, No.388, July 1983 (An important piece of research on the divisions between the trades and their relationships as organized unions with the Chartist movement after 1848)

906   Belchem, John   'English Working-Class Radicalism and the Irish, 1815-1850', *Eiré-Ireland,* Vol.XIX, No.4, 1984 (For the growing political links, despite Daniel O'Connell's proscriptions)

907   Belchem, John   'The Politics of Chartism', *History Sixth,* Vol.1, No.1, October 1987 (Article on Chartist ideology in a journal for school sixth formers studying 'A' level)

908   Belchem, John   'Radical Language and Ideology in Early Nineteenth-Century England: The Challenge of the Platform', *Albion,* Vol.20, No.2, Summer 1988 (A contribution to the debate initiated by Gareth Stedman Jones. Argues that the Chartists adopted the language of popular constitutionalism and employed it through a mass platform to intimidate government)

909   Belchem, John   'The Neglected "Unstamped": The Manx Press of the 1840s', *Albion,* Vol.14, No.4, Winter 1992

910   Belchem, John   'Image, Myth and Implantation: The Peculiarities of Liverpool, 1800-1850', *Het Tijdschrift voor Sociale Geschiedenis* (Amsterdam), Vol.18, Nos.2/3, July 1992 (A special issue on the 'Regional Implantation of the Labour Movement in Britain and the Netherlands'. Includes the Chartist dimension in Liverpool's history 1800-1850)

911   Belchem, John   'Radical Entrepreneur: William Shirrefs and the Manx Free Press of the 1840s', *Proceedings of the Isle of Man Natural History and Antiquarian Society,* Vol.IX, No.1, 1992

912   Bell, Phyllis   'International Women's Year : Helen MacFarlane, Chartist and Marxist', *Quarterly Bulletin of the Marx Memorial Library,* No.74, April/June 1975

913   Berridge, Virginia   'The Language of Popular and Radical Journalism: The Case of *Reynolds's Newspaper*', Conference Report in *Bulletin of the Society for the Study of Labour History,* No.44, Spring 1982 (Founded in 1850, the paper is shown to be the meeting place of two tendencies - backwards to the unstamped and Chartist press and forwards to the commercialism of the early twentieth century)

914   Bisceglia, Louis R.   'The Threat of Violence: Irish Confederates and Chartists in Liverpool in 1848', *The Irish Sword,* Vol.14, Summer 1981 (Explores the links between Irish Confederates and Chartists during the first part of 1848)

915   Brandl, A.   'Chartisten, Sozialisten und Carlyle', *Deutsche Rundschau,* Vol.XXXVIII, 7 April, 1912 (In German. Copy available in Cambridge University Library)

916   Brown, Brian R.   'Lancashire Chartism and the Mass Strike of 1842: the Political Economy of Working Class Contention', *Centre for Research on Social Organization, University of Michigan, Working Paper*, No.203, August 1979

917   Buch, Irina   'Engels and the Place of Chartism in the Formation of Marxism', *Bulletin of the Institute of Marxism-Leninism*, No.19, November 1970 (Moscow. In Russian)

918   Challinor, Raymond   'Peter Murray McDouall and "Physical Force Chartism"', *International Socialism*, Series 2, No.12, Spring 1981

919   Challinor, Raymond   'Chartism and Co-operation in the North East', *North East Labour History Bulletin*, No.16, 1982 (Explores the relationships between Chartists and Owenite Socialists 1839/1840, and the Chartist co-operative retail trading ventures of 1840)

920   Challinor, Raymond   'The German Doctor and His Contradictions', *North East Labour History Bulletin*, No.16, 1982 (In April 1856 James Watson, a prominent Newcastle Chartist, shared with Karl Marx the platform at a London rally to celebrate the fourth anniversary of the publication of the *People's Paper*. The article also reflects on the changing political and cultural scene, 1838-1858, on Tyneside, the growth of reformism and the successful professional careers of local ex-Chartist leaders in conditions of relative stability)

921   Challinor, Raymond   'W.P. Roberts, the Miners' Attorney', *North East Labour History Bulletin,* No.20, 1986

922   Chase, Malcolm   'The Chartist Land Plan and the Local Historian', *Local Historian*, Vol.18, No.2, May 1988 (Examines the Chartist Co-operative Land Society in the late 1840s and early 1850s on Teesside and in Middlesbrough)

923   Chase, Malcolm   'Chartism 1838-1858: Responses in Two Teesside Towns', *Northern History*, Vol.XXIV, 1988 (Traditionally viewed as non-political, Middlesbrough and Stockton are shown to have produced a significant Chartist movement and local leadership)

924   Chase, Malcolm   'Chartism and the "Prehistory" of Politics in Middlesbrough', *Bulletin of the Cleveland and Teesside Local History Society*, No.55, Autumn 1988

925   Chase, Malcolm   'The Concept of Jubilee in late Eighteenth and Nineteenth Century England', *Past and Present*, No.129, November 1990 (Deals with the Chartist movement and activities in the final section of the article)

926   Chase, Malcolm   'Out of Radicalism: The Mid-Victorian Freehold Land Movement', *English History Review*, Vol.CVI, No.419, April 1991   (A major article on the development of small-scale land-holding in England after the initiatives of the Chartist Land Plan)

927   Chase, Malcolm   'The Implantation of Working-Class Organisations on Teesside, 1830-1874' *Het Tijdschrift voor Sociale Geschiedenis*, Vol.18, Nos.2/3, July 1992 (A special Issue on the 'Regional Implantations of the Labour Movement in Britain and the Netherlands'. Includes the Chartist dimension in the social history of the region)

928   Chase, Malcolm   'The Teesside Irish in the Nineteenth Century. The Irish in British Labour History', *Institute of Irish Studies University of Liverpool, Conference Proceedings in Irish Studies*, No.1, 1993 (Includes a section on the Irish and Chartism on Teesside)

929   Christodoulou, Joan   'The Glasgow Universalist Church and Scottish Radicalism from the French Revolution to Chartism: A Theology of Liberation', *Journal of Ecclesiastical History*, Vol.43, Part 4, 1992 (Includes a consideration of moral-force Christian Chartism in Glasgow, 1840-1841, under the leadership of John Fraser)

930   Church, Roy   'Chartism and the Miners: A Reinterpretation', *Labour History Review*, Vol.56, Part 3, 1991 (Argues that for most colliery workers, sectional interests reinforced by a trade union consciousness, rather than ideology or class interests, explain the minimal links between the miners and Chartism)

931   Claeys, Gregory   'A Utopian Tory Revolutionary at Cambridge: The Political Ideas and Schemes of James Bernard, 1834-1839', *The Historical Journal*, Vol.25, No.3, June 1982 (Important for Bernard's political views - Toryism and radicalism - and influence on the early Chartist movement, and on Bronterre O'Brien and Feargus O'Connor)

932   Claeys, Gregory   'The *Chartist Pilot:* Feminist and Socialist Chartism in Leicester, 1843-4', Notes on the Labour Press, *Bulletin of the Society for the Study of Labour History*, No.45, Autumn 1982

933   Claeys, Gregory   'The Political Ideas of the Young Engels, 1842-45: Owenism, Chartism and the Question of Violence in the Transition from "Utopian" to "Scientific" Socialism', *History of Political Thought*, Vol.6, No.3, Winter 1985 (In the early 1840s Engels attacked Owenism and hoped to see it moulded to Chartism)

934   Claeys, Gregory   'Mazzini, Kossuth and British Radicalism, 1848-1854', *Journal of British Studies*, Vol.28, Part 3, July 1989 (For the popularity of the anti-socialist republicanism of Mazzini and Kossuth amongst Chartists, particularly W.E. Adams, Joseph Cowen jr., W.J. Linton and Isaac Ironside's Sheffield-based Anti-Centralization Union)

935   Clark, Anna   'The Rhetoric of Chartist Domesticity: Gender, Language and Class in the 1830s and 1840s', *Journal of British Studies*, Vol.31, Part 1, January 1992 (A contribution to, and extension of, the debate initiated by Gareth Stedman Jones, about the nature of Chartism)

936   Clark, Arthur   'Monmouthshire Chartists', *Presenting Monmouthshire*, No.39, 1975 (A narrative history restating the events of 1839 and the march on Newport)

937   Clayson, Jim   'Some Chartist Poetry of North West England', *North West Labour History Bulletin*, No.17, 1992/93 (Mainly anonymous, but includes one by a Mr. Curran and another by Mr. Heims, both of Manchester)

938   Cordell, Alexander   'Vanguard of Victory', *Newport 600, Supplement to the Western Mail*, Thursday, April 25 1985, pp.24 (Article on John Frost and the Newport Rising to mark the 600th anniversary of Newport's existence. See p.14)

939   Cordell, Alexander   'The Making of a Chartist', *Newport Local History News, Chartist Special*, Local History Society, Newport, 1986 (No pagination; pp.12; one page article on John Frost's life)

940   Corrigan, J.V.   'Strikes and the Press in the North East, 1815-44: A Note', *International Review of Social History*, Vol.XXIII, Part 3, 1978 (Short article arguing for the value to the researcher of the Chartist newspaper, the *Northern Liberator*, 1837-1840, in the press' treatment of industrial disputes by ten newspapers on Tyneside in the period)

941   Courtenay, Adrian   'Cheltenham Spa and the Berkeleys, 1832-1848: Pocket Borough and Patron?', *Midland History*, Vol.XVIII, 1992 (Includes a lengthy consideration of the Chartists' political challenge to the power of the Berkeley family)

942   Cule, John   'The Eccentric Doctor William Price of Llantrisant (1800-1893)', *Morgannwg*, VII, 1963

943   Cullen, Michael   'The Chartists and Education', *New Zealand Journal of History*, Vol.10, 1976 (Argues that the Chartist leadership and both male and female supporters shared views on the role of education with contemporary middle class reformers)

944   Cunningham, Hugh   'The Language of Patriotism 1750-1914', *History Workshop Journal*, Issue 12, Autumn 1981 (For Radical and Chartist patriotism 1793-1850 and its demise into jingoism by 1878. Article also appears in Raphael Samuel (ed.) *The Making and Unmaking of British National Identity*, Routledge, London and New York, 1989, Vol.I History and Politics, pp.362; see pp.57-89)

945   Cunningham, Hugh   'The Nature of Chartism', *Modern History Review*, Vol.1, No.4, April 1990 (Update on recent contributions in a journal directed at schools and undergraduates)

946   Cunliffe, John   'Marx, Engels and the Party', *History of Political Thought*, Vol.11, No.2, June 1981 (Examines those types of working-class political organization with which Marx and Engels were involved, primarily the Communist League and the First International, but also Chartism)

947   D'Anieri, Paul, Ernst, Clare and Kier, Elizabeth   'New Social Movements in Historical Perspective', *Comparative Politics*, Vol. 22, Part 4, July 1990 (Highly theoretical; compares Chartism with mid-twentieth century protest movements)

948   Dare, Eddy   'Chartism in Deptford and Greenwich', *South London Record*, No.3, 1988 (A one-page summary)

949   Darwent, Charles   'Mansions for Workers', *Country Life*, September 22, 1988 (Article about the Chartist Land Plan)

950   Davis, Mary   'The Forerunners of the First International - The Fraternal Democrats', *Marxism Today*, No.15, 1971 (Reviews the activities, leadership, role and internationalism of the Chartist society from its formation in 1845 until its end in 1852)

951   Davis, Noel   'The Chartists', *Gwent Leisureline Monthly Magazine*, November 1991   (A brief heritage type article linking the Gwent Chartists' spirit of the nineteenth century with the unveiling of a number of inspirational pieces of modern sculpture in Newport in November 1991)

952   Dekar, Paul R.   'Baptist Peacemakers in Nineteenth-Century Peace Societies', *The Baptist Quarterly, Journal of the Baptist Historical Society*, Vol.XXXIV, No.1, January 1991 (Contains a section on the Christian Chartist leader in Birmingham, Arthur O'Neill, who came to Baptist convictions in 1846 and was the third Baptist to become Secretary of the British Peace Society)

953   Driver, F.   'Tory Radicalism? Ideology, Strategy and Locality in Popular Politics during the Eighteen-Thirties' *Northern History*, Vol.XXVII, 1991 (Radicalism and radical leaders in Huddersfield from co-operation with Richard Oastler into Chartism in 1839)

954   Duncan, Robert   'Artisans and Proletarians: Chartism and Working Class Allegiance in Aberdeen 1838-1842', *Northern Scotland*, Vol.IV, Nos.1-2, 1981

955   Dutton, H.I. and King, J.E.   'The Limits of Paternalism: the Cotton Tyrants of North Lancashire, 1836-54', *Social History*, Vol.7, No.1, January 1982 (Looks at Chartism in Preston and Blackburn as one aspect of the working class' continuous challenge to employer domination in the period)

956   Edsall, Nicholas C.   'A Failed National Movement: the Parliamentary and Financial Reform Association, 1848-54', *Bulletin of the Institute of Historical Research*, Vol.XLIX, No.119, May 1976 (Details the Chartist leaders' differing responses - compromise and opposition - to the overtures made after 1848 by the movement's middle class radicals, particularly Joseph Hume and Sir Joshua Walmsley)

957   Edwards, Michael S.   'Methodism and the Chartist Movement', *London Quarterly and Holborn Review*, October 1966

958   Edwards, Michael S.   'Joseph Rayner Stephens, 1805-1879', *Wesley Historical Society, Lancashire and Cheshire Branch, Occasional Publication*, No.3, 1968

959   Edwards, Michael S.   'Joseph Rayner Stephens (1805-1879)', *The Expository Times*, February, 1993

960   Epstein, James   'Radical Dining, Toasting and Symbolic Expression in Early Nineteenth-Century Lancashire: Rituals of Solidarity', *Albion*, Vol.20, No.2, Summer 1988 (Includes Chartist conviviality in Ashton-under-Lyne; also useful for the local Chartist leader, William Aitken)

961   Epstein, James   'Understanding the Cap of Liberty: Symbolic Practice and Social Conflict in Early Nineteenth Century England', *Past and Present*, No.122, February 1989 (A detailed and extensive analysis of the changing meaning of one particular symbolic practice in radical discourse and iconography between the 1790s and 1840s)

962   Epstein, James   'The Constitutional Idiom in Radical Reasoning, Rhetoric and Action in Early Nineteenth Century England', *Journal of Social History*, Vol.23, No.3, Spring 1990 (Shows how the Chartists in 1838-9 pushed the boundaries of constitutionalist action as far as they could and posed a revolutionary challenge through a radicalized constitutionalism)

963   Erofeev, N.A.   'Chartism and British Colonial Policy', *Novoya i noveistaya istorya (Recent and Most Recent History)*, No.1, 1957 (In Russian)

964   Everard, Nick   'Three Angry Men Who Changed History: Welshmen Who Shook The Government of Queen Victoria', *In View*, 1987 (Magazine of the Centre for Journalism Studies, University College Cardiff. Brief one page synopsis of the Newport Rising, the part played by Frost, Williams and Jones, and the commemorative activities that have taken place in Newport since the late nineteenth century. Copy available in Newport Central Library)

965   Faherty, Ray   'Bronterre O'Brien's Correspondence with Thomas Allsop', *European Labour and Working Class History Newsletter*, No.8, November 1975

966   Faherty, Ray   'The Memoir of Thomas Martin Wheeler, Owenite and Chartist', *Bulletin of the Society for the Study of Labour History*, No.30, Spring 1975

967   Finn, Margot   'A Vent Which Has Conveyed Our Principles: English Radical Patriotism in the Aftermath of 1848', *The Journal of Modern History*, Vol.64, No.4, December 1992 (Considers Chartist efforts to reshape in a radical patriotic direction the meaning of continental nationalism in the Hungarian agitation of 1849, the Haynau incident of 1850, and the Kossuth welcome of 1851, thus underlining the class differences at this time between middle and working class radicals, rather than their common ground)

968   Flett, Keith   'But the Chartist Principles Did Not Die', *North East Labour History Bulletin*, No.21, 1988 (Examines the increased political activity of the Chartists on Teesside and in South Durham 1848-1858)

969   Flett, Keith   'Coercion and Consent', *Bulletin of the Society for Study of Labour History*, Vol.53, Part No.3, Winter 1988 (One page 'Communication' note on what role the state played repressively after 1848, how it was viewed by the Chartists, and a call for a detailed study of the Radical/Chartist press in the 1850s to extend our understanding of Chartism in decline)

970.   Flett, Keith   'Progress and Light: Secularism and Radicalism on Teesside after 1848', *Bulletin of the Cleveland and Teesside Local History Society*, No.56, 1989

971   Flett, Keith   'Sex or Class: the Education of Working Class Women 1800-1870', *History of Education*, Vol.18, Part 2, 1989 (Relates to debates in the 1850s)

972   Flett, Keith   'To Make That Future Now: The Land Question in Nineteenth Century Radical Politics', *The Raven: Anarchist Quarterly*, Vol.5, Part 1, January-March 1992 (Explores the land question both during and after Chartism)

973   Foster, John   'South Shields Labour Movement in the 1830s and 1840s, *North East Labour History Society Bulletin*, No.4, 1970 (Includes a study of Chartism)

974   Fox, Ralph   'Marx, Engels and Lenin on the British Workers' Movement', *Communist Review*, March 1931; reptd. in *Quarterly Bulletin of the Marx Memorial Library*, Vol.108, Autumn/Winter 1986/87 (Includes a consideration of how Marx and Engels regarded Chartism, and their views on O'Connor, O'Brien, Harney and Jones)

975   Frame, Richard   'The Search for John Frost's Grave', *Newport Local History News, Chartist Special*, Local History Society, Newport, 1986 (No pagination; pp.12; one page article on the detective-work that went into the search for Frost's grave in Horfield, Bristol)

976   Frow, Edmund and Frow, Ruth   'Karl Marx and the Labour Parliament 1854', *Quarterly Bulletin of the Marx Memorial Library*, No.37, January/March 1966 (The Labour Parliament was called by the Chartist leader Ernest Jones to discuss how best to aid striking power-loom weavers in Preston)

977   Frow, Edmund and Frow, Ruth   'James Leach', *Quarterly Bulletin of the Marx Memorial Library*, No.39, July/September 1966

978   Frow, Edmund and Frow, Ruth   'Women in the Early Radical and Labour Movement', *Marxism Today*, April 1968 (Looks at the involvement of women from Peterloo in 1819 through to Chartism in the 1840s)

979   Frow, Edmund and Frow, Ruth   'The General Strike of 1842', *Labour Monthly*, vol.88, No.2, February 1976

980   Frow, Edmund and Frow, Ruth   'Biographies of Irish Chartists', *North West Labour History Bulletin*, No.16, 1991/92 (Article on Christopher Doyle, power-loom weaver, Chartist and Land Plan director; and James Leach, factory-worker, newsagent, bookseller, author and Chartist)

981   Frow, Edmund and Frow, Ruth   'Frederick Engels in Manchester. A Commemoration of The Centenary of the Publication of *The Condition of the Working Class in England in 1844*, *Communist Review*, No.14, 1992 (Communist Party of Britain publication, Third Series. Looks at Engels' involvement with Manchester Chartists and their activities 1839-1842)

982   Gadian, D.S.   'Class Consciousness in Oldham and Other North-West Industrial Towns, 1830-1850', *The Historical Journal*, Vol.21, No.1, March 1978

983   Gagnier, Regenia   'Social Atoms: Working-Class Autobiography, Subjectivity and Gender', *Victorian Studies*, Vol.30, Part 3, Spring 1987 (Draws on the Chartists W.E. Adams', James D. Burns', Thomas Cooper's and B. Wilson's personal testimonies to indicate the variety of forms, rhetorical functions, structuring of gender and subjectivity in working class autobiography)

984   Geary, Laurence M.   'O'Connorite Bedlam: Feargus and his Grand-Nephew, Arthur', *Medical History*, Vol.34, No.2, April 1990 (Details the medical decline of Feargus O'Connor from 1852, his committal to and life in Tuke's asylum, and death at his sister's home in 1855 amidst family squabbles over the inheritance of his estate. The article also suggests a possible link between the Chartist leader's mental illness and that of his grand-nephew, Arthur, a Fenian sympathiser who attacked Queen Victoria in 1872 in the courtyard of Buckingham Palace)

985   Godfrey, Christopher   'The Chartist Prisoners, 1839-41', *International Review of Social History*, Vol.XXIV, Part 2, 1979 (A major article, based on the extremely valuable HO 20/10 material. Covers occupations, ages, religion of prisoners and their experiences in jail)

986   Godfrey, Christopher and Epstein, James   'H.O. 20/10: Interviews of Chartist Prisoners, 1840-41', *Bulletin of the Society for the Study of Labour History*, No.34, Spring 1977

987   Goodway, David   'The Métivier Collection and the Books of George Julian Harney', *Bulletin of the Society for the Study of Labour History*, No.49, Autumn 1984 (Notes on Sources. A collection of 1,600 books in 2,100 volumes, the bulk of which come from Harney's personal library which was bequeathed by Professor James Métivier, Harney's stepson, to Vanderbilt University Library, Nashville, Tennessee)

988   Gossman, Norbert J.   'British Aid to Polish, Italian and Hungarian Exiles 1830-1870', *The South Atlantic Quarterly*, Vol.68, Spring 1969 (Acknowledges the role played both by the Fraternal Democrats and that of individual Chartist leaders such as Joseph Cowen, G.J. Holyoake and W.J. Linton in the struggles of continental exiles for national self-determination)

989   Gossman, Norbert J.   'William Cuffay, London's Black Chartist', *Phylon*, Vol.XLIV, 1983 (A U.S.A. journal)

990   Gray, Robert   'Medical Men, Industrial Labour and the State in Britain, 1830-50', *Social History*, Vol.16, No.1, January 1991 (Looks at medical intervention in debates about industrial labour and state regulation. Includes a section on the views on social and economic issues, particularly the factory system, of Matthew Fletcher and Peter McDouall, both Bury practitioners and leading Chartists)

991   Greenall, R.L.   'Baptist as Radical: The Life and Opinions of the Rev. John Jenkinson of Kettering (1799-1876)', *Northamptonshire Past and Present*, Vol.8, No.3, 1991-2 (Jenkinson was a teetotal advocate, political pamphleteer and very active Kettering Chartist leader)

992   *Griffin, C.P.   'Chartism and Opposition to the New Poor Law in Nottinghamshire: The Basford Union Workhouse Affair of 1844', *Midland History*, Vol.11, No.4, Autumn 1974

993   Guan, Shijie   'Chartism and the First Opium War', *History Workshop*, Issue 24, August 1987 (Examines Chartist opposition to the Opium War pursued by the British government against China and its people 1839-1842, in order to protect the British merchants' lucrative but illegal trade of smuggling Indian opium into China)

994   Guan, Shijie   'Yingguo Dazhong Fandin Znenggu Jinxing Yapian Zhanzheng' *Shijie Lishi (World History)*, Vol.4, 1990 (In Chinese. Title translation: 'The British People's Opposition to the Government's Engagement in the Opium War'. Looks at the opposition from all classes, but particularly at the way in which the Chartists headed that of the working class, to the immorality of the Opium War in the early 1840s)

995   Hardy, Dennis   'Unsubversive Plots at Snigs End', *Gloucestershire and Avon Life*, July 1980 (On the Chartist Land Plan at Snigs End, Gloucestershire)

996   Harris, Keith   'Joseph Cowen - The Northern Tribune', *North East Labour History Bulletin*, No.5, 1971 (A short article indicating Cowen's associations with Chartism in the North East in the late 1840s and 1850s. The article is accompanied by a select bibliography of primary and secondary sources on Cowen's early years)

997   Harris, Ruth-Ann   'The Failure of Republicanism among Irish Migrants to Britain 1800-1840', *Eire-Ireland*, Vol.21, Winter 1986 (Contribution to the debate about the Irish presence in Chartism. Argues that in the pre-famine period, the main objectives of Irish short-term migrants tended to be material and economic rather than political)

998   Harrison, Brian   "Kindness and Reason": William Lovett and Education', *History Today*, Vol.37, Part 3, March 1987

999   Harrison, J.F.C.   'The Portrait', *History Workshop Journal*, Issue 10, Autumn 1980 (In the 'Historian's Notebook' section. An account of the discovery by the author of a portrait of the Loughborough Chartist leader, John Skevington, in the summer of 1955. Reprint from 'The Portrait', *Manchester Guardian*, 9 January 1957)

1000   Hastings, R.P.   'Chartism in South Durham and the North Riding of Yorkshire, 1838-1839', *Durham County Local History Society Bulletin*, No.22, November 1978

1001   Hewitt, John   'The Bradford Rising', *Bradford Telegraph and Argus*, 25 January 1968 (Concerning events in January 1840)

1002   Hewitt, Martin   'Radicalism and the Victorian Working Class: The Case of Samuel Bamford', *The Historical Journal*, Vol.34, No.4, December 1991 (In 1848 Bamford enrolled as a special constable to help keep down the Chartists who had assembled on Kennington Common)

1003   Hobsbawm, E.J. and Scott, Joan Wallach 'Political Shoemakers', *Past and Present*, No.89, November 1980 (A broad survey which emphasizes that of the persons active in Chartism, whose occupation is known, shoemakers formed much the largest single group, after the weavers and unspecified labourers. Article also appears in E.J. Hobsbawm, *Worlds of Labour. Further Studies in the History of Labour*, Weidenfeld and Nicolson, London, 1984, pp.369; see pp.103-130)

1004   Howell jr., Roger 'Cromwell and the Imagery of Nineteenth Century Radicalism: The Example of Joseph Cowen', *Archaeologia Aeliana*, 5th Series, Vol.10, 1982 (Shows how Cowen, a champion of the Chartist cause, utilized Cromwell as a radical image in his writings, speeches and activities)

1005   Huch, Ronald K. 'Francis Place and the Chartists: Promise and Disillusion', *The Historian: A Journal of History*, Vol.45, August 1983 (A U.S.A. periodical. Focuses on Place's attempt to bring about co-operation between free-trade reformers and Chartists)

1006   Hudson, Keith 'The Chartists-Contemporary Political Songwriting', *Planet: The Welsh Internationalist*, No.70, August/September 1988 (Brief article about a group of twentieth century musicians in South Wales known as "The Chartists", whose material draws heavily on the nineteenth century political movement in South Wales, particularly the Newport Rising 1839)

1007   Humpherys, Anne 'G.W.M. Reynolds: Popular Literature and Popular Politics', *Victorian Periodicals Review*, Vol.16, Part 3/4, Fall, 1983 (The article also appears in Joel H. Wiener (ed.) *Innovators and Preachers: The Role of the Editor in Victorian England*, Westport, Connecticut, 1985, pp.332; see pp.3-21).

1008   Jackson, Frank 'The European Hyena', *Quarterly Bulletin of the Marx Memorial Library*, No.31, July/September 1964 (For G.J. Harney and the Chartist reaction to the visit of the Austrian General Haynau, who had suppressed the 1848 revolutions in Italy and Hungary)

1009   Jackson, T.A. 'Eighteen Forty-Eight', *Our Time. Chartist Centenary Issue*, Vol.7, No.7, April 1948 (Brief overview of the course of Chartism in 1848 in the context of the wave of revolutions on the continent and the development of events in Ireland. Makes the point that Chartism began to grow more formidable after April 10 1848 when the authorities proceeded with fierce repression)

1010   James, Les 'The People's Charter', *Newport Local History News, Chartist Special*, Local History Society, Newport, 1986 (No pagination; pp.12; one page article on the events in Newport on Nov.3 1839)

1011   James, W.L.G. 'Two Lincolnshire Writers. A Study of the Lives of Thomas Cooper (1805-1892) and Thomas Miller (1807-1874)' *Lincolnshire Historian*, Vol.2, 1963 (Reflects on Cooper's novels, short stories and, briefly, the *Purgatory of Suicides*)

1012   Jenkin, Alfred   'The Cornish Chartists', Journal of the Royal Institution of
        Cornwall, New Series, Vol.IX, Part 1, 1982

1013   Jenkins, Mick   'The Councils of Action as a Form of Struggle', *Marxism Today*,
        May 1976 (Looks at the history of the trade union movement's strategy to call
        General Strikes 1832-1926. Includes a discussion of the 'Plug Plot' Riots of
        August 1842 and the predisposition of the trade representatives gathered in
        Manchester in 1842 to join the Chartist movement)

1014   Jones, D.J.V.   'Women and Chartism', *History*, Vol.68, No.222, February 1983
        (An important piece on the wide-ranging part women played in the Chartist
        movement)

1015   Jones, D.J.V.   'The Newport Rising and The Chartist Movement', *Newport
        Local History News, Chartist Special*, Local History Society, Newport, 1986
        (No pagination; pp.12; short article on the significance of the rising)

1016   Jones, Ieuan Gwynedd   'The Anti-Corn Law Letters of Walter Griffiths',
        Bulletin of the Board of Celtic Studies, Vol.XXVIII, Part 1, 1978 (For Griffith's
        recording of Chartist opposition experienced at his meetings in Mid and South
        Wales, circa 1840-1842)

1017   Journès, Hugues   'Le Chartisme vu à travers les écrivains chartistes', *La pensée
        politique au XIXe*, Communications presêntées au Colloque de Grenoble, 22-
        23 Mars 1980, Cahiers du C.R.E.C.I.B. (In French. Chartism as seen through
        Chartist writers. A paper presented at the Grenoble Colloquium in March
        1980)

1018   Journès, Hugues   'Sur un poème chartiste, ou la Révolution comme passage
        d'un désordre ancien à un ordre nouveau', *Cahiers Victorians and Edouardians*,
        Montpellier, No.27, Avril 1988, (Actes du Colloque de Paris de la S.F.E.V.E. de
        Janvier 1987 sur la thème, 'Ordre et Désordre'. (In French. In Papers of the
        S.F.E.V.E. Paris Colloquium, January 1987 on the theme 'Order and Disorder'.
        An article on *Ernest, or Political Regeneration* by Capel Lofft)

1019   Kaijage, F.J.   "Poor Law Catechism": Religious Parody and Social Protest',
        Bulletin of the Society for the Study of Labour History, No.42, Spring 1981
        (Short article putting into context an accompanying document entitled *Poor
        Law Catechism*, which was part of the literary barrage produced and
        disseminated during 1836-38 in protest against the introduction of the New
        Poor Law of 1834 in the industrial North of England)

1020   Kemnitz, Thomas Milton   'The Chartist Convention of 1839', *Albion*, Vol.10,
        No.2, Summer 1978 (Presents some of the basic facts about the Chartist
        Convention of 1839 and the strategies it considered in order to enact the
        Charter)

1021   Kennedy, James G.   'Examples of Class Feeling in Victorian Poetry',
        Zeitschrift für Anglistik und Amerikanistik, Vol.29, 1981 (Includes a discussion
        of poems by Ernest Jones)

1022   Kent, Christopher   'Presence and Absence: History, Theory and the Working Class', *Victorian Studies*, Vol.29, No.3, Spring 1986 (Includes a consideration of the place of Chartism and its decline in recent debates on structuralist and cultural theory, and historiography)

1023   Kett, Christine   'The *Uxbridge Spirit of Freedom* 1849: A Rare Radical Periodical Recently Acquired by Uxbridge Library', *The Uxbridge Record*, No.32, Autumn 1979

1024   Kingsford, P.W.   'Thomas Slingsby Duncombe 1796-1861', *Quarterly Bulletin of the Marx Memorial Library*, April 1982 (Brief article which includes a consideration of the contribution Duncombe made to the Chartist cause)

1025   Kirk, Neville   'The Decline of Chartism in South East Lancashire and North East Cheshire 1850-1870', *North West Labour History Society Bulletin*, No.1, 1973

1026   Koga, Hideo   Ernest Jones no Tuioku to Hyóden', *Journal of the Faculty of Liberal Arts, Yamaguchi University*, Vol.15, October 1981 (In Japanese. 'Memorials and Biographies of Ernest Charles Jones: Chartist')

1027   Koga, Hideo   'Chartist no Shakaiteki Kósei - Zenkoku Kenshó kyókai "Katudóka" no Shodugyó Bunseki', *Journal of the Faculty of Liberal Arts, Yamaguchi University*, Vol.16, October 1982 (In Japanese. 'Social Composition of the Prominent Chartists - an Analysis of Occupations of the Members of the General Council of the National Charter Association')

1028   Koga, Hideo   '1848 nen niokeru London no Shokushu Kumiai to Chartism', *Journal of the Faculty of Liberal Arts, Yamaguchi University*, Vol.19, February 1986 (In Japanese. 'London Trades and Chartism in 1848')

1029   Koga, Hideo   'Cold Bath Fields Jiken - 1833 nen no Minshú Kyúshinshugi Undó to Shuto Keisatu', *Journal of the Faculty of Liberal Arts, Yamaguchi University*, Vol.21, February 1988 (In Japanese. 'The Cold Bath Fields Affair in May 1833 - Working Class Radicalism and the Metropolitan Police'. Includes a consideration of the meaning of an intended Convention and the intentions of the Metropolitan Police)

1030   Koga, Hideo   '*Times*, Hoshuha to Chartist Undo', *Seiyoshigaku Ronshú/Studies in Western History*, Vol.XXVI, July 1989 (In Japanese. Deals with the attitude of *The Times*, and the Conservative and Whig governments to the Chartist movement 1838-1848, and their influence on Chartism)

1031   Koga, Hideo   'Some Notes on Evaluations and Materials of Ernest Charles Jones:Chartist', *Journal of the Faculty of Liberal Arts, Yamaguchi University*, Vol.23, February 1990 (In English. Looks at some obscure source material to throw fresh light on Jones' activities as a Chartist)

1032   Koga, Hideo   'The Chartists and Marx-Engels', *Journal of the Faculty of Liberal Arts, Ymaguchi University*, Vol.26, February 1993 (In English)

1033   Koseki, Takashi   'The Chartist Movement in Ireland', *Studies in Western History*, No.148, March 1988 (In Japanese. Osaka, Japan)

1034   Koseki, Takashi   'Chartism and the London Irish in 1848' *Rekishigaku Kenkyu/Journal of Historical Studies*, No.590, February 1989 (In Japanese. Tokyo, Japan)

1035   Koseki, Takashi   '*The Times* and Its Arguments in Defence of the British Constitution in 1848', *Yachiyo Journal of International Studies*, Vol.3, No.1, April 1990 (In Japanese. Chiba, Japan)

1036   Koseki, Takashi   'Liverpool Irish and the Threat of Physical Force in 1848', *Studies in Western History*, No.157, June 1990 (In Japanese. Osaka, Japan)

1037   Koseki, Takashi   'Patrick O'Higgins and Irish Chartism', *Hosei University Ireland-Japan Papers*, No.2, October 1990 (In English. Examines the contribution Irish Chartists made to the realization of a Chartist-Irish alliance; comment by L.M. Cullen; pp.33)

1038   Koseki, Takashi 'London in 1848: the Chartist "Conspiracy" and Agents Provocateurs', *Hitotsubashi Review*, Vol.107, No.2, February 1992 (In Japanese, Tokyo, Japan)

1039   Koseki, Takashi 'Ruling Ireland: Lord Clarendon and the Repeal Movement in 1848', *Bulletin of the Faculty of General Education, Tokyo University of Agriculture and Technology*, Vol.28, March 1992 (In Japanese, Tokyo, Japan)

1040   Koseki, Takashi 'Dublin Confederate Clubs and the Repeal Movement' *Hosei University Ireland-Japan Papers*, No.10, April 1992 (In English. Includes references to some of the Irish Chartists in 1848; comment by Dorothy Thompson; pp.49)

1041   Kovalev, Yuri V.   'Article on Petöfi in the Chartist Journal *Friend of the People*', *Le Messager de l'Université de Leningrad*, No.1, 1951 (In Russian)

1042   Kovalev, Yuri V.   'Charles Dickens and the Chartists', *Le Messager de l'Université de Leningrad*, No.20, 1962, 4th edition (In Russian)

1043   Kunina, Valeria   'Former Chartists' Later Associations with Karl Marx', *Bulletin of the Institute of Marxism-Leninism*, Moscow, No.21, January 1972 (In Russian)

1044   Little, Alan   'Thomas Winters: Chartist and Trade Unionist', *Bulletin of the Society for the Study of Labour History*, No.49, Autumn 1984 (Notes and Queries Section. Brief one page profile)

1045   Lloyd, T.H.   'Chartism in Warwick and Leamington' *Warwickshire History*, Vol.4, Part 1, Summer 1978

1046   Louvre, Alf   'Reading Bezer: Pun, Parody and Radical Intervention in Nineteenth Century Working Class Autobiography', *Literature and History*, Vol.14, No.1, Spring 1988 (A literary and political analysis of some of the radical political views and language expressed by the Chartist, J.J. Bezer, in his *Autobiography of one of the Chartist Rebels of 1848*, published in 1851)

1047   Lowe, R.A.   'Mutual Improvement in the Potteries', *North Staffordshire Journal of Field Studies*, Vol.12, 1972 (On the Chartist People's Hall in Hanley)

1048   Lowe, W.J.   'The Chartists and the Irish Confederates: Lancashire, 1848', *Irish Historical Studies*, Vol.XXIV, No.94, November 1984 (Focuses on the growth of branches of the Irish Confederation in urban-industrial Lancashire and their co-operative efforts, open and conspiratorial, with the local Chartists especially in Manchester, Salford, Ashton and Oldham)

1049   McCaffrey, John F.   'Irish Immigrants and Radical Movements in the West of Scotland in the Early Nineteenth Century', *The Innes Review*, Vol.XXXIX, No.1, Spring 1988 (Points up the Irish dimension in terms of support and personnel in Chartism in Scotland in 1847/48)

1050   McCalman, Iain   'Ultra-Radicalism and Convivial Debating Clubs in London, 1795-1838', *English Historical Review*, Vol.C11, No.403, April 1987 (Such clubs helped ultra-Radicalism to survive from the mid 1790s through to Chartism)

1051   McColgan, Michael   'Georg Weerth's Bradford Poems and the Poetry of the Chartists', *Gulliver. Deutsch-Englische Jahrbücher/German-English Yearbooks*, Vol.9, 1981

1052   McNulty, David   'Samuel Jacobs', *Bulletin of the Society for the Study of Labour History*, No.38, Spring 1979 (Letter to the editor, briefly outlining some aspects of the career of the influential Bath and Bristol Chartist leader)

1053   McNulty, David   'Class and Politics in Bath 1832-1848', *Southern History*, Vol.8, 1986 (Examines the parliamentary reform movement, radicalism and Chartism in Bath)

1054   Malmgreen, Gail   'Anne Knight and the Radical Subculture', *Quaker History*, Vol.71, Part 2, Fall 1982 (Knight was a feminist, radical and abolitionist who took a friendly interest in Chartism)

1055   Marinicheva, Maria P.   'The Translation of the Communist Manifesto and Helen MacFarlane', *Bulletin of the Institute of Marxism-Leninism*, Moscow, No.20, April 1971

1056   Marinicheva, Maria P.   'Mare's nest of a Marxologist', *Quarterly Bulletin of the Marx Memorial Library*, No.81, January/March 1977 (Article on Helen MacFarlane)

1057   Markham, John   'The East Riding House of Correction, Beverley and Robert Peddie, Its Most Famous Prisoner', *Journal of Local Studies*, Vol.1, No.1, Summer 1980

1058   Marwick, W.H.   'The Beginnings of the Scottish Working Class Movement in the Nineteenth Century', *International Review of Social History*, Vol.III, 1939 (A section on 'Early Forms of Political Action' includes a seven page consideration of the impact of Scottish Chartism, its leaders and the 'moral force' character of the movement in Scotland 1838-1852)

1059   Mitchell, Julian   'Nathan Rogers and the Wentwood Case: A Continuing Issue in Monmouthshire Politics from Charles I to the Chartists', *Welsh History Review*, Vol.14, No.1, June 1988 (Considers the controversy around the seventeenth century enclosure of Wentwood forest in South East Wales which had roots in religious issues as far back as before the English Civil War and repercussions as late as the Chartist movement of the 1830s. Nathan Rogers's book *Memories of Monmouthshire* (1708) was an attack on the violent enclosure undertaken by the royalist Marquis of Worcester, the Duke of Beaufort, after 1682. The book was reprinted by the radical Chartist printer Samuel Etheridge in 1826 in Newport as part of an ongoing political campaign against the local power of the Beauforts)

1060   Montgomery, Fiona A.   'Glasgow and the Movement for Corn Law Repeal', *History*, Vol.64, No.212, October 1979 (An indepth study of the relationships between Glasgow Repealers and the Glasgow Chartists 1839-1842)

1061   Morris, E. Ronald   'Thomas Powell - Chartist, c.1802-1862', *The Montgomeryshire Collections, Journal of the Powysland Club*, Vol.80, 1992 (Biographical article of a leading figure in mid-Wales Chartism)

1062   Morris, R.J.   'Samuel Smiles and the Genesis of Self-Help; The Retreat to a Petit Bourgeois Utopia', *The Historical Journal*, Vol.24, No.1, March 1981 (For the links between the petit-bourgeois radicalism of the 1840s, the Complete Suffrage Union, the Leeds Parliamentary Reform Association and the Chartists)

1063   Moss, D.J.   'A Study in Failure: Thomas Attwood M.P. for Birmingham 1832-9', *The Historical Journal*, Vol.21, No.3, September 1978 (Includes Attwood's involvement in both Birmingham radical politics and national Chartist affairs 1836-1839)

1064   Munden, A.F.   'Radicalism versus Evangelicalism in Victorian Cheltenham', *Southern History*, Vol.5, 1983 (Considers the hostile position that the Evangelist, the Rev. Francis Close, the incumbent of Cheltenham Parish Church, took on a range of local issues, particularly the appearance of Chartism and Owenite Socialism)

1065   Newens, Stan   'Thomas Edward Bowkett: Nineteenth Century Pioneer of the Working-Class Movement in East London', *History Workshop Journal*, Issue 9, Spring 1980 (Brief article on the East End London Chartist and friend of Bronterre O'Brien)

1066   Okamoto, Mitsuhiro   '1848 nen no Chartism-Kokumin Taikai Kara Kokumin Shúkai ni itarumade', *Shisô*, No.645, March 1978 (In Japanese. 'Chartism in 1848 - from the National Convention to the National Assembly')

1067   Osburn, John D.   'The Full Name of Lloyd Jones: Reflections of Nineteenth-Century Working Class Religion and Politics', *Bulletin of the Institute of Historical Research*, Vol.XLVI, 1973 (Interesting for his contacts with Joseph Cowen jr. and G.J. Holyoake)

1068   Osmond, David   'A Gravestone At Last For John Frost', *Newport Local History News, Chartist Special*, Local History Society, Newport, 1986 (No pagination; pp.12; brief account of the unveiling of a new gravestone to John Frost by Neil Kinnock, October 9th 1986, at Horfield Parish Church Yard, Bristol)

1069   Osmond, David   'Mad Edwards The Baker : A Forgotten Newport Chartist', *Newport Local History News, Chartist Special*, Local History Society, Newport, 1986 (No pagination; pp.12; one page article on the Chartist activist in South Wales arrested in May 1839 and subsequently imprisoned in August for 9 months. He played an important role in rebuilding the local movement after his release)

1070   Parsons, Frederick   'The Monmouth Treason Trials', *Presenting Monmouthshire*, No.11, 1961 (Short article on the trial of Frost, Williams and Jones)

1071   Perry, George   'Found - the World's First Crowd Photograph', *Sunday Times Colour Supplement Magazine*, 5 June 1977 (Ephemera piece with very brief commentary on the discovery at Windsor of the first crowd photograph - that of the Chartist crowd - gathered at Kennington Common, London on 10 April 1848)

1072   Pickering, Paul   'Class Without Words: Symbolic Communication in the Chartist Movement', *Past and Present*, No.112, August 1986 (Looks at aspects of the Chartists' concern with visual as well as oral communication e.g. colours, modes of appearance and symbolic accessories such as Feargus O'Connor dressed as a working man)

1073   Pickering, Paul   'Chartism and the "Trade of Agitation" in Early Victorian Britain', *History*, Vol.76, No.247, June 1991 (Shows how historians have neglected the wide range of goods and services that were paraded under the banner of Chartism, how some of the leaders made a living from the sale of Chartist goods and products, and how such transactions provided a culture of mutuality which underpinned the Chartist struggle)

1074   Porter, Thomas W.   'Ernest Charles Jones and the Royal Literary Fund', *Labour History Review*, Vol.57, No.3, Winter 1992 (Documentary Essay. Details two successful requests for grants by Ernest Jones - one in 1854 for £50, the other in 1859 for £25 - to the Royal Literary Fund to relieve his personal distress whilst still active in Chartism and radical politics. Also included are a small selection of letters from supporters in literary and social circles, such as Bulwer Lytton, R. Monckton Milnes and Archer Gurney)

1075   Postgate, R.W.   'History in the Dock: the Last Insurrection', *The New Leader*, 20 March 1925 (Article on John Frost's trial)

1076   Prothero, Iorwerth J.   'Chartism in the North West', *North West Labour History Bulletin*, No.1, 1973

1077   Purvis, M.   'Co-operative Retailing in England, 1835-1850: Developments Beyond Rochdale', *Northern History*, Vol.XXII, 1986 (Looks in part at both the dialogue and dual membership between Owenite and Chartist organizations in the North of England which extended nearly twenty years to the writings of Ernest Jones, and to the debates with Lloyd Jones in the early 1850s)

1078   Quinault, Roland '1848 and Parliamentary Reform', *The Historical Journal*, Vol.31, No.4, December 1988

1079   Reaney, Bernard 'Irish Chartism in Britain and Ireland: Rescuing the Rank and File', *Saothar, Journal of the Irish Labour History Society*, No.10, 1984 (Examines the role of the Irish in Chartism and also traces the history of the Irish Universal Suffrage Association, established in 1841, as the Irish Chartist Association)

1080   Reay, Barry 'The Last Rising of the Agricultural Labourers: The Battle of Bossenden Wood, 1838', *History Workshop Journal*, Issue 26, Autumn 1988 (Reveals Chartists' sympathy for the agricultural labourers' rising at the Battle of Bossenden Wood, 31 May 1838 in Kent)

1081   Rees, Bryan 'The Lost Years: Northumberland Miners 1844-1862', *North East Labour History Bulletin*, No.19, 1985 (Includes reference to attempts in the 1849 strikes by Benjamin Embleton, an old union and Chartist activist, to form a union of the miners of Durham and Northumberland)

1082   Reid, T.D.W. and Reid, Naomi 'The 1842 "Plug Plot" in Stockport', *International Review of Social History*, Vol.XXIV, Part 1, 1979

1083   Roberts, Stephen 'Thomas Cooper in Leicester, 1840-1843', *Transactions of the Leicestershire Archaeological and Historical Society*, Vol.61, 1987

1084   Roberts, Stephen 'Thomas Cooper: Radical and Poet, c.1830-1860', *Bulletin of the Society for the Study of Labour History*, Vol.53, No.1, Spring 1988 (Thesis Report)

1085   Roberts, Stephen 'The Later Radical Career of Thomas Cooper, c.1845-55', *Transactions of the Leicestershire Archaeological and Historical Society*, Vol.64, 1990 (Examines Cooper's break with Feargus O'Connor and his advocacy of co-operation with middle class radicals, home colonization and freethought)

1086   Roberts, Stephen 'Thomas Cooper: A Victorian Working Class Writer', *Our History Journal*, Vol.16, 1990 (Looks at the *Purgatory of Suicides* and Cooper's novels)

1087   Roberts, Stephen 'Joseph Barker and the Radical Cause, 1848-51', *Publications of the Thoresby Society*, Second Series, No.1, 1990

1088   Rogers, Gareth 'Henry Vincent: The Young Demosthenes', *Presenting Monmouthshire*, No.30, 1970

1089   Rogers, Gareth 'Henry Vincent: The Idol Removed', *Presenting Monmouthshire*, No.31, 1971

1090   Rose, Arthur G.   'Truckling Magistrates of Lancashire in 1842', *Transactions of the Lancashire and Cheshire Antiquarian Society*, Vol.83, 1985 (Examines the involvement of both Chartists and Anti-Corn Law Leaguers in the 1842 riots and strikes, and the responses of the authorities)

1091   Rössler, Horst   'Charles Dickens und seine Rezeption in der Chartistenpresse', *Gulliver. Deutsch-Englische Jahrbücher/German-English Yearbooks*, Vol.9, 1981 (In German)

1092   Rössler, Horst   'Literatur und politische Agitation im Chartismus: Eine Studie zu Thomas Doubleday's "Political Pilgrim's Progress', *Englisch Amerikanische Studien (EASt)*, No.3, 1981 (In German. Doubleday's work was serialised in the *Northern Liberator* January 19 to March 30 1839)

1093   Rössler, Horst   'Labour is Peace. Anmerkungen zu den Friedensbestrebungen der Chartisten', *Englisch Amerikanische Studien (EASt)*, No.7, 1985 (In German)

1094   Rössler, Horst and Watson, Ian   'Literatur und Arbeiterbewegung in England: Zwei Traditionslinien aus dem 19 Jahrhundert', *Englische Amerikanische Studien (EASt)*, No.4, 1982 (In German. Includes a discussion of Shelley's influence on Chartist literary perceptions as well as on poems by William S. Villiers Sankey, Edwin Gill and Ernest Jones)

1095   Rössler, Horst and Watson, Ian   'In Defence of Ernest Jones', *Gulliver. Deutsch-Englische Jahrbücher/German-English Yearbooks*, Vol.12, 1982

1096   Roth, H.   'My Quest for Binns', *New Zealand Monthly Review*, October 1961 (Brief account of Binns' life in Nelson, New Zealand, 1842-7, where he worked for a time as a baker)

1097   Rotherham, Donald   'Chartism in Burnley', *Retrospect: The Burnley and District Historical Society Journal*, Vol.1, 1980

1098   Rothstein, Theodore   'Aus der Vorgeschichte der Internationale', *Ergänzungshefte zur Neuen Zeit*, No.17, 1913 (In German. Article on the origins of the Society of Fraternal Democrats in the mid 1840s)

1099   Rowe, D.J.   'Francis Place and the Historian', *The Historical Journal*, Vol.16, No.1, 1973

1100   Royle, Edward   'Mechanics' Institutes and the Working Classes, 1840-1860', *The Historical Journal*, Vol.14, No.2, June 1971 (Includes a consideration of Chartist infiltration and control of several Institutes)

1101   Royle, Edward   'The *Star* that Charted Good Radical Fortune', *Journalism Studies Review*, No.6, July 1981 (Article on the *Northern Star*)

1102   Royle, Edward   'Reading History: Chartism', *History Today*, Vol.35, Part 12, December 1985

1103   Royle, Edward *'Chartism', ReFresh (Recent Findings of Research in Economic and Social History)*, No.2, Spring 1986 (Intended for teachers, pupils and undergraduates, the article surveys the changing interpretations of Chartism from the economic to the political, from leaders to followers, and to a rehabilitation of Feargus O'Connor. A revised edition also appears in A. Digby and C.H. Feinstein (eds.) *New Directions in Economic and Social History*, Macmillan, London, 1989, pp.203; see pp.157-169 'Chartism')

1104   Royle, Edward 'The Origins and Nature of Chartism', *History Review*, No.13, September 1992

1105   Rozhkov, B.A. 'Ernest Jones - One of the first Proletarian Revolutionaries', *Novaya i noveishaja istoriya*, No.2, 1959 (In Russian)

1106   Rozhkov, B.A. 'Obschchie printsipy Chartizma', *Voprosy Istorii*, No.9, 1987 (In Russian. Article on the 'General principles of Chartism' in a journal translated as 'Questions of History'. Author argues for the independent working class character of the movement, rather than one dependent on the bourgeoisie. Its independence made it a powerful force in the face of which the ruling class made concessions)

1107   Rule, John 'Richard Spurr - Small Town Radical', *Journal of the Institute of Cornish Studies*, Vol.4/5, 1976/77, (Chartist cabinet-maker and local leader in Truro)

1108   Rule, John 'Update: Popular Protest in Britain c.1811-1850', *The Historian*, No.25, Winter 1989/90 (Includes some consideration of books and articles on Chartism since 1980)

1109   Russell, Dave 'Some Early Irish Movements in South London', *South London Record*, No.2 1987 (Includes a section on 'Chartism and the Irish Confederates')

1110   Russell, David 'The Leeds Rational Recreation Society, 1852-9: "Music for the People" in a Mid-Victorian City', *The Thoresby Society*, Vol.LVI, Part 3, 1980, No.126 (Contains references to Leeds Chartism and radicalism)

1111   Ruston, Alan 'The Omnibus Radical: Rev. Henry Solly (1813-1903)', *Transactions of the Unitarian Historical Society*, Vol. XIX, No.2, 1988

1112   *Rüter, A.J.C. 'William Benbow's Grand National Holiday and Congress of the Productive Classes', with an introduction by Dr. A.J.C. Rüter, *International Review of Social History*, Vol.1, 1936

1113   Sager, E.W. 'The Working-Class Peace Movement in Victorian England', *Histoire Sociale-Social History*, Vol.XII, May 1979 (For the links between Chartists and peace-campaigners between the 1840s and 1870s)

1114   Sager, E.W. 'The Social Origins of Victorian Pacifism', *Victorian Studies*, Vol.23, No.2, Winter 1980 (For attempts by the Peace Society to make common cause with the Chartists against militarism and despotism 1840-1852)

1115   Salt, John   'Isaac Ironside and the Hollow Meadows Farm Experiment',
        Yorkshire Bulletin of Economic and Social Research, Vol.12, No.1, 1960
        (Considers Ironside, the Sheffield Chartist, and his campaign between 1848-
        1854 to secure improved treatment for paupers in the Sheffield workhouse)

1116   Salt, John   'Experiments in Anarchism, 1850-1854', *Transactions of the Hunter
        Archaeological Society,* Vol.10, 1971 (Looks at various attempts by Isaac
        Ironside, the Sheffield Chartist, to secure power for radical activists through
        the local government machinery of Sheffield, 1850-1854)

1117   Salt, John   'Isaac Ironside 1808-1870: The Motivation of a Radical Educationist',
        British Journal of Educational Studies, Vol.XIX, 1971 (Looks at the interplay
        between Ironside's support for Chartism, his educational experiences, his
        promotion of popular educational schemes and involvement in the local
        government of Sheffield)

1118   Scheckner, Peter   'Chartism, Class and Social Struggle: A Study of Charles
        Dickens, *The Mid-West Quarterly,* Vol.29, Part 1, 1987 (Through a brief
        examination of the fiction Dickens wrote in the Chartist years - *The Old
        Curiosity Shop*, the Christmas story, *The Chimes*, and *Hard Times* - argues
        that, for all his ideological contradictions, Dickens advocated the rule of law
        and order against the radical demonstrators)

1119   Schwarzkopf, Jutta   'The Sexual Division in the Chartist Family', *Bulletin of the
        Society for the Study of Labour History*, Vol.54, Part 1, Spring 1989
        (Conference Report. Brief article on how the Chartists opposed women's
        waged labour, reaffirmed male hegemony and women's family-centredness,
        but are not to be confused with the increasingly dominant middle-class ideal
        of female domesticity)

1120   Scott, Joan Wallach   'On Language, Gender and Working-Class History,
        International Labour and Working-Class History, No.31, Spring 1987 (With
        particular reference to Gareth Stedman Jones' work on Chartism, the author
        re-reads Chartism and argues for using both the force of language and the
        dimension of gender as a means of uncovering the formation of class. The
        article also appears revised and slightly expanded in her *Gender and the
        Politics of History*, Columbia University Press, New York, 1988, pp.242. See
        Chapter 3, eponymous title pp.53-67)

1121   Scott, Susan   'The *Northern Tribune*: A North East Radical Magazine', *North
        East Labour History Bulletin*, No.19, 1985 (Joseph Cowen's *Northern Tribune*
        1854-1855, edited by G.J. Harney, was a focal point for Chartist and republican
        activity on Tyneside in the last years of Chartism)

1122   *Searby, Peter   'Chartists and Freemen in Coventry 1838-1860', *Social History*,
        No.6 October 1977

1123   Searby, Peter   'Update: Chartism', *The Historian*, No.10, Spring 1986 (A
        valuable brief guide to the most important publications on Chartism between
        1973 and 1986)

1124   Seehase, Georg   '*Sunshine and Shadow* and the Structure of Chartist Fiction', *Zeitschrift für Anglistik und Amerikanistik*, Vol.21, 1974 (Thomas Martin Wheeler was the Chartist author of *Sunshine and Shadow*)

1125   Shanley, J.R.   'The Chartist Contribution to Marxist Theory', *Quarterly Bulletin of the Marx Memorial Library*, No.85, January/March 1978

1126   Shepherd, Michael A.   'The Origins and Incidence of the term "Labour Aristocracy"', *Bulletin of the Society for the Study of Labour History*, No.37, Autumn 1978 (Notes and Queries Section. On the influential personality and activities of the cabinet-maker and Bath and Bristol Chartist leader, Samuel Jacobs)

1127   Shepherd, Michael A.   'Labour Aristocracy: A Reply', *Bulletin on the Society for the Study of Labour History*, No.40, Spring 1980 (Letter to the editor: A reply to David McNulty 'Samuel Jacobs, Bath and Bristol Chartist', *Bulletin of the Society for the Study of Labour History*, No.38, Spring 1979; and to John Baxter 'Chartist Notions of "Labour Aristocracy" in 1839', *Bulletin of the Society for the Study of Labour History*, No.40, Spring 1980)

1128   Shestoperova, L.A.   'Pedagogicheskii vzglyady proletarskogo revolyutsionnera Ernsta Dzhonsa, *Soveskaya Pedagogika*, No.4, 1986 (In Russian. 'The Pedagogical Views of the Proletarian Revolutionary Ernest Jones', *Soviet Pedagogy*, Moscow, No.4, 1986)

1129   Shikanyan, I.N.   'K voprosu ob ispolzovanii molodym Engelsom chartistskoi gazetoi *Norzern Star*', *Nauchno-informatsionny byulletin Instituta Marxisma-Leninisma pri TsK KPSS*, No.30, 1977 (In Russian. 'The Young Engels' use of the Chartist newspaper the *Northern Star*', *Scientific Information Bulletin of the Institute of Marxism-Leninism attached to the Central Committee of the Communist Party of the Soviet Union*, No.30, 1977)

1130   Shraepler, Ernst   'Der Bund der Gerechten. Seine Tätigkeit in London 1840-1847, *Archiv Für Sozialgeschicte*, Vol.II, 1962 (In German. Article on the 'League of the Just. Its Operation in London'. Includes a section on the Fraternal Democrats, G.J. Harney and their connections with the revolutionary League's branch in London, and particularly with one of the leaders, Karl Schapper)

1131   Sinnott, Diana   'This Strange Interlude', *Our Time. Chartist Centenary Issue*, Vol.7, No.7, April 1948 (Short article which discusses bias and ignorance in a random selection of history text books concerning the Chartists since the late nineteenth century)

1132   Smith, F.B.   'Great Britain and The Revolutions of 1848', *Labour History Australia*, Vol.33, November 1977 (For Chartism and the reactions of the authorities in Britain during and immediately after 1848. A near identical version also appears in Eugene Kamenka and F.B. Smith (eds.) *Intellectuals and Revolution: Socialism and the Experience of 1848*, Edward Arnold, London, 1979, pp.165. See Chapter 7 "The View from Britain 1: Tumults Abroad, Stability at Home", pp.94-120)

1133   Smith, Paul A   'Chartism in Loughborough', *Leicestershire Historian*, Vol.2, No.6, 1975

1134   *South Wales Argus*   'The Chartists 1839-1989, 150th Anniversary Supplementary Edition', *South Wales Argus*, 15 August 1989, pp.20 (Features short commemorative pieces on aspects of the Newport Rising by local journalists, Alexander Cordell, Brian Davies and Neil Kinnock)

1135   Storch, R.D.   'The Plague of Blue Locusts: Police Reform and Popular Resistance in Northern England 1840-57', *International Review of Social History*, Vol.XX, Part 1, 1975 (Shows how the hostility towards the new police derived from the perception of the force not as crime-fighters, but as agents of a tyrannical state intent on breaking trade unions and Chartism)

1136   Sykes, R.A.   "Some Aspects of Working-Class Consciousness in Oldham 1830-1842', *The Historical Journal*, Vol.23, No.1, March 1980

1137   Sykes, R.A.   'Physical-Force Chartism: the Cotton District and the Chartist Crisis of 1839', *International Review of Social History*, Vol.XXX, Part 2, 1985 (Assesses Chartist tactics, support for confrontational strategies and the extent of arming amongst the rank and file Chartists in the cotton districts of South Lancashire in 1839)

1138   Tate, W.E.   'A Battle Long Ago', *Indoors, The Trust House Review*, No.27, April 1956 (General account of the Newport Rising in an hoteliers' journal with illustrations and featuring the Westgate Hotel)

1139   Taylor, James   'The Life and Times of Thomas Attwood', *Blackcountryman*, Vol.17, Winter 1984 (A very basic three page introduction)

1140   Taylor, Miles   'Imperium et Libertas? Rethinking the Radical Critique of Imperialism during the Nineteenth Century', *Journal of Imperial and Commonwealth History*, Vol.19, No.1, January 1991 (Includes Ernest Jones' criticism of British government policy in India in 1857)

1141   Thomas, W.E.S.   'Francis Place and Working-Class History' *The Historical Journal*, Vol.5, No.1, 1962

1142   Thornes, Robin   'Co-operation and the English Working-Class Movement 1816-44', *Bulletin of the Society for the Study of Labour History*, No.43, Autumn 1981 (Conference Report. Argues that the resurgence of and interest in co-operative societies in 1839 was due to Chartism and the advocacy of a policy of exclusive dealing)

1143   Tiller, Kate   'Charterville and the Chartist Land Company', *Oxoniensia*, Vol.L, 1985

1144   Todd, Nigel   '"His Majesty The Chief Constable": Tyneside's Chartist Policeman, John Elliott 1863-1891', *North East Labour History Bulletin*, No.26, 1992 (Biographical article on a leading Tyneside Chartist who went on to become the Chief Constable of Police in Newcastle-upon-Tyne)

1145   Tomlinson, V.I.   'Postcript to Peterloo', *Manchester Region History Review, Special Issue: Peterloo Massacre*, Vol.III, No.1, Spring/Summer 1989 (Through an examination of the life of Rev. Dr. James Scholefield (1790-1855), a Radical and Chartist sympathiser, the author charts the connections from Peterloo to Chartism)

1146   Troup, Colin   'Chartism in Dumfries 1830-50', *Dumfriesshire and Galloway Natural History and Antiquarian Society Transactions*, Vol.56, 1981 (Also useful for the profile of a local Chartist leader, Andrew Wardrop)

1147   Tucker, Clifford   'The Prisoner in Monmouth Gaol: A Study of Henry Vincent', *Presenting Monmouthshire*, No.20, 1965

1148   Turner, William   'Gifted Orator Fought to Give Workers A Fair Deal', *Accrington Observer*, 12 October 1985 (Report by Jack Broderick, local journalist, of a talk given by William Turner to Hyndburn Local History Society on the life of William Beesley, the Accrington Chartist leader and secretary to W.P. Roberts of the national Miners' Association. A useful thumb-nail sketch)

1149   Tyrrell, Alex.   'Personality in Politics: The National Complete Suffrage Union and Pressure Group Politics in Early Victorian Britain', *Journal of Religious History*, Vol.XII, Part 4, December 1983 (A case study of Joseph Sturge and the origins and development of his Complete Suffrage Union, which emphasizes the importance of personality as a means of understanding his moral radical party's policies and actions towards the Chartists in 1842)

1150   Vincent, David   'Love and Death and the Nineteenth Century Working Class', *Social History*, Vol.5, No.2, May 1980 (Takes examples from the autobiographies of various Chartist leaders including J.J. Bezer, Thomas Cooper, J.B. Leno, W. Lovett, James Myles and William Thom. Subsequently incorporated as Chapter 3 in his book *Bread, Knowledge and Freedom. A Study of Nineteenth Century Autobiography*, Europa, London, 1981)

1151   Wallace, Ryland   'The Anti-Corn Law League in Wales', *Welsh History Review*, Vol.13, No.1, June 1986 (For relationships between the Anti-Corn law League and the Chartists)

1152   Walsh, David   'Working Class Development and Class Relationships in the Industrial North-West, 1820-1850: A Theoretical and Historical Dimension', *University of Salford Occasional Paper*, No.14, 1988 (From the Department of Politics and Contemporary History. The paper suggests that working class political sectionalization was taking place in the industrial North West even before 1838)

1153   Weisser, Henry   'Chartism in 1848: Reflections on a Non-Revolution', *Albion*, Vol.13, No.1, Spring 1981

1154   Wells, Roger   'Southern Chartism', *Rural History*, Vol.2, No.1, April 1991

1155   Whitehead, Andrew   'The *New World* and the O'Brienite Colony in Kansas', *Bulletin of the Society for the Study of Labour History*, Vol.53, Part No.3, Winter 1988 (Notes on the Labour Press: An account of the colonisation company to which many of the London supporters of Bronterre O'Brien devoted much of their energies, its journal and their colonisation scheme in April 1869 to North East Kansas. The paper was extant in 1871)

1156   Wilks, Ivor   'Insurrections in Texas and Wales: the careers of John Rees', *Welsh History Review*, Vol.11, No.1, June 1982 (Article on the part played by the peripatetic Tredegar Chartist leader, who first became prominent in the Newport Rising of 1839)

1157   Wilson, Keith   'Chartism in Sunderland', *North East Labour History Society Bulletin*, No.16, 1982 (The article first appeared in the *May Day Magazine of Sunderland Trades Council*, centenary edition, 1981. Particularly useful for the careers of loçal Chartist leaders, James Williams and George Binns)

1158   Wilson, Keith   'Sunderland Chartists', *Journal of the Sunderland Antiquarian Society*, No.4, 1986 (More information on local Chartist leaders including Thomas Thompson, James Williams and George Binns)

1159   Williams, Chris   'History, Heritage and Commemoration: Newport 1839-1989', *Llafur, Journal of Welsh Labour History*, Vol.6, No.1, 1992 (Explores and evaluates the traditions of commemoration surrounding the Newport Rising of 1839: for example, John Frost's return in 1856; the 1939 centenary; and intense celebrations in 1988/89)

1160   Williams, David   'The Chartist Centenary', *Welsh Review*, November 1939 (An outline of the significance of the events surrounding the Chartist march on Newport 1839)

1161   Winstanley, Michael   'News from Oldham: Edwin Butterworth and the Manchester Press, 1829-1848', *Manchester Region History Review*, Vol.iv, No.1, 1990 (Although concerned primarily with the reliability of the press reports of a local, self-styled and appointed journalist, the article does have references to Chartist activity in Oldham 1838-1840)

1162   Winstanley, Michael   'Oldham Radicalism and the Origins of Popular Liberalism, 1830-52', *The Historical Journal*, Vol.36, No.3, September 1993 (Argues that continuities in personnel, values, motivation, policies and strategies suggest that militant grass-roots Liberalism of the 1850s, and the culture of self-improvement which pervaded it, were essentially continuations of a radical platform of the 1830s which was preserved, even enhanced, through the Chartist period)

1163   Working Class Movement Library Staff   'Reginald John Richardson 1808-1861', *Working Class Movement Library Bulletin*, No.2 Salford, 1992 (Brief outline of Richardson's life as a Chartist)

1164   Working Class Movement Library Staff   'The Round House in Ancoats', *Working Class Movement Library Bulletin*, No.3, Salford, 1993 (Brief history of the Rev. Dr. James Scholefield's house in Manchester, a focal point for Manchester Chartism particularly during the 1842 General Strike)

1165   Working Class Movement Library Staff   'The Ernest Jones Memorial',
        Working Class Movement Library Bulletin, No.3, Salford, 1993 (Article on his
        career and memorials to him in Manchester and Salford)

1166   Working Class Movement Library Staff   'General Strike!', *Working Class
        Movement Library Bulletin*, No.3, Salford, 1993 (A brief article on the concept
        of the General Strike as advocated by William Benbow in 1831 and debated
        and utilized by some Chartists in 1839)

1167   Wright,Sarah A.   'Joseph Barker - Seeker of the Truth? A Comparison of Two
        Sources', *The Wesley Historical Society, Yorkshire Branch(Bulletin)* No.32,
        April 1978 (Much of the article is based upon Barker's *Reformers' Almanac*
        and *Companion to the Almanacs* published in the late Chartist period)

1168   Yeo, Eileen 'Christianity in Chartist Struggle 1838-1842', *Past and Present*,
        No.91, May 1981 (An important publication on a neglected theme)

Unpublished Secondary Material

1169   Anderson, Duane Charles   'English Working-Class Internationalism 1846-1864', PhD thesis; University of Oklahoma, 1976 (Includes a consideration of the Chartists' Democratic Friends of All Nations and the Society of Fraternal Democrats)

1170   Andrew, Alison   'The Working Class and Education in Preston, 1830-70: A Study of Social Relations', PhD thesis; University of Leicester, 1987 (Includes in Chapter 3 'Education by Collision: 1. Trade Union Activity: The 1842 Turn-out and the Plug Plot Riots; 2. The 1853/4 Strike and Lock-Out in Preston; 3.Chartism and other Forms of Agitational Association'. See particularly pp.60-84)

1171   Archer, John E.   'Rural Protest in Norfolk and Suffolk 1837-70', PhD thesis; University of East Anglia, 1982, 2 Vols. (See Chapter 7 'Collective Protest 1830-70', particularly pp.465-474, for the brief appeal of Chartism to farm workers in East Suffolk, but less so in Norfolk)

1172   Ashton, Owen R.   'Radicalism and Chartism in Gloucestershire, 1832-1847', PhD thesis; University of Birmingham, 1980.

1173   Barnes, J.C.F.   'Popular Protest and Radical Politics: Carlisle, 1780-1850', PhD thesis; University of Lancaster, 1981 (Carlisle had a strong radical tradition. Chapter 7 'The Chartist Years, 1836-1850', pp.323-393, looks at the Chartist contribution to that tradition)

1174   Barnett, C.A.   'Fears of Revolution, Finality and the Re-opening of the Question of Parliamentary Reform in England, 1832-67', DPhil thesis; University of Oxford, 1981 (From a national perspective and chronologically, the thesis looks at the fears of revolution aroused in Britain between 1832-1867 in connection with the attempts made to re-open the question of parliamentary reform. Chapters 3-6 relate closely to the agitation of the Chartists 1839-1848. The author, however, did not utilize the Chartist press as source material)

1175   Barnsby, George J.   'Social Conditions in the Black Country in the Nineteenth-Century', PhD thesis; University of Birmingham, 1969 (Includes a consideration of Chartism)

1176   Bebb, Carol S.   'The Origins of Chartism in Dundee', BPhil thesis; University of St Andrews, 1977

1177   Behagg, Clive   'Radical Politics and Conflict at the Point of Production: Birmingham 1815-1845. A Study in the Relationship between the Classes', PhD thesis; University of Birmingham, 1982 (Includes Chartism in Birmingham)

1178   Berridge, Virginia   'Popular Journalism and Working-Class Attitudes. A Study of *Reynolds's Newspaper, Lloyd's Weekly Newspaper,* and *Weekly Times,* 1854-1886', 3 Vols. PhD thesis; University of London, 1976 (G.W.M. Reynolds, the London Chartist)

1179   Blaszak, Barbara J.   'George Jacob Holyoake: An Attitudinal Study', PhD thesis; State University of New York at Buffalo, 1978

1180   Brooke, Alan J.   'The Social and Political Responses to Industrialization in the Huddersfield Area, c.1790-1850', PhD thesis; University of Manchester, 1988 (For Chartism in Huddersfield)

1181   Bryson, C.A.   'Riot and Its Control in Liverpool, 1815-60', MPhil thesis; The Open University, 1990 (Includes a Chartist dimension)

1182   Cameron, Kenneth J.   'Anti-Corn Law Agitations in Scotland with Particular Reference to the Anti-Corn Law League', PhD thesis; University of Edinburgh, 1971 (For the Scottish Chartists' attitude to and relationships with the Anti-Corn Law League, see pp.243-251)

1183   Campbell, A.B.   'Honourable Men and Degraded Slaves: A Social History of Trade Unionism in the Lanarkshire Coalfield, 1775-1874, with Particular Reference to the Coatbridge and Larkhall Districts', PhD thesis; University of Warwick, 1976 (For a discussion of the Chartist influence among the Lanarkshire leaders and the rank and file during the 1840s and particularly 1842, see pp.368-377)

1184   Chase, Malcolm   'The Land and the Working-Classes: English Radical Agrarianism, c.1775-1851', DPhil thesis; University of Sussex, 1984 (Particularly valuable for the Chartist Land Plan)

1185   Christodoulou, J.P.   'The Universalists: Radical Sectarianism (1760-1850)', MPhil thesis; The Open University, 1988 (Looks at the theological and intellectual origins of the Universalist faith, which believed in the certainty of salvation for all men, human emancipation and progress through reason. Their millenarian vision of a just and equal society formed the basis of moral-force, Christian Chartism. See Chapter 9 'British Universalist Societies and Chartism', pp.242-281, for a case study of Glasgow Chartism)

1186   Claeys, Gregory R.   'Owenism, Democratic Theory and Political Radicalism: An Investigation of the Relationship between Socialism and Politics in Britain, 1820-1852', PhD thesis; University of Cambridge, 1983 (For the relationship between Owenism and Chartism)

1187   Clark, Anna   'Womanhood and Manhood in the Transition from the Plebeian to Working-Class Culture: London 1780-1845', PhD thesis; Rutgers University, 1987 (For Chartism, women and gender relations)

1188   Clinton, J.R.   'The National Charter Association and Its Role in the Chartist Movement, 1840-58', MPhil thesis; University of Southampton, 1980

1189   Cole, John   'Chartism in Rochdale', MA thesis; Manchester Polytechnic (CNAA), 1986

1190   Coles, S.D.   'Chartism and Radical Politics in Devon and Exeter, 1790-1848', MA thesis; University of Exeter, 1979

1191   Collier, A.B.   'Some Aspects and Some Determinants of Popular Politics in Bury, 1838-58', MA dissertation; University of Lancaster, 1983 (For the rise and demise of Chartism in Bury)

1192   Colls, R.M.   'Work, Culture and Protest in the North-East Mining Community in the Eighteenth and Nineteenth Centuries', DPhil thesis; University of York, 1980 (See Part Three: 'Protest' - Chapter 6 'Chartists and the National Miners' Association', pp.428-459, which explores the extensive Chartist influence in the pit-villages, 1838-1844)

1193   Cordery, Simon C.E.   'Voice of the West Riding: Joshua Hobson in Huddersfield and Leeds, 1831-1845', MA thesis; University of York, 1984 (Hobson was the Chartist printer and publisher of the *Northern Star*)

1194   Cotsworth, Violet Gwilt   'Chartism in Wigan and District', MA thesis; University of Liverpool, 1935 (Copy in Wigan Public Library)

1195   Courtenay, Adrian   'Parliamentary Representation and General Elections in Cheltenham Spa, 1832-1848: A Study of a Pocket Borough', MPhil thesis; Open University, 1991 (Includes a detailed consideration of the Chartist challenges at election times, 1838-1848)

1196   D'Arcy, F.A.   'Charles Bradlaugh and the World of Popular Radicalism, 1833-91', PhD thesis; University of Hull, 1978 (Chapter 1 looks at the roles of G.J. Holyoake, Thomas Cooper and Joseph Barker in Chartism and the early growth of Secularism, circa 1848-1858)

1197   Devereux, Stephen   'Working Class Heroes: A Comparison of Chartist and Communist fictions as Proletarian texts', MPhil thesis; University of Manchester, 1991 (Looks at Chartist novels as popular and political fiction)

1198   Dinwiddy, J.R.   'Parliamentary Reform as an Issue in English Politics, 1800-1860', PhD thesis; University of London, 1971

1199   Duncan, Robert   'Popular Radicalism and Working Class Movements in Aberdeen, 1790-1850, MLitt thesis; University of Aberdeen, 1976

1200   Elliott, Adrian   'The Establishment of Municipal Government in Bradford 1837-1857', PhD thesis; University of Bradford, 1976 (Includes a consideration of the Chartists' increasing involvement by 1850 in the work of the newly formed municipal town council; see Chapter 8 for Chartism)

1201   Epstein, James A.   'Feargus O'Connor and the English Working-Class Radical Movement, 1832-41: a Study in National Chartist Leadership', PhD thesis; University of Birmingham, 1977

1202   Ferguson, K.M.   'Carlyle's Chartism: Its Origins and Reception' MLitt thesis; University of Edinburgh, 1980

1203   Finn, Margot C.   'After Chartism: Nationalist Sentiment in English Popular Radicalism, 1848-1871', PhD thesis; University of Columbia, 1987 (Emphasizes the persistence of radical agitation and class politics in the last decade of the Chartist movement and beyond)

1204   Fowler, R.   'John Collins, A Working Class Chartist in Birmingham', MA thesis; Wolverhampton Polytechnic (CNAA), 1987

1205   *Fyson, Robert   'Chartism in North Staffordshire, 1838-1842', MA dissertation; University of Lancaster, 1975

1206   Gadian, David   'The Social History of Oldham Radicalism in the 1830s', MA dissertation; University of Lancaster, 1970 (For early Chartism in Oldham)

1207   Gadian, David   'A Comparative Study of Popular Movements in North-West Industrial Towns, 1830-1850', PhD thesis; University of Lancaster, 1977 (Includes a lengthy consideration of Chartism)

1208   Goodway, David J.   'Chartism in London', PhD thesis; University of London (Birkbeck College), 1979

1209   Granath, Andrew   'The Irish in Mid-Nineteenth Century Lancashire, 1830-81', MA thesis; University of Lancaster, 1975 (Chapter 4 argues for the minimal role of the Irish in Chartism and political activity until the emergence of Irish nationalism in the 1850s and 1860s)

1210   Grant, Maureen C.   'Education for the Working Class: the Views of the British Radical Press, 1815-50', PhD thesis; Drew University, Madison, New Jersey, 1981 (Looks at popular responses to educational reform proposed by working class leaders, including Bronterre O'Brien, Feargus O'Connor and William Lovett. See Chapter 5: 'William Lovett and Feargus O'Connor: a Conflict of Ideals', and Chapter 6 'A Matter of High Moment: Education in the Period of Chartism's Decline')

1211   Groth, Eileen L.   'Religion and Politics in Birmingham: The Case of the Chartist Church 1838-1846', MSocSc thesis; University of Birmingham, 1989 (Examines the development of Christian Chartism with specific focus on Arthur O'Neill)

1212   Groth, Eileen L.   'Christian Radicalism in Britain 1830-1850', PhD thesis; University of Cambridge, 1993 (Examines the relationship between religion and radical politics, asserting the importance of religious motivation and rhetoric in radical campaigns)

1213   Hackett, Nancy A.   'The Evolution of Nineteenth-Century Working-Class Autobiography', PhD thesis; University of Iowa, 1983 (Includes literary critical studies of the autobiographies of James Dawson Burn, Samuel Bamford, Thomas Cooper, G.J. Holyoake, William Lovett, Francis Place and Alexander Somerville)

1214   Hall, R.G.   'Work, Class and Politics in Ashton-under-Lyne, 1830-1860', PhD thesis; Vanderbilt University, Nashville, Tennessee, 1991 (Explores the nature of radical politics in this major stronghold of Chartism)

1215   Haynes, J.B.   'A Study of Social Perceptions and Attitudes in the Context of Class Relationships in Mid-Victorian Leicester', MPhil thesis; University of Leicester, 1988 (For the collective, self-help activities - friendly societies, co-operatives, trade unions and political organizations - of some of the ex-Chartist leaders in Leicester in the 1850s and 1860s)

1216   Herbert, D.   'Chartism and the Churches', MPhil thesis; University of Manchester, 1992

1217   Hewitt, Martin   'Structures of Accommodation: The Intellectual Roots of Social Stability in Mid Nineteenth-Century Manchester', DPhil thesis; University of Oxford, 1991 (Explores, through the case-study of Manchester, the intellectual world of the working class in the Chartist and post-Chartist period. Despite middle class moral imperialism, the attempt to mould working class culture and consciousness from the Manchester evidence suggests that there was considerable persistence of radical class consciousness amongst the working classes in the 1850s and 1860s; see particularly Chapters 7&8 for the continuation of working class consciousness)

1218   Hobby, Martin   'Chartism and the Land Plan in Gloucestershire', MA dissertation; University of Wales (Swansea), 1980

1219   Holden, Grayson G.   'Respectable Militants: The Lancashire Textile Machinery Makers, c.1800-1939', PhD thesis; University of Salford, 1987 (Demonstrates how the engineering artisans' respectability and independence could be the basis of a consistent militancy and radicalism. Includes Alexander Hutchinson, the Manchester Chartist, and his United Trades Association, 1841-2)

1220   Holmes, J.D.S.   'The Role of Education Among Popular Working Class Movements with Particular Reference to the Chartists, 1780-1860', MA dissertation; Institute of Education, London, 1987.

1221   Hooper, Alan   'Mid-Victorian Radicalism: Community and Class in Birmingham, 1850-1880', PhD thesis; University of London, 1978 (Small section in Chapter IV 'Liberalism and Labour Representation', pp.376-381, deals with Chartism, political reform and foreign affairs - the Crimean War - c. 1850-1858)

1222   Howell, A.R.   'Patrick Brewster. Scottish Chartist and Minister of the Second Charge of Paisley Abbey', Typescript, 1943 (Copy in Paisley Public Library)

1223   Hugman, Joan   'Joseph Cowen of Newcastle and Radical Liberalism', PhD thesis; University of Northumbria at Newcastle, 1993 (Early chapters consider Tyneside Chartism)

1224   Huxhorn, Sieglinde   'United We Stand, Divided We Fall! Chartist celebrations in Ashton-under-Lyne in the 1840s', Typescript, 1981, pp.72 (In Tameside Local Studies Library, Stalybridge)

1225   Kaijage, F.J. 'Labouring Barnsley, 1815-56: A Social and Economic History',
        PhD thesis; University of Warwick, 1975

1226   Kirk, Neville 'Class and Fragmentation: Some Aspects of Working Class Life
        in South-East Lancashire and North-East Cheshire, 1850-1870', PhD thesis;
        University of Pittsburgh, 1974 (For Chartism in the 1850s in the industrial
        North-West)

1227   Koditschek, Theodore 'Class Formation and the Bradford Bourgeoisie', PhD
        thesis; University of Princeton, 1981 (Includes a consideration of Bradford
        Chartism)

1228   Koseki, Takashi 'Chartism and Irish Nationalism, 1829-1848: Bronterre
        O'Brien, the London Irish and Attempts at a Chartist-Irish Alliance', MPhil
        thesis; University of Birmingham, 1988

1229   Lawrence, J.M. 'Party Politics and the People: Continuity and Change in the
        Political History of Wolverhampton, 1815-1914', PhD thesis; University of
        Cambridge, 1989 (Chapters 1 and 2 analyse popular radicalism in
        Wolverhampton 1815-1880 and argue that historians have greatly under-
        estimated the continuity between Chartism and mid-Victorian radicalism in
        such industrial areas)

1230   Little, Alan D. 'Chartism and Liberalism: Popular Politics in Leicestershire,
        1842-74' PhD thesis; University of Manchester, 1989

1231   Llewellyn-Williams, G.D. 'Plutocrats and Proletarians: An Examination of the
        Background to Social, Political and Industrial Unrest in South-East Wales, 1815-
        1850', MA thesis; University of Wales (Swansea), 1984

1232   Lowe, J.E.B. 'Women in the Chartist Movement', MA thesis; University of
        Birmingham, 1984

1233   McGuire, John 'Chartism in the Paisley Area', MA thesis; University of
        Strathclyde, 1974

1234   McNulty, David 'Working-Class Movements in Somerset and Wiltshire, 1837-
        48', PhD thesis; University of Manchester, 1981

1235   Martin, Caroline E. 'Female Chartism: a Study in Politics', MA thesis;
        University of Wales (Swansea), 1974

1236   Mitchell, John B. 'The Ragged Trousered Philanthropists and the Aesthetic
        Maturity of the British Working-Class Novel', PhD thesis; University of Berlin,
        1964 (Includes a discussion of novels by Thomas Martin Wheeler and Ernest
        Jones)

1237   Montgomery, F.A. 'Glasgow Radicalism, 1830-48', PhD thesis; University of
        Glasgow, 1974 (Includes aspects of Scottish Chartism and the career of
        prominent Scottish Chartists such as James Moir)

1238   Moore, Kevin   "This Whig and Tory-Ridden Town": Popular Politics in Liverpool 1815-50', MPhil thesis; University of Liverpool, 1988 (Includes a Chartist dimension)

1239   Morgan, Carol Edyth   'Working-Class Women and Labour and Social Movements in Mid-Nineteenth Century England', PhD thesis; University of Iowa, 1979 (Includes women and Chartism)

1240   Moss, D.J.   'Thomas Attwood: The Biography of a Radical', D.Phil thesis; University of Oxford, 1973 (See Chapter 9: 'Member of Parliament and Chartist')

1241   Murphy, Paul Thomas   'Defining a Working-Class Literature: Views of Literature in British Working-Class Periodicals, 1816-1858', PhD thesis; University of Colorado at Boulder, 1989 (Chapter 3 looks at Chartist periodicals; Chapter 4 on Chartist views of fiction, and Chapter 4 has a lengthy section on Chartist poetry and the influence of Shelley, Byron and Burns on Chartists)

1242   Murray, Norman   'A Social History of the Scottish Handloom Weavers, 1790-1850', PhD thesis; University of Strathclyde, 1976 (Chapter 5: 'Radical Attitudes and Activities', pp.398-407, includes a consideration of the Scottish handloom weavers' involvement in Chartism)

1243   Nadorf, Bernhard   'Die Chartistenbewegung in Manchester von 1838 bis 1842. Eine strukturgeschichtliche Untersuchung', 1975 (In German. 'Chartism in Manchester 1838-42. A structural, historical investigation'. Typescript, pp.310. Presented to Manchester Central Library. Local Studies Unit, 1975)

1244   Obaidi-Ford, K.   'The Radical Career of John Goodwyn Barmby, 1838-1848', MPhil thesis; Manchester Polytechnic (CNAA), 1986 (Based on a wide selection of Barmby's letters)

1245   Osburn, John D.   'Lloyd Jones, Labour Journalist 1871-1878. A Study in British Working-Class Thought', PhD thesis; University of Oklahoma, 1969 (Chapter 1 includes brief, but useful, insights into Jones' relationships with Chartism)

1246   Patterson, I.R.   'Chartism in Devon, 1838-65', MPhil thesis; University of Exeter, 1987

1247   Pickering, Paul   'The Fustian Jackets: Aspects of the Chartist Movement in Manchester and Salford to 1842', PhD thesis; La Trobe University, Melbourne, 1992

1248   Porter, T.W.   'The Political Thought of Ernest Charles Jones', PhD thesis; Northern Illinois University, 1972

1249   Powys, Robert W.   'From Alienation to Accommodation: Merthyr Tydfil Industrial Relations, 1842-1870', MA dissertation; University of Wales (Swansea), 1989 (Examines the changing nature of industrial relations in Merthyr during the mid nineteenth-century and the growth of moderate reformism, observable, it is argued here, as early as 1842. Chapter 5 is particularly useful for the effect of Chartist thought and leadership on the development of non-violent working class attitudes in the town in the 1840s and 1850s)

1250   Randall, Adrian J.   'Labour and the Industrial Revolution in the West of England Woollen Industry', PhD thesis; University of Birmingham, 1979 (Chapter 9: 'The Woollen Workers and Radical Politics 1789-1839: The Legacy of the Moral Economy', pp.598-642. Looks at the precursors and the beginnings of Chartism in Wiltshire and Gloucestershire, and the relative speed of the demise of a deep-rooted moral economy)

1251   Reid, C.A. Naomi   'The Chartist Movement in Stockport', MA thesis; University of Hull, 1976

1252   Reid, Douglas A.   'Labour, Leisure and Politics in Birmingham, c.1800-1875', PhD thesis; University of Birmingham, 1985 (Chapter 4: 'Artisans and Rational Recreation', pp.180-197,includes a consideration of Chartist rational recreation in the 1840s as an offshoot of political radicalism. The chapter also contains useful information on the Birmingham Chartist, John Mason)

1253   Rickard, M.T.   'Chartism and Trade Unionism: A Study of the Inter-Relationships of Aims, Organisations and Individuals, 1837-1860', MPhil thesis; University of Sheffield, 1981

1254   Roberts, Stephen   'Thomas Cooper: Radical and Poet, c.1830-1860', MLitt thesis; University of Birmingham, 1986

1255   Rose, D.J.   'Chartism and the Education of the People', MEd thesis; University of Newcastle, 1979

1256   Rössler, Horst   'Literatur und Arbeiterbewegung. Studien zur Literatur-Kritick und Frühen Prosa des Chartismus', PhD thesis; University of Bremen, 1984 (In German. 'Literature and the Labour Movement. Studies in the Literary Criticism and Early Prose of Chartism')

1257   Rowley, J.J.   'Drink and Temperance in Nottingham, 1830-60', MA dissertation; University of Leicester, 1974 (Chapter 3: 'Temperance activists and objectives', pp.46-59, and Chapter 4: 'Temperance, class and conflict', pp.60-67, look at the relationship between the temperance movement and Chartism)

1258   Rule, John G.   'The Labouring Miner in Cornwall, c.1740-1870', PhD thesis; University of Warwick, 1971 (See 'Chartism and the Cornish Miners', pp.362-374 for the years 1838-1840)

1259   Ryan, John   'Radicalism and Christianity in Early Victorian Birmingham; A Study in Rhetoric and Institutions', MLitt thesis; University of Birmingham, 1979

1260   Salt, John   'Isaac Ironside and Education in the Sheffield Region in the First
         Half of the Nineteenth Century', MA thesis; University of Sheffield, 1960

1261   Sanders, John R.   'Working-Class Movements in the West Riding Textile
         District 1829 to 1839, with Emphasis upon Local Leadership and Organization',
         PhD thesis; University of Manchester, 1984

1262   Seary, Edgar Ronald   Ebenezer Elliott: A Study, Including an Edition of his
         Works. 2 Vols. in 3, PhD thesis; University of Sheffield, 1932 (Vol.1
         Biography, see Chapter IV 'Corn Laws, Reform and Chartism 1824-1840',
         pp.63-95, for an understanding of Elliott's switch to the Anti-Corn Law League
         from Chartism by the end of 1839. Vol.2: Political works, Parts I & II)

1263   Seehase, Georg   'Die Widerspiegelung des Chartistischen Volkskampfs in der
         Englischen Literatur in der Zeit von 1840 bis 1855', Habil Schrift (Post-
         Doctoral thesis); University of Leipzig, 1965 (In German. 'The Chartist
         Struggle as Reflected in English Literature from 1840 to 1855')

1264   Shaaban, Bouthaina   'Shelley's Influence on the Chartist Poets, with Particular
         Emphasis on Ernest Charles Jones and Thomas Cooper', PhD thesis;
         University of Warwick, 1981

1265   Sharratt, Bernard   'Autobiography and Class Consciousness: An Attempt to
         Characterize Nineteenth-Century Working Class Autobiography in the Light of
         the Writer's Class', DPhil thesis; University of Cambridge, 1973 (A literary,
         critical analysis of both text and context of the working class autobiographies
         of Samuel Bamford, James Dawson Burn, Thomas Frost and Alexander
         Somerville)

1266   Shiach, Morag E.   'A Critical Account of Historical Developments in the
         Analysis of Popular Culture in Britain since the Eighteenth Century', PhD
         thesis; University of Cambridge, 1987 (Chapter 3: 'Popular Culture and the
         Periodical Press 1830-1870', pp.102-144 which includes a discussion of Chartist
         journals such as the *Northern Star, Democratic Review, Notes to the People,
         People's Paper*)

1267   Silver, A.B.   'Chartism in the Localities: Culture and Community', MLitt thesis;
         University of Edinburgh, 1987

1268   Simmonds, A.   'George Jacob Holyoake and the Struggles of Working-Class
         Education, 1836-1898', MA dissertation; Institute of Education, London, 1989

1269   Simpson, Roy I.   'The Significance of Education within the Scottish Chartist
         Movement', MEd thesis; University of Glasgow, 1987

1270   Smith, Dennis   'A Comparative Study of Class Relationships and Institutional
         Orders in Birmingham and Sheffield between 1830 and 1895, with Particular
         Reference to the Spheres of Education, Industry and Politics', PhD thesis;
         University of Leicester, 1981

1271   Smith, Jonathan P.   'Politics and Ideology in Early Nineteenth Century Bradford: Conflict and Compromise, 1825-1852', MPhil thesis; University of York, 1983 (Examines the development and nature of a 'physical force' Chartist movement in Bradford, which emerged from the trade union struggles of the 1820s and 1830s. Also considers Chartist decline after 1848 through liberalization by important sections of the local middle class)

1272   Smith, L.D.   'The Carpet Weavers of Kidderminster, 1800-50', PhD thesis; University of Birmingham, 1982 (Looks at the weavers' involvement in Chartism)

1273   Spraggon, E.D.   'The Radicalism of Joseph Cowen', MA thesis; Newcastle-upon-Tyne Polytechnic (CNAA), 1985 (For Cowen and Tyneside Chartism in the 1850s)

1274   Strange, Keith   'The Condition of the Working Classes in Merthyr Tydfil, circa 1840-1850', PhD thesis; University of Wales (Swansea), 1982 (Chapter VII, pp.393-424 for Merthyr Chartism 1838-1858 and its political legacy down to 1867)

1275   Sykes, Robert   'Popular Politics and Trade Unionism in South-East Lancashire, 1829-42', PhD thesis; University of Manchester, 1982 (For the close connections between Chartism and Trade Unionism in the region)

1276   Taylor, Antony D.   'Ernest Jones: His Later Career and the Structure of Manchester Politics, 1861-9', MA thesis; University of Birmingham, 1984

1277   Taylor, Antony D.   'Modes of Political Expression and Working-class Radicalism 1848-1874: The London and Manchester examples', PhD thesis; University of Manchester, 1992 (Pinpoints the reasons for the success of a broadly based popular Liberalism in the provinces on the one hand and, on the other, those factors which caused the continuation of Chartism and a related independent tradition of working class political activity in London down to the 1870s)

1278   Taylor, Miles   'Radicalism and Patriotism, 1848-59', PhD thesis; University of Cambridge, 1989 (For aspects of Chartism in the 1850s)

1279   Taylor, P.F.   'Popular Politics and Labour-Capital relations in Bolton, 1825-50', PhD thesis; University of Lancaster, 1992

1280   Thomas, K.J.   'Chartism in Monmouthshire and the Newport Insurrection, 1837-39', MA dissertation; University of Wales (Swansea), 1980

1281   Thomas, M.P.   'Friends of Democracy: A Study of Working Class Radicalism in Derbyshire, 1790-1850', MPhil thesis; University of Sheffield, 1985

1282   Thornes, R.C.N.   'The Early Development of the Co-operative Movement in West Yorkshire, 1827-1863', DPhil thesis; University of Sussex, 1984 (Includes co-operation and democracy in the Chartist associations)

1283   Tiller, K.   'Working Class Attitudes and Organization in Three Industrial Towns, 1850-75', PhD thesis; University of Birmingham, 1975 (For a study of late Chartism in Halifax, Wigan and Kidderminster)

1284   Todd, F.A.   'The Condition of the Working Class in Preston, 1791-1855', MLitt thesis; University of Lancaster, 1975 (See Chapter 5: 'Trade Unions, Early Radicalism and Chartist Politics in Preston')

1285   Tosney, B.C.   'Educational Chartism: An Exploration into Its Influence on the Development of Adult Education in Great Britain', MEd dissertation; University of Nottingham, 1983

1286   Turner, C.M.   'Politics in Mechanics' Institutes, 1820-50: A Study in Conflict', PhD thesis; University of Leicester, 1982 (Explores the differing degree of Chartist and Owenite affiliation in a wide-range of Mechanics' Institutes including Ashton-under-Lyne, Birmingham, Brighton, Cheltenham, Coventry, Dundee, Sheffield and Stroud)

1287   Valentine, G.R.   'The Development of Independent Working Class Educational Activity, 1800-1860', MA dissertation; Institute of Education, London, 1987 (See Chapter 3: 'The Educational Activity of the Chartists', pp.69-105)

1288   Vernon, N. James   'Politics and the People: A Study in English Political Culture and Communication, 1808-68', PhD thesis, University of Manchester, 1991 (Includes a lengthy consideration of Chartism)

1289   Wallace, Ryland D. 'Political Reform Societies in Wales, 1832-84', PhD thesis; University of Wales (Aberystwyth), 1978 (Includes Chartism in Wales)

1290   Walmsley, P.   'Political, Religious and Social Aspects of the Stroud Parliamentary Borough, 1830-52', MLitt thesis; University of Bristol, 1990 (Explores aspects of the Stroud Chartists' involvement in local politics)

1291   Walsh, David   'Working-Class Development, Control and New Conservatism: Blackburn 1820-50', MSc thesis; University of Salford, 1986 (For Chartism in Blackburn, see Chapter 2: 'Working Class Development and Class Consciousness', pp.127-151. Includes the mass protest of 1839, the 'Plug Plots' of 1842 and subsequent trials, factory politics and the Land Plan)

1292   Walsh, David   'Working-Class Political Integration and the Conservative Party: A Study of Class Relations and Party Political Development in the North West, 1800-1870', PhD thesis; University of Salford, 1991, 2 vols (Chapter 7 considers how Chartist success in the North West built upon the traditions of paternalistic Tory-Radicalism. Case studies include Chester, Clitheroe, Lancaster, Preston, Bolton and Blackburn)

1293   Watch, Thomas Richard   'A Lack of Co-operation: the Evangelicals, the Christian Socialists and the Chartist Movement', MA thesis; Eastern Michigan University, 1989

1294   Weaver, M.K.   'Crime, Chartism, Community and the Police: The Birmingham Police Act, 1839-1842', PhD thesis; University of North Carolina at Chapel Hill, 1989

1295   Weaver, S.A.   'The Politics of Popular Radicalism: John Fielden and the Progress of Labour in Early Victorian England', PhD thesis; University of Stanford, 1985

1296   Webb, R.F.   'Birmingham and the Chartist Movement', PhD thesis; University of Birmingham, 1926

1297   Weiland, Steven   'Chartism and English Literature, 1838-50', DPhil thesis; University of Chicago, 1971

1298   Wilson, Gordon M.   'The Miners of the West of Scotland and Their Trade Unions 1842-74', PhD thesis; University of Glasgow, 1977 (For the Clyde Valley Miners' various links with Chartism, see Chapter 5: 'Narrative Account of Trade Unionism among the Miners of West Central Scotland, 1842-55' These include the strike activities of 1842, 1844, 1847, 1850 and 1855 in Ayrshire, Lanarkshire, Renfrewshire and Stirlingshire)

1299   Wilson, Keith   'Political Radicalism in the North East of England, 1830-1860: Issues in Historical Sociology', PhD thesis; University of Durham, 1987 (Looks at the growth and decline of working class political radicalism, 1830-60, in three case studies - Sunderland, Darlington and the Durham miners. Argues for a greater theoretical debate, via a fusion of History and Sociology, to explore the factors of cultural ideology, work regimes and labour processes in influencing class formation and development)

1300   Winn, Sharon A.   'Friends of the People: Chartism in Victorian Social Protest Fiction', PhD thesis; University of Tulsa, 1989

1301   Worrall, Brian G.   'Self-Taught Working Men: The Culture of Autodidaction, with Special Reference to Lancashire, c.1790-1930', PhD thesis; University of Manchester, 1985 (See Chapter 5: 'The Culture of the Autodidact: Institutional and Political Collectivism c. 1820-1850', pp.127-155, which focuses on the relationship between autodidacts and Chartism)

Anthologies

1302   Ashraf, Mary (ed.) *Political Verse and Song from Britain and Ireland*, Lawrence and Wishart, London, 1975, pp.440 (Includes a wide selection of Chartist poets and poetry; such as George Binns, Thomas Cooper, Ernest Jones, Ebenezer Jones, William Jones, J.B. Leno)

1303   Behagg, Clive (ed.) *Chartism*, Longman, Harlow, London, 1993, pp.116 (A valuable classroom resource pack of 33 Chartist documents with comments, interpretations and historiography by historians. The pack is part of the publisher's series called ETHOS - Enquiry into Teaching History to Over-Sixteens)

1304   Benn, Tony (ed.) *Writings on the Wall: A Radical and Socialist Anthology 1215-1984*, Faber and Faber, London,1984, pp.318 (Selections of writings, speeches and songs for justice, freedom and equality. Draws on thirteen pieces of Chartist source material including extracts from William Lovett, Bronterre O'Brien, J.R. Stephens, Robert Lowery, Ernest Jones)

1305   Brown, Richard and Daniels, Christopher *The Chartists*, Macmillan, London, 1984, pp.138 (Documents and Debates; for VI Formers; covers the period 1836-1848; Introduction pp.4 and extensive commentary on the documents)

1306   Finn, Joe (ed.) *Chartists and Chartism*, Hodder and Stoughton, London, 1992, pp.124 (Publisher's 'History at Source Series' for 'A' Level and university students. A wide-ranging collection of documents on the Chartist movement with interpretation and commentary. Includes a historiography of Chartism setting out major areas of debate)

1307   Firth, G., Laybourn, K. and O'Connell, J. (eds.) *Yorkshire Labour Movements c.1780-1926: A Guide to Historical Sources and their Value*, University of Leeds School of Education, Leeds, 1981, pp.126 (A collection of documents intended to assist history teachers in the classroom on the subject of labour movements in the county. See pp.31-42 for documents on the local factory movement, the anti-poor law agitation and Chartism)

1308   Fyson, Robert (ed.) *Chartism in North Staffordshire*, Staffordshire Study Book 12, Staffordshire County Council Education Department, Stafford, 1981, pp.46 (Documents for use in schools and colleges relating to the beginnings of Potteries Chartism, the riots of 1842, and events up to 1844)

1309   Haywood, Ian *The Literature of Struggle: An Anthology of Chartist Fiction*, Scolar Press Aldershot, 1995, pp.210 (Includes an introduction surveying radical fiction accompanied by lenthy extracts from little noticed texts)

1310   Hepplewhite, Peter (ed.) *Tyneside Chartism*, Tyne and Wear Archive Services, Newcastle-upon-Tyne, 1988, pp.9 (Small collection of local documents for 1839, produced as an education pack)

1311   Hollis, Patricia (ed.) *Women in Public: The Women's Movement 1850-1900*, George Allen and Unwin, London, 1980, pp.336 (See pp.287-289 for documents relating to women and Chartism)

1312   James, Louis (ed.) *Print and the People*, Allen Lane, London, 1976 and
       Peregrine Books, Harmondsworth, 1978, pp.368 (An anthology of popular
       literature with an Introduction and extensive commentary on the documents.
       It includes several pieces on Chartism and some extracts from the fiction of
       Thomas Frost and G.W.M. Reynolds. There is also a document by Samuel
       Smiles on the life of Gerald Massey)

1313   Lapides, Kenneth (ed.) *Marx and Engels on the Trade Unions*, Praeger
       Publishers, New York, 1987, pp.239 (With introduction and notes. Chapter 1:
       'Trade Unions and Revolution 1844-1848', pp.1-37 includes extracts from
       articles by Engels in the *Northern Star* and extensive commentary by both
       men on Chartism, the General Strike of 1842, the Miners' strike of 1844 and
       'Workers' Disturbances')

1314   Lindsay, Jack and Rickword, Edgell (eds.) *A Handbook of Freedom: A
       Record of English Democracy Through Twelve Centuries*, Lawrence and
       Wishart, London, 1939, pp.408 (See particularly Chapter VI 'The Tide of
       Chartism 1826-1860', pp.275-333, for poems and passages by John Bramwich,
       Thomas Cooper, Bronterre O'Brien, G.J. Harney, Henry Hetherington, G.J.
       Holyoake, W.J. Linton, Ernest Jones, William Jones)

1315   No entry

1316   Maidment, Brian (ed.) *The Poorhouse Fugitives: Self-Taught Poets and Poetry
       in Victorian Britain*, Carcanet Press, Manchester, 1987 pp.374 (An anthology
       of nineteenth-century artisan verse from, amongst others, the Chartists,
       Thomas Cooper, Ebenezer Jones, Ernest Jones, Gerald Massey, E.P. Mead and
       Willie Thom)

1317   Mather, F.C. (ed.) *Chartism and Society*, Bell and Hyman, London, 1980,
       pp319 (A wide-ranging collection of documents)

1318   Mulgan, John (ed.) *Poems of Freedom*, Victor Gollancz, London, 1938,
       pp.192 (An anthology of protest poems from 1381 to Stephen Spender. See
       pp.65-121 for poems by Ebenezer Elliot and Ernest Jones; and for Ralph
       Waldo Emerson's 'The Chartist Complaint')

1319   Royle, Edward (ed.) *The Infidel Tradition. From Paine to Bradlaugh*,
       Macmillan, London, 1976, pp.228 (For a number of documents on Chartism
       and Republicanism in the 1850s)

1320   Ryan, Michael (ed.) *Chartism*, Factpack No.8, Elm Publications, Kings Ripton,
       Huntingdon, 1987 (No pagination. A well-produced factpack of 27 Chartist
       documents covering aspects between 1838-1849. Intended for GCSE and 'A'
       Level use)

1321   Scheckner, Peter (ed.) *An Anthology of Chartist Poetry: Poetry of the British
       Working Class, 1830s-1850s*, Associated University Presses, London and
       Toronto, 1989, pp.353 (Introduction pp.15-58; poems by Thomas Cooper,
       Ernest Jones, W.J. Linton, Gerald Massey, W. Rider, W. Thom, W.J. Vernon,
       T.M. Wheeler, J. Athol Wood; many are reprinted from Y.V. Kovalev (ed.) *An
       Anthology of Chartist Literature*, Moscow, 1956)

1322   Simkin, John (ed.)   *Chartism*, Spartacus, Brighton, 1986, pp.16 (A short
collection of documents in the publisher's 'Voices from the Past' series of
publications for GCSE pupils)

Literary Forms Concerned
with Chartism

1323   Bentley, Phyllis *Inheritance*, Gollancz, London, 1932, pp.592; 28th
        impression 1950; Reptd., 1979 (A novel set in part against a Luddite and
        Chartist background in the West Riding of Yorkshire)

1324   Cordell, Alexander *Land of My Fathers*, Hodder and Stoughton, London,
        pp.300. Reptd. Coronet, London, 1985 (A novel set largely in Dowlais,
        Merthyr, during 1838-1840. Includes the activities of Merthyr Chartists and
        their involvement in the march on Newport in November 1839)

1325   Cordell, Alexander *Requiem for a Patriot*, Weidenfeld and Nicolson, London,
        1988, pp.318 (A novel on the life and activities of the Newport Chartist leader,
        John Frost)

1326   Davies, Idris "The Sacred Road" in Islwyn Jenkins (ed.) *The Collected Poems
        of Idris Davies*, Gomerian Press, Llandysul, 1972, pp.190. Reptd., Gomerian
        Press, 1980 (See p.22. This political poem has contributed to the popular
        memory of the Gwent Chartists in Wales)

1327   Lindsay, Jack *Men of Forty-Eight*, London, 1948, pp.448; Reptd., Cedric
        Chivers, Portway, Bath, 1971 (A novel of Chartism and the European
        revolutions of 1848 set chiefly in London, Paris and Vienna)

1328   Red Ladder *Taking Our Time*, Pluto Plays, London, 1979, pp.52 (With an
        Introduction by Julian Harber. A play about Chartism and the strike
        movement in and around Halifax in 1842)

1329   Schofield, Stephen *The Chartist: A Play*, Samuel French Limited, London,
        1936, pp.28 (Set in a working-class cottage in 1848. Copy in Nuffield College
        Library, Oxford)

1330   Webb, Harri "The Stars of Mexico (An Old Chartist Remembers)" in Harri
        Webb, *Rampage and Revel*, Gomer Press, Llandysul, 1977, pp.63 (A poem
        about the Newport Rising of 1839; see pp.41-42)

1331   Williams, Mari *Cyffro Yn Y Cwm*, Gwasg Gomer Press, Llandysul, 1990, pp.58
        (Children's stories in Welsh. Commissioned by the Welsh Arts Council as
        part of the Welsh History Project. Published in English and entitled *Revolt in
        the Valley*, Gomer Press, Llandysul, 1991, pp.56. A children's story about the
        Newport Rising of 1839 as experienced by a ten year old boy)

Biographical Dictionaries

1332   Banks, Olive *The Biographical Dictionary of British Feminists, Vol.I, 1800-1930*, New York University Press, New York, 1985 (Includes an entry for Catherine Barmby and for Anne Knight)

1333   Barrows, Floyd and Mock, David B. *A Dictionary of Obituaries of Modern British Radicals*, Harvester Wheatsheaf, London, 1989 (Includes entries for Thomas Attwood; Samuel Bamford; Joseph Cowen jr.; William Cuffay; T.S. Duncombe; R.G. Gammage; Henry Hetherington; Abel Heywood; G.J. Holyoake; Joseph Hume; Isaac Ironside; Ernest Jones; Patrick Lloyd Jones; William Lovett; John McAdam; Feargus O'Connor; Arthur O'Neill; G.W.M. Reynolds; Alexander Somerville; Joseph Sturge)

1334   Baylen, Joseph O. and Gossman, Norbert J. (eds.) *Biographical Dictionary of Modern British Radicals Since 1770*, Harvester Press, Brighton, 3 Vols. Vol.I 1770-1832 (1979); Vol.II 1830-1870 (1984); Vol.III 1870-1914 (1988)

(See **Vol. I** for entries on Allen Davenport; Joseph Hume; Francis Place; Thomas Preston; Thomas Perronet Thompson.
Vol. II for entries on William Henry Ashurst senior; Thomas Attwood; Joseph Barker; Augustus H. Beaumont; George Binns; Robert Blakey; J.F. Bray; Patrick Brewster; William Carpenter; John Cleave; John Collins; Samuel Cook; Thomas Cooper; Joseph Cowen jr; William Cuffay; Thomas Doubleday; Abram Duncan; T.S. Duncombe; George Edmonds; Ebenezer Elliott; John Fielden; R.G. Gammage; G.J. Harney; Robert Hartwell; Thomas Hepburn; Henry Hetherington; Abel Heywood; Joseph Hickin; Charles Hindley; G.J. Holyoake; Thornton Leigh Hunt; Isaac Ironside; Ernest Jones; Patrick Lloyd Jones; Anne Knight; W.J. Linton; J.H.B. Lorymer; William Lovett; Robert Lowery; John McAdam; Peter McDouall; Gerald Massey; Charles Neesom; C.F. Nicholls; H.R. Nicholls; Bronterre O'Brien; Feargus O'Connor; Arthur O'Neill; Richard Oastler; John Humffreys Parry; Lawrence Pitkethly; Richard B. Reed; G.W.M. Reynolds; R.J. Richardson; William Rider; J.A. Roebuck; William Shaen; Samuel Smiles; Caroline Ashurst Stansfeld; Sir James Stansfeld; J.R. Stephens; Joseph Sturge; John Taylor; James Turner; David Urquhart; Henry Vincent; Thomas Wakley; Sir Joshua Walmsley; James Watson; James Whittle; James Williams
Vol. III for entries on W.E. Adams; George Howell, John Kane; F.R. Lees; A.J. Mundella; John Murdoch; Henry Solly)

1335   Bellamy, Joyce M. and Saville, John (eds.) *Dictionary of Labour Biography*, Macmillan, London, 1976 - Vols. IV, V, VI, VII, VIII, IX

(See **Vol. IV** for entries on Jonathan Barber; Samuel Holberry; Robert Lowery; Richard B. Reed; Benjamin Stott; James Sweet.
Vol. V for entries on Joseph Gurney; David William Heath; John McAdam.
Vol. VI for entries on Catherine Barmby and John Goodwyn Barmby; William Benbow; John Chance; Thomas Clark; John Cleave; Samuel Cook; Samuel Quartus Cook; William Cuffay; Robert George Gammage; William Peck Hemm; Abel Heywood; George Keadall; Joseph Linney; William Lovett; William Henry Mott; Arthur George O'Neill; Richard Pilling; Daniel Wallwork; Thomas Martin Wheeler. **Vol. VII** for entries on William Edwin Adams; William Henry Chadwick; Benjamin Lucraft; John West.

Vol. VIII for entries on Thomas Allsop; Daniel Chatterton; Allen Davenport; Joshua Hobson; Richard Marsden; Charles Hodgson Neesom; Thomas Preston.
Vol. IX for entries on Thomas Cooper; John Knight; James Leach; John Vallance; Jeremiah Yates)

1336   Lloyd, J.E. and Jenkins, R.T. (eds.) *The Dictionary of Welsh Biography Down to 1940*, The Honourable Society of the Cymmrodorion, London, 1959 (There are entries for the following Chartists: John Frost; David John; Thomas Powell; William Price; Hugh Williams; Morgan Williams; Zephaniah Williams)

1337   Nicholls, C.S. (ed) *The Dictionary of National Biography: Missing Persons*, Oxford University Press, Oxford, 1993 (Entry for Henry Solly)

1338   Stephens, Leslie and Lee, Sidney (eds.) *The Dictionary of National Biography*, Vol.XXII, Supplement, Oxford University Press, Oxford, 1901 (Entry for Joseph Cowen jr.)

Index

The references in this index are to ITEM NUMBERS, not to page numbers. Entries in the final section (Biographical Dictionaries) have not been indexed here.

257,328,625,679,727-8,753,
770,795-6,822,825,831,881,
884,912,932,935,943,971,978,
983,1014,1054-6,1119-20,
1150,1187,1232,1235,1239,
1311
Wood, J. Athol 1321
Wood, Thomas 365
wool 160,649,686,1250
Wooler, Thomas J. 46
Worcester, Marquis of (Duke of,
  Beaufort 1059
Worcestershire 3,188,323,557,
  810,1272,1283
Working Men's Associations
  23.1,24.3,29,34,103,274-9,
  305,379; in Germany 607;
  international 713
Wroe, James 623

Yates, Jeremiah 23.13,878
Yeovil 28
Yorkshire 23.1,24.10,32,36,39,
  51,53-4,56-7,69,84,91,97,
  136-7,159,167-8,246,253,287,
  328A,355,365,375.6,375.14,
  375.17,375.23,375.26,504-5,
  532,538,560,608,643,649-50,
  652,726,773,953,1000,1051,
  1057,1077,1110,1115-17,1180,
  1193,1200,1227,1261,1270-1,
  1282-3,1286,1307,1323,1328